# THE INTEGRATION OF INTERNATIONAL CAPITAL MARKETS

*To Kutadgu*

# The Integration of International Capital Markets

## Theory and Empirical Evidence

Haluk Akdogan
*Bilkent University*
*and Boston University*

**Edward Elgar**
Cheltenham, UK • Northampton, MA, USA

Published by
Edward Elgar Publishing Limited
8 Lansdown Place
Cheltenham
Glos GL50 2HU
UK

Edward Elgar Publishing, Inc.
6 Market Street
Northampton
Massachusetts 01060
USA

Reprinted 1998

**British Library Cataloguing in Publication Data**
Akdogan, Haluk
Integration of International Capital
Markets: Theory and Empirical Evidence
I. Title
332.042

**Library of Congress Cataloguing in Publication Data**
Akdogan, Haluk, 1959–
The integration of international capital markets : theory and empirical evidence / Haluk Akdogan.
p. cm.
Includes bibliographical references and index.
1. Capital market. 2. International finance. 3. International economic integration. I. Title.
HG4523.A38 1995
332'.042—dc20 94-2754
CI

ISBN 1 85898 131 X

Printed in Great Britain by The Ipswich Book Company, Suffolk

# Contents

# Tables

# Preface

The subject matter of this book is currently of enormous public and scholarly interest. Global financial issues are very much at the core of major changes throughout the world. Economists frequently speak about globalization of financial services and integration of international money and capital markets. Markets all over the world have undergone major structural changes. A variety of financial instruments has been introduced to the investors. Recent developments in telecommunications technology and computers have fostered the expansion of international financial markets even further. As a result, investors from many countries have started following and utilizing on-line business news. Increasingly financial and economic news deals with such matters of interest as behaviour of stock prices, exchange rate movements, performances of international funds, and monetary announcements made by the central bank governors or finance ministers. Institutional developments toward financial integration have taken place so rapidly that one could not have even imagined ten or fifteen years ago.

The book addresses the issue of international capital market integration both theoretically and empirically. It aims to combine financial theory with the theory of integration. Empirical models that deal with the testing whether world capital markets are integrated are also explored. The book differs fundamentally in two important respects from others treating the topic of integration. First, it is based entirely on financial theory, unlike many other books where integration is studied in the context of pure theory of international trade. Second, it develops several models and empirically tests the issue of integration of capital markets – in particular the European markets using modern capital asset-pricing approach.

The basic motivation of the author in writing this book is the absence of a volume in the bookshelves in which can be found a financial-theoretical examination of integration. In a convenient book form we have not seen any work addressing the tests of international capital market integration. Several journal articles are available in the topic of international integration of capital markets, yet they are fairly specialized in certain aspects of financial theory and hence not easily usable by most students of finance and economics.

The principal theory examined in this volume is the international capital asset-pricing model, including the arbitrage pricing theory dimension. Its intended audience are graduate and advanced undergraduate students majoring in finance, international business or economics. Researchers interested in international capital markets and the financial theory of integration will also find useful material, for its substance is not normally covered in a book form. Although we do not particularly aim at professionals, the book can also serve international portfolio managers as a reference in international capital markets. Some material, especially Chapter 2, is of much use to professionals. Some knowledge of economics, financial theory, asset pricing, statistics and econometrics would be helpful.

Topics in many of the chapters are drawn largely from the earlier works of the author, including a doctoral dissertation. I am grateful to my many professors, friends and acquaintances, at the City University of New York Graduate School, Bilkent University, the International House of New York, the New York Chapter of the Fulbright Association and the Morgan Bank of New York. Bilkent University, the International House of New York and the New York Chapter of the Fulbright Association have provided financial assistance that has directly or indirectly helped me in writing this book. I have written most of it at Bilkent University, however.

I should like to thank Edward Elgar who encouraged me to complete the manuscript and have it ready for publication when I first met him in New York and Dymphna Evans who supported the idea. My thanks also go to the Edward Elgar staff involved in preparing and marketing the book, in particular Julie Leppard, Jo Perkins, Susan Howard and Charlotte Kitchen. I acknowledge the generosity of the International Monetary Fund which has granted me the permission to reprint some of the tables which appeared in its annual publications.

I thank Nedim Alemdar, Yaman Asikoglu, Michael Edelstein, Thomas J. Gardner, Michael Grossman, Salih Neftci, Andreas Pericli and Subidey Togan for their help and advice. I also thank David Maslin of Morgan Bank, who provided data on government bond yields and interest rates. I thank Ismail Saglam, who provided research assistance and forbearingly prepared most of the tables. Nihat Dilek also provided research assistance. Finally, my deepest thanks go to my wife Nevin, with whom I have discussed finance and economics over the past several years, for her enormous patience and love.

I solely bear the responsibility of all remaining errors and shortcomings.

HALUK AKDOGAN

# Abbreviations

| | |
|---|---|
| APM | Arbitrage pricing model |
| APT | Arbitrage pricing theory |
| CAC | French (Paris) Stock Price Index |
| CAPM | Capital asset-pricing model |
| EC | European Community |
| ECU | European Currency Unit |
| EEA | European Economic Area |
| EEC | European Economic Community |
| EES | European Economic Space |
| EFTA | European Free Trade Association |
| EMS | European Monetary System |
| ERISA | Employee Retirement Income Security Act |
| ERM | Exchange Rate Mechanism |
| EU | European Union |
| GATT | General Agreement on Tariffs and Trade |
| GDP | Gross Domestic Product |
| GNP | Gross National Product |
| IAPM | International asset-pricing model |
| IAPT | International arbitrage-pricing theory |
| ICAPM | International capital asset-pricing model |
| IFC | International Finance Corporation |
| IFS | International Financial Statistics |
| IMF | International Monetary Fund |
| LDC | Less-developed country |
| LOOP | Law of one price |
| MCC | Marginal cost of capital |
| OECD | Organization for Economic Co-operation and Development |
| P/BV | Price–book-value ratio |
| P/E | Price–earnings ratio |
| S&P | Standard & Poor (price index) |
| UK | United Kingdom |
| US | United States |

# PART I

# STATISTICS AND INSTITUTIONS

# 1 Introduction

## Definition

The word integration refers literally to the state of being integrated. Once objects or entities become integrated they are treated as one. Integration does not only imply the combination of once-independent beings, however. Its extent is far greater than a simple mixture or association of separate economies. Yet integration may not be full and complete. The state of affairs might very well be such that it shows neither integration nor segmentation; then we can speak of *degree of integration*. Indeed, the word is also used to refer to a process that is expected to lead to integration in the future.

Theoretically, integration is associated with equalization of product and factor prices across the relevant markets so that the *law of one price* (LOOP) holds. That is, when transportation costs are not taken into account, identical goods and services should carry the same price across all places where such goods and services are traded. If people are well informed of what is marketed elsewhere and the relevant prices of all tradeable goods and services, prices should be equalized. This is what is known as the law of one price in economic theory.

Integration, when defined as a process, involves several strategic stages before and after a customs union is actually reached. Indeed, existing examples of economic integration portray some degree of international economic co-operation based on reciprocity and, with a possible exception of the European Union (EU), they can hardly be identified as customs unions. Yet many have accomplished a great deal towards integration. People have realized the potential gains associated with fewer controls and less intervention. The examples of the EU and the European Free Trade Association (EFTA) are enough to make others take the issue seriously. So, a customs union ought to be thought of as an intermediate step towards a more complete state of integration. The generally accepted stages of an economic integration process are, in increasing degree of sophistication, (a) free trade areas, (b) customs unions, (c) common markets, (d) economic unions, and finally as the last stage of affairs (e) unification. The important issue here is whether these steps towards economic integration are taken internationally. In practice, all these stages are more regional than they are international. Indeed, integration attempts across the world are more of a geographical nature. The most important among the geographical integration attempts are the European Union (EU), the European Free Trade Association (EFTA), and the North American Free Trade Association (NAFTA).

### Trade integration and economic theory

The pioneers of classical economic theory did not specifically address the issues relevant to a segmented or an integrated world economy. This is perhaps due to the fact that there were physical barriers against integration of any kind at that time. Markets were clearly segmented. Activities of trade and finance took place in different parts of the world without much interaction.

Many classical writers, starting with Adam Smith and including John Stuart Mill, however, did speak about the virtues and benefits of free trade and commercial activities. A free market was the essential focus in their works on political economy. Although international trade and finance were perceived as important to the economic welfare of states, national economies were at the core of classical writing. It was not until the 1940s that the issue was given more serious thought. The theory of economic integration can be traced back to the famous series of factor price equalization articles of Paul Samuelson. When Samuelson wrote, ironically, the orientation of economies and markets was fairly domestic and segmented from each other.

There is now a rich body of economic theory literature on the integration aspects of international trade theory. Much of the literature deals with the trade creation and trade diversion features of integration. The first comprehensive treatment of the theory is the Balasa's (1961) well-known book, *The Theory of Economic Integration*, in which he broadly defines integration as both a process and a state of affairs. What Balasa and many others stressed later is that the theory of economic integration is a customs union theory and hence should be investigated as a natural part of international economics. This approach undermines some very important aspects of integration, such as fiscal and monetary policy co-ordination, the issues related to the measurement of integration, and international factor movements. The theory of international factor movements in particular deserves better attention. It involves basically the movement of labour and capital from one place to another.

### Plan and organization of the book

The scope of this book is to contemplate the existing financial theory of international capital market integration *vis-à-vis* capital movements. We address the issues relevant for international financial integration, more specifically the issue of the international integration of capital markets. Models are developed to test the status of capital market integration. A number of empirical techniques are employed and cross-country tests of integration are carried out.

Although the book is specifically about the integration of capital markets, it does not by any means attempt to test or validate existing theories of international asset-pricing. It utilizes these theories to test integration and not the pricing theories themselves. We combine the existing theory of capital market integration with research that the author has completed on this topic over the past several years. Empirical models use the data from international capital markets that include developing as well as developed capital markets. Special emphasis is given to the European, in particular the European Union, markets. One other aspect is that several methodologies to test regional financial integration, in addition to worldwide integration, are suggested.

There are several reasons for employing European capital markets as the principal data source. First, and most importantly, the European Union (EU hereafter) capital markets are in the process of institutional integration. Most legal barriers have been either removed or are scheduled to be removed. The process of legal integration is nearly complete. Hence, the EU markets can serve as an excellent sample to test for integration. Second, the EU capital markets are fairly well established compared to most markets in the world. Third, they are not of huge size, unlike the US and Japanese markets. In terms of market values, European capital markets are comparable to most of the existing less-developed markets. This characteristic makes them a better sample upon which to base reasonable generalizations. Fourth, whether the EU capital markets are integrated is still unclear from an empirical standpoint, despite the institutional process being almost complete. Fifth, data on many European markets are readily available.

The book is organized as follows. It is divided into three parts, the first of which is devoted to the descriptive aspects and institutional developments concerning international capital markets. In this part, the first chapter is introductory; the second supplies some basic statistics about the world financial markets; and the third introduces the concept of integration.

In Part II asset-pricing theories are studied. First, the standard capital asset-pricing model is reviewed and the concept of the international mean variance efficiency of a given portfolio is explored. Second, international asset pricing *à la* Sharpe–Lintner is investigated. Third, Roll–Ross arbitrage pricing theory is studied and the international dimensions of arbitrage pricing are examined in detail. International asset pricing theories are then modified in order to address the issue of capital market integration.

Part III is devoted to empirical tests of international capital market integration. Both regional and international financial integration are investigated using stock market data from several world capital markets. These empirical chapters are self-contained, and the reader, with little or no reference to other chapters of the book, may follow the material presented there.

# 2 World capital markets: statistics and institutions

## Capital markets

Capital markets are exchange places where long-term claims are traded. This definition is a little erratic. A precise distinction between short- and long-term lending or borrowing in terms of the length of time period does not exist. Although long-term arrangements are established for a period of several years, any such definition of the long-term as 'commitments extending over a period of time greater than one year' is arbitrary. Indeed, it is difficult, and rarely necessary, to distinguish capital markets from money markets where short-term obligations are exchanged.

It has been recognized that the most important elements of capital markets are equity capital and debt capital. Claims that represent ownership stem from equity capital. Claims that identify one party who borrows and another who lends represent what we call debt capital. Indeed, investors trade equity and debt capital in capital markets. More recently, investors have started trading state-contingent claims such as futures and options. These too should be taken as elements of capital markets even though their presence has to do with speculative motives. Such claims or, to use their more popular name, derivatives do expand the capital markets where their underlying instruments are traded. Hence, whether they are or are not part of the capital markets, their existence affect the dynamics of debt and equity exchanges.

The size of capital markets is measured either by the *stock of outstanding claims* held at any specific point in time by different agents or the *flows of funds* between different economic groups over a given period of time. The practical way to measure the size of a capital market, in particular a stock market, is to look at the market capitalization at any point in time. Market capitalization is the outstanding value of all securities traded in a given market based on observed market-determined prices. The size can also be measured based on book-values. This second way is not of much use in empirical works because bids and asks change the prices of all exchange-traded instruments almost continuously. Tables 2.1 to 2.4 report several size aspects of international capital markets.

The existence of international capital markets can be traced back to the 1800s because international investment in equity capital dates back to the eighteenth century when European merchants founded the East India Company. In the nineteenth century, international equity investors, particularly the British, established ventures such as the South American railways, and French investment began. Substantial flows of investment capital have been seen throughout the twentieth century. In the first half of the century international investment consisted mainly of debt capital. From the 1970s, and especially since the 1980s, equity capital has become a major part of international investment.

*Table 2.1: World markets: how they are valued (as at February 1992)*

| Country | P/E | % yield | Price/book ratio | Mrkt cap ($ bn) | Number of assets[a] |
|---|---|---|---|---|---|
| Austria | 17.4 | 1.7 | 1.91 | 18.1 | 29 |
| Belgium | 12.0 | 5.0 | 1.48 | 39.6 | 76 |
| Denmark | 132.4 | 1.6 | 1.78 | 26.7 | 44 |
| Finland | 68.8 | 2.3 | 0.73 | 3.4 | 42 |
| UK | 15.7 | 5.1 | 1.89 | 609.7 | 329 |
| France | 15.0 | 3.2 | 1.68 | 208.7 | 185 |
| Germany | 16.2 | 3.4 | 2.00 | 231.5 | 145 |
| Ireland | 13.7 | 2.4 | 1.59 | 10.2 | 17 |
| Italy | 15.9 | 3.5 | 1.15 | 77.1 | 150 |
| Netherlands | 13.0 | 4.3 | 1.48 | 100.4 | 68 |
| Norway | 9.9 | 1.9 | 1.88 | 9.5 | 36 |
| Spain | 10.9 | 4.4 | 1.26 | 77.1 | 69 |
| Sweden | 17.6 | 3.1 | 1.61 | 21.8 | 77 |
| Switzerland | 17.5 | 2.0 | 1.65 | 102.3 | 124 |
| **Europe total** | | | | **1536.3** | **1324** |
| India[b] | 16.8 | 1.9 | 3.10 | 25.0 | – |
| Pakistan[b] | 9.0 | 7.0 | 1.90 | 2.4 | 429 |
| Greece[b] | 3.5 | 4.2 | 3.50 | 6.7 | 119 |
| Korea[b] | 39.7 | 1.3 | 2.70 | 140.0 | 586 |
| Malaysia[b] | 31.6 | 2.2 | 3.30 | 33.8 | 245 |
| Mexico[b] | 9.7 | 2.1 | 1.00 | 139.1 | 255 |
| Philippines[b] | 19.6 | 1.1 | 4.70 | 11.9 | 142 |
| Portugal[b] | 23.7 | 1.7 | 4.20 | 10.0 | 176 |
| Taiwan[b] | 49.6 | 0.6 | 7.40 | 243.7 | 167 |
| Thailand[b] | 18.2 | 2.5 | 5.70 | 17.8 | 159 |
| Turkey[b] | 12.0 | 5.7 | 4.50 | 4.3 | 50 |
| Venezuela[b] | 5.6 | 2.4 | 1.30 | 1.2 | 60 |
| **Emerging markets total** | | | | **635.9** | **2388** |
| Canada | 41.7 | 3.1 | 1.44 | 154.8 | |
| USA | 24.5 | 3.0 | 2.29 | 2190.7 | 1547 |
| **North America total** | | | | **2345.5** | |
| Japan | 31.9 | 0.9 | 2.15 | 1474.9 | 1161 |
| **World Total** | | | | **5992.6** | |

*Notes:*

[a] As of January 1990

[b] As of September 1989

*Sources*: Morgan Stanley Capital International, Geneva. International Finance Corporation, *Quarterly Review of Emerging Stock Markets*, various issues, and author's calculations.

*Table 2.2: Gross international equity flows, 1986–first quarter 1991[a] (US$bn)*

| | 1986 | 1987 | 1988 | 1989 | 1990 | 1991 |
|---|---|---|---|---|---|---|
| Investor from: | | | | | | |
| United States[b] | 128.5 | 263.3 | 191.8 | 275.5 | 297.4 | – |
| Japan[c] | 34.8 | 125 0 | 150.1 | 176.2 | 147.3 | – |
| United Kingdom[d] | 173.6 | 232.9 | 224.1 | 324.1 | 333.8 | – |
| Continental Europe | 258.3 | 369.9 | 332.6 | 368.1 | 332.7 | – |
| of which: Germany[e] | 42.9 | 59.4 | 42.3 | 65.0 | 49.1 | – |
| Rest of world | 205.6 | 380.4 | 314.0 | 454.1 | 330.1 | – |
| Equity from: | | | | | | |
| United States | 277.5 | 481.9 | 363.8 | 416.8 | 360.9 | – |
| Japan | 189.6 | 354.5 | 327.1 | 432.9 | 268.6 | – |
| United Kingdom | 84.3 | 144.1 | 120.8 | 141.3 | 151.6 | – |
| Continental Europe | 185.5 | 208.9 | 244.2 | 343.3 | 425.5 | – |
| of which: Germany | 77.9 | 76.8 | 60.7 | 109.2 | 158.6 | – |
| Rest of World | 60.9 | 155.0 | 156.7 | 263.8 | 234.6 | – |
| **Total** | **800.8** | **1344.5** | **1212.6** | **1598.1** | **1441.2** | **1475.0[f]** |

*Notes:*
[a] Gross flows are defined as the sum of equity purchases and sales associated with international portfolio investment.
[b] Includes US Employee Retirement Income Security Act (ERISA) funds.
[c] Including purchase of Japanese Euro-warrants.
[d] Including only pension funds, insurance companies, and open- and closed-end mutual funds.
[e] Excluding investment certificates.
[f] Estimate.
*Source*: International Monetary Fund, *International Capital Markets, Developments and Prospects*, 1991 and 1992.

An international new issue equity market emerged in the early 1980s. One important aspect of this market was that offerings were internationally syndicated. As a result of this development a variety of instruments derived from equities, such as convertible bonds, new stock options and warrants, have been introduced to international investors. Those who invest internationally and benefit from global risk diversification have much wider opportunities than they had ten years ago.

Institutional investors have also played an important role in the recent growth in world capital markets. These investors entered into the equity markets immediately after the general deregulation of capital controls. Most of those who emerged in the early 1980s were of UK origin. The US and Japanese equity investors followed after the mid-1980s. Before the stock market crash of 1987 and the subsequent crisis, the international equity market had already grown remarkably.

*Table 2.3: Net international equity flows, 1986–first quarter 1990[a] (US$bn)*

| | 1986 | 1987 | 1988 | 1989 | 1990 | 1991[e] |
|---|---|---|---|---|---|---|
| Investor from: | | | | | | |
| United States | 2.4 | –1.1 | –0.6 | 20.9 | 11.9 | 26.3 |
| Japan[b] | 7.1 | 16.9 | 3.0 | 17.9 | 6.3 | 7.4 |
| United Kingdom[c] | 9.5 | –0.3 | 7.2 | 29.8 | –0.8 | –4.2 |
| Continental Europe | 12.0 | 6.8 | 8.1 | 16.4 | 3.8 | 16.1 |
| of which: Germany[d] | 2.3 | –0.2 | 2.8 | 1.6 | 0.1 | – |
| Rest of world | 0.8 | –18.3 | 3.4 | 7.4 | –10.2 | 5.5 |
| Equity from: | | | | | | |
| United States | 18.7 | 16.2 | –1.8 | 11.5 | –15.1 | 14.2 |
| Japan | –15.8 | –42.8 | 6.8 | 7.0 | –13.3 | 31.6 |
| United Kingdom | 4.3 | 10.0 | 4.3 | 3.1 | 4.9 | 7.4 |
| Continental Europe | 20.3 | 8.7 | 13.0 | 42.1 | 15.5 | –1.6 |
| of which: Germany | 6.9 | –1.0 | 3.0 | 12.4 | –2.0 | – |
| Rest of world | 4.1 | 11.9 | –1.2 | 28.6 | 18.9 | –0.5 |
| **Total** | **31.7** | **4.0** | **21.1** | **92.3** | **10.9** | **51.1** |

*Notes:*

[a] Net flows are defined as purchases minus sales of equity associated with international portfolio investment.

[b] Including purchase of Japanese Euro-warrants.

[c] Including only pension funds, insurance companies, and open and closed-ended mutual funds.

[d] Excluding investment certificates.

[e] Estimates.

*Source*: As Table 2.2.

Indeed, facts clearly indicate the rapid expansion in world capital markets, an expansion that includes not only the markets in the developed part of the world but also less-developed countries' (LDCs) capital markets. Fostered by the rapid expansion in the world economy in the 1980s, the total market value of the securities traded in world capital markets has increased to almost US$6 trillion by February 1992 (Table 2.1) from a figure of less than US$2 trillion in 1980 (Ibbotson *et al.*, 1982). International gross equity flows defined as the sum of equity purchases and sales associated with portfolio investment doubled between 1986 and 1989 (Table 2.2). Similarly, net equity flows measured as purchases minus the sales of equities associated with international portfolio investment tripled between 1984 and 1989 (Table 2.3). Interbank claims have quadrupled in the same period (Table 2.4).

*Table 2.4: Change in interbank claims and liabilities*[a] *(US$bn)*

| | 1984 | 1985 | 1986 | 1987 | 1988 | 1989 | 1990 | 1991 |
|---|---|---|---|---|---|---|---|---|
| **Total change in claims**[b] | **155** | **217** | **449** | **663** | **480** | **651** | **466** | **–169** |
| Industrial countries | 120 | 184 | 375 | 468 | 393 | 449 | 359 | –154 |
| of which: United States | 25 | 33 | 69 | 83 | 69 | 59 | 23 | –16 |
| Japan | 22 | 40 | 149 | 192 | 185 | 136 | 47 | –130 |
| Developing countries[c] | 5 | 8 | 4 | 16 | –3 | – | 12 | 15 |
| Offshore centres[d] | 26 | 19 | 81 | 164 | 82 | 171 | 118 | –16 |
| Other transactors[e] | 4 | 7 | –11 | 15 | 8 | 30 | –23 | –14 |
| *Memorandum items* | | | | | | | | |
| Capital-importing developing countries[c,f] | 7 | 8 | 4 | 14 | –7 | –2 | 12 | 16 |
| Non–oil developing countries[c,g] | 7 | 6 | 4 | 14 | –10 | –3 | 11 | 17 |
| 15 heavily indebted countries | –1 | – | –1 | 2 | –10 | –3 | –9 | –1 |
| **Total change in liabilities**[h] | **152** | **213** | **464** | **625** | **444** | **655** | **441** | **–154** |
| Industrial countries | 110 | 168 | 363 | 439 | 326 | 467 | 371 | –121 |
| of which: United States | 14 | 8 | 56 | 35 | 63 | 60 | –3 | 15 |
| Japan | 11 | 40 | 111 | 145 | 147 | 127 | 58 | –44 |
| Developing countries[c] | 23 | 1 | –10 | 33 | 19 | 38 | 57 | 31 |
| Offshore centres[d] | 18 | 37 | 117 | 138 | 9 | 135 | 34 | –55 |
| Other transactors[e] | 1 | 8 | –5 | 16 | 4 | 12 | –21 | –9 |
| *Memorandum items* | | | | | | | | |
| Capital-importing developing countries[c,f] | 23 | 5 | 2 | 25 | 12 | 37 | 53 | 35 |
| Non–oil developing countries[c,g] | 22 | 2 | 9 | 25 | 13 | 33 | 44 | 32 |
| 15 heavily indebted countries | 12 | –3 | –7 | 5 | –1 | 7 | 16 | 2 |
| **Change in total net claims**[i] | **3** | **5** | **–15** | **38** | **35** | **–4** | **25** | **–15** |
| Industrial countries | 10 | 16 | 13 | 30 | 70 | –18 | –12 | –33 |
| of which: United States | 11 | 25 | 13 | 48 | 6 | –2 | 26 | –31 |
| Japan | 11 | –1 | 37 | 47 | 39 | 12 | –11 | –86 |
| Developing countries[c] | –18 | 6 | 14 | –16 | –21 | –39 | –46 | –16 |
| Offshore centres[d] | 9 | –18 | –36 | 26 | –14 | 37 | 84 | 40 |
| Other transactors[e] | 3 | –1 | –5 | –1 | 4 | 18 | –2 | –5 |
| *Memorandum items* | | | | | | | | |
| Capital-importing developing countries[c,f] | –16 | 3 | 2 | –10 | –19 | –39 | –41 | –19 |
| Non–oil developing countries[c,g] | –15 | 4 | –5 | –11 | –23 | –37 | –33 | –15 |
| 15 heavily indebted countries | –10 | 3 | 6 | –3 | –8 | –10 | –25 | –3 |
| Net errors and omissions[j] | –3 | –4 | 15 | –39 | –39 | 6 | –25 | 15 |

*Notes:*

[a] Data on changes in claims and liabilities are derived from stock data on the liabilities and assets of the countries reporting to the International Monetary Fund, excluding changes attributed to exchange rate movements.

[b] As measured by differences in the outstanding liabilities of borrowing countries, defined as cross-border interbank accounts by residence of borrowing bank.

[c] Excluding offshore centres.

[d] Consisting of the Bahamas, Bahrain, the Cayman Islands, Hong Kong, the Netherlands Antilles, Panama and Singapore.

[e] Transactors included in IFS measures for the world, to enhance global symmetry, but excluded from IFS measures for 'all countries'. The data comprise changes in the accounts of the Bank for International Settlements with banks other than central banks and changes in identified cross-border interbank accounts of centrally planned economies (excluding the IMF members).

[f] Consisting of all developing countries except the eight Middle Eastern oil exporters (the Islamic Republic of Iran, Iraq, Kuwait, the Libyan Arab Jamahiriya, Oman, Qatar and the United Arab Emirates) for which external debt statistics are either not available or are small in relation to external assets.

[g] Consisting of all developing countries except the Middle Eastern oil exporters (listed in [f]), Algeria, Indonesia, Nigeria and Venezuela.

[h] As measured by differences in the outstanding assets of developing countries, defined as cross-border interbank accounts by residence of lending banks.

[i] Difference between changes in claims and liabilities.

[j] Calculated as the difference between global measures for cross-border changes in interbank claims and liabilities.

*Source*: As Table 2.2.

The growth in securitization in some relatively less-developed economies is partially due to the emergence of country funds. These are mutual funds that invest in the securities listed on LDC exchanges. Most of them are closed-end and managed by prestigious brokerage firms. The closed-end country funds are traded basically in three international exchanges, namely London, New York and Tokyo. Some country funds were initiated by the International Finance Corporation, others are privately managed. These funds grew remarkably after the stock market crash of October 1987. The funds of Korea, Taiwan, Turkey and Brazil became very popular, especially among US pension investors, in the late 1980s.

Japanese investors have also contributed to the growth and performance of these country mutual funds. The funds have somewhat lost their popularity due to the overall world recession in the early 1990s. Most LDC capital markets have been considerably liberalized, however, and this makes investment in the LDCs much easier. International investors no longer need a mechanism such as that offered by the closed-end, country-specific mutual funds listed outside a developed exchange country in order to enter the developing capital markets. Rather, they can directly invest in the LDC securities.

Increasing preference towards the LDC capital markets has changed the distribution of financial funds across world capital markets. The market value of the securities traded in the so-called emerging capital markets increased in 1992 to over US$500 billion from almost nothing in 1980 (Table 2.1).[1] The share in terms of market capitalizations of LDC equities in the total world market now amounts to 9 per cent. The domination of US equities has gradually decreased in relative terms due to the fast growth in the Japanese securities markets and rapid securitization in the less-developed capital markets. The share of US securities decreased to some 30–35 per cent in 1992 (Table 2.1) from over 60 per cent before 1980 (Ibbotson *et al.*, 1982).

**Further descriptive statistics**

In this section we provide several important statistics about the price, risk and return characteristics of major world capital markets. The statistics computed, using a fairly long data set, will shed light on our understanding of international capital markets. The means, cross-correlation coefficients, variances and auto-correlation coefficients of share price indices in 26 world capital markets are reported.

*Table 2.5: Correlation coefficients of share prices*[a]

| | UK | Germany | France | Netherlands | Belgium | Denmark |
|---|---|---|---|---|---|---|
| Germany | 0.372911 | | | | | |
| France | 0.316738 | 0.362513 | | | | |
| Netherlands | 0.303303 | 0.423391 | 0.282755 | | | |
| Belgium | 0.292644 | 0.376825 | 0.261819 | 0.359381 | | |
| Denmark | 0.402805 | 0.398021 | 0.182763 | 0.300292 | 0.201237 | |
| Italy | 0.209281 | 0.182632 | 0.209181 | 0.123805 | 0.210962 | 0.273615 |
| Spain | 0.272833 | 0.283019 | 0.266616 | 0.265013 | 0.182761 | 0.152831 |
| Switzerland | 0.426338 | 0.530165 | 0.425092 | 0.327707 | 0.299072 | 0.300053 |
| Austria | 0.380921 | 0.356271 | 0.337903 | 0.220321 | 0.263590 | 0.202039 |
| Norway | 0.299834 | 0.270513 | 0.192872 | 0.302736 | 0.255402 | 0.190254 |
| Sweden | 0.393875 | 0.429288 | 0.297206 | 0.333848 | 0.201055 | 0.144077 |
| Ireland | 0.434248 | 0.234893 | 0.323866 | 0.249453 | 0.198003 | 0.240815 |
| Japan | 0.390603 | 0.375052 | 0.369622 | 0.376628 | 0.290919 | 0.339758 |
| Canada | 0.502947 | 0.435573 | 0.403816 | 0.307609 | 0.260712 | 0.278541 |
| Australia | 0.448603 | 0.245901 | 0.276042 | 0.301171 | 0.276000 | 0.243099 |
| USA | 0.590253 | 0.302912 | 0.365205 | 0.382064 | 0.354087 | 0.403761 |
| Finland | 0.329730 | 0.351844 | 0.368072 | 0.187531 | 0.162509 | 0.188002 |
| India | 0.202981 | 0.110413 | 0.130292 | 0.092312 | 0.062917 | 0.057918 |
| N. Zealand | 0.361033 | 0.280083 | 0.283701 | 0.163617 | 0.199922 | 0.209714 |
| Pakistan | 0.207329 | 0.141704 | 0.92855 | 0.079341 | 0.160803 | 0.115056 |
| S. Africa | 0.373509 | 0.299513 | 0.303832 | 0.440981 | 0.258534 | 0.330352 |
| Venezuela | −0.23908 | −0.17265 | −0.07172 | −0.27360 | −0.18732 | −0.39180 |
| Peru | 0.145799 | 0.100093 | 0.005243 | 0.075486 | 0.034725 | 0.096905 |
| Philippines | −0.23159 | −0.30611 | −0.17097 | −0.25536 | −0.39907 | −0.25520 |
| Colombia | 0.124497 | 0.38093 | 0.070854 | 0.179038 | 0.005470 | 0.003284 |

| | Italy | Spain | Switzerland | Austria | Norway | Sweden |
|---|---|---|---|---|---|---|
| Spain | 0.238877 | | | | | |
| Switzerland | 0.267000 | 0.197293 | | | | |
| Austria | 0.230760 | 0.093022 | 0.450011 | | | |
| Norway | 0.182634 | 0.134917 | 0.223398 | 0.186145 | | |
| Sweden | 0.101184 | 0.082773 | 0.440821 | 0.287505 | 0.269020 | |
| Ireland | 0.140802 | 0.209131 | 0.090777 | 0.095640 | 0.108572 | 0.132382 |
| Japan | 0.192681 | 0.155193 | 0.209205 | 0.101615 | 0.120174 | 0.195063 |
| Canada | 0.202013 | 0.038506 | 0.183030 | 0.09277 | 0.170344 | 0.220818 |
| Australia | 0.117506 | 0.082711 | 0.160603 | 0.099028 | 0.120761 | 0.160043 |
| USA | 0.383740 | 0.287903 | 0.525031 | 0.302089 | 0.277272 | 0.390942 |
| Finland | 0.136243 | 0.103066 | 0.140215 | 0.106970 | 0.206959 | 0.328515 |
| India | 0.100625 | 0.004221 | 0.150572 | 0.033073 | 0.093531 | 0.140347 |
| N. Zealand | 0.112580 | 0.068619 | 0.199007 | 0.85211 | 0.096594 | 0.140418 |
| Pakistan | 0.005245 | –0.00314 | 0.021563 | 0.092759 | 0.052478 | 0.102355 |
| S. Africa | 0.127260 | 0.092053 | 0.240336 | 0.141901 | 0.101882 | 0.133729 |
| Venezuela | –0.23084 | 0.090742 | –0.08273 | 0.125271 | –0.00053 | –0.09037 |
| Peru | 0.019237 | –0.00202 | 0.107688 | 0.027829 | 0.092681 | 0.070619 |
| Philippines | –0.06519 | –0.28076 | –0.29610 | –0.09582 | –0.06627 | –0.30738 |
| Colombia | 0.098274 | –0.27051 | 0.091721 | 0.005253 | 0.023879 | 0.118013 |

| | Ireland | Japan | Canada | Australia | USA | Finland |
|---|---|---|---|---|---|---|
| Japan | 0.142803 | | | | | |
| Canada | 0.167219 | 0.190384 | | | | |
| Australia | 0.140715 | 0.256018 | 0.206917 | | | |
| USA | 0.292740 | 0.376102 | 0.597203 | 0.438195 | | |
| Finland | 0.130288 | 0.121192 | 0.086237 | 0.100210 | 0.192039 | |
| India | 0.102834 | 0.158302 | 0.058644 | 0.180552 | 0.130571 | 0.070953 |
| N. Zealand | 0.179031 | 0.220833 | 0.149739 | 0.330298 | 0.283655 | 0.052654 |
| Pakistan | 0.172680 | 0.097373 | 0.167209 | 0.139724 | 0.190504 | 0.020513 |
| S. Africa | 0.160044 | 0.148028 | 0.230255 | 0.258590 | 0.290453 | –0.01408 |
| Venezuela | –0.22799 | –0.00481 | –0.31066 | –0.20894 | 0.075512 | –0.40720 |
| Peru | –0.20917 | 0.105932 | 0.207338 | 0.170235 | 0.149903 | 0.091837 |
| Philippines | –0.25054 | –0.01873 | –0.16614 | –0.33961 | –0.30286 | –0.17409 |
| Colombia | 0.162352 | 0.109381 | 0.119516 | 0.092830 | 0.149207 | 0.005218 |

| | India | N. Zealand | Pakistan | S. Africa | Venezuela | Peru | Philippines |
|---|---|---|---|---|---|---|---|
| N. Zealand | 0.19438 | | | | | | |
| Pakistan | 0.16092 | 0.09276 | | | | | |
| S. Africa | 0.24873 | 0.16044 | 0.18904 | | | | |
| Venezuela | –0.0947 | –0.1840 | –0.3049 | –0.2700 | | | |
| Peru | 0.00625 | 0.00049 | 0.07952 | 0.09333 | 0.13741 | | |
| Philippines | –0.3146 | –0.0375 | –0.0990 | –0.1827 | 0.00279 | –0.4592 | |
| Colombia | 0.02873 | 0.10794 | 0.00022 | 0.00459 | –0.0732 | 0.17503 | –0.088 |

*Note:* The correlation coefficients reported here are computed using the monthly country share price data published by the IMF in its IFS. The period based on which cross correlations are computed is from January 1972 to January 1990 (187 observations).

Table 2.5 reports the cross-correlation coefficients computed using monthly data from January 1972 to January 1990. The cross-correlation coefficient between any two developed markets has been found to be in the range between 0.2 and 0.5. The USA, the UK, Germany, Switzerland, the Netherlands, Japan, Canada and France have considerably high correlation coefficients among themselves and other developed markets, exceeding in many cases 0.4. Developing capital markets, on the other hand, have low correlations to their developed counterparts. Venezuela and the Philippines have consistently negative correlations to the other markets.[2]

Unconditional means, i.e. the average monthly rates of return to national markets that we listed in Table 2.5, are provided in Table 2.6. The rates of return in this table are computed as depreciation or appreciation in monthly share prices for the period January 1972–January 1990. The highest mean returns are observed in Austria, Sweden, Finland, Italy and Denmark. The lowest mean returns among all countries in the table are observed in the Philippines, Venezuela, Germany and Belgium.

Variances and autocorrelations of the monthly excess returns are displayed in Table 2.7. The largest variances are reported in Austria, the UK, France, Norway, Ireland, South Africa, Peru, the Philippines and Colombia. On the other hand, monthly excess returns in Japan, India, Germany, the Netherlands, Switzerland and Pakistan display small volatility. They have the lowest variances in the sample.

*Table 2.6: Summary statistics: computed average monthly rates of return to market indices*[a]

| Market | Average rate of return(%)[b] |
|---|---|
| United Kingdom | 1.0611 |
| Germany | 0.06166 |
| France | 1.1068 |
| Netherlands | 0.07304 |
| Belgium | 0.06582 |
| Denmark | 1.2693 |
| Italy | 1.2821 |
| Spain | 0.06486 |
| Switzerland | 0.03353 |
| Austria | 1.8217 |
| Norway | 0.09109 |
| Sweden | 1.3945 |
| Ireland | 1.0544 |
| Japan | 1.1659 |
| Canada | 0.07236 |
| Australia | 0.08566 |
| United States | 0.05506 |
| Finland | 1.3529 |
| India | 0.07909 |
| New Zealand | 1.1979 |
| Pakistan | 0.07849 |
| South Africa | 1.0703 |
| Venezuela | 0.03314 |
| Peru | 0.07494 |
| Philippines | 0.00934 |
| Colombia | 0.09772 |

*Notes:*

[a] Average monthly rates of return are computed as appreciation or depreciation in country share price indices as published by the International Monetary Fund in its International Financial Statistics. The computation period is from January 1972 to January 1990 (187 observations).

[b] Computed as appreciation or depreciation in national stock market price indices.

*Table 2.7: Summary statistics for country excess returns*

| Market | $\sigma^2(R_i)$ | $\rho_1$ | $\rho_2$ | $\rho_3$ | $\rho_4$ | $\rho_{12}$ | $\rho_{24}$ |
|---|---|---|---|---|---|---|---|
| UK | 0.00515 | 0.06905 | 0.00049 | 0.08533 | 0.03515 | –0.0048 | 0.0480 |
| Germany | 0.00116 | 0.23259 | 0.11095 | 0.17065 | 0.04274 | 0.01118 | 0.1828 |
| France | 0.00676 | –0.1489 | –0.1238 | –0.1455 | –0.0297 | 0.00105 | 0.0658 |
| Netherlands | 0.00146 | 0.30564 | 0.12431 | 0.07309 | –0.0267 | 0.19676 | 0.1655 |
| Belgium | 0.00249 | –0.0268 | 0.00113 | 0.05637 | –0.0103 | 0.17475 | 0.1116 |
| Denmark | 0.00292 | 0.17016 | 0.19093 | 0.21274 | 0.17152 | –0.0733 | –0.012 |
| Italy | 0.00492 | 0.29117 | –0.0092 | 0.07086 | 0.09128 | 0.14930 | 0.0915 |
| Spain | 0.00351 | 0.14728 | 0.08344 | 0.09676 | 0.09313 | 0.01590 | 0.0695 |
| Switzerland | 0.00148 | 0.16698 | –0.0719 | 0.02827 | 0.12047 | 0.10734 | 0.1368 |
| Austria | 0.03840 | –0.0624 | –0.0080 | –0.0008 | 0.00729 | –0.0047 | 0.0004 |
| Norway | 0.00479 | 0.00805 | –0.0036 | 0.14143 | 0.01875 | 0.02787 | 0.0490 |
| Sweden | 0.00258 | 0.14274 | 0.01024 | 0.24441 | 0.12617 | 0.06222 | 0.0554 |
| Ireland | 0.00469 | 0.11979 | 0.04078 | 0.13975 | 0.00515 | –0.1683 | 0.0476 |
| Japan | 0.00108 | 0.34335 | 0.13268 | 0.10681 | –0.0009 | –0.0765 | –0.024 |
| Canada | 0.00322 | –0.0479 | –0.0187 | 0.14735 | –0.0060 | –0.0289 | –0.035 |
| Australia | 0.00255 | 0.25759 | – 0.433 | 0.05996 | 0.08082 | 0.05386 | 0.0031 |
| USA | 0.00255 | 0.25759 | –0.0205 | 0.04909 | 0.10854 | –0.0478 | –0.089 |
| Finland | 0.00482 | –0.1974 | 0.17201 | 0.06800 | 0.07664 | 0.02993 | 0.0711 |
| India | 0.00118 | 0.42032 | 0.03882 | –0.1162 | –0.6755 | –0.0681 | 0.0148 |
| N. Zealand | 0.00159 | 0.45449 | 0.19783 | 0.10735 | 0.05544 | –0.0038 | –0.023 |
| Pakistan | 0.00145 | 0.12543 | 0.09178 | –0.0436 | –0.0451 | –0.0436 | 0.0381 |
| S. Africa | 0.00758 | –0.1329 | –0.9773 | –0.0598 | 0.04809 | –0.0855 | 0.0338 |
| Venezuela | 0.00154 | 0.16256 | 0.23073 | 0.09728 | 0.12334 | 0.14247 | 0.0356 |
| Peru | 0.00482 | 0.00978 | 0.08143 | 0.6353 | –0.0417 | –0.0150 | 0.0823 |
| Philippines | 0.00770 | 0.11535 | 0.01168 | 0.05042 | –0.1008 | 0.08203 | 0.0777 |
| Colombia | 0.00722 | 0.10902 | –0.0695 | –0.0318 | 0.07438 | 0.17046 | 0.1244 |

*Note:* The country excess returns are computed in excess of the short term time deposit rates reported in the IFS.

Most countries in the sample exhibit high positive first-order autocorrelations. High positive autocorrelations of virtually all degrees are reported for the UK, Germany, the Netherlands, Denmark and Italy. Meanwhile, negative autocorrelations of both low and high degrees are observed in Austria, South Africa and France. Negative autocorrelations seen in these three markets may be due to price over-reaction to value changes or transitory price disturbances such as bid–ask spreads and pricing errors.

**Recent growth in financial derivatives and securitization**

World capital markets have grown both in volume and in the variety of instruments traded. The underlying aspect of this growth is that the markets now offer numerous alternatives to suit all tastes. Financial derivatives markets have also become easily usable areas where one can hedge and diversify. Derivatives have also activated the growth in the markets of their underlying instruments. Options, futures, warrants and convertibles have become widespread, especially since the liberalization of financial markets that started in the early 1980s. The underlying factor playing a crucial role in the recent growth of the derivative markets is the increased volatility in asset prices, exchange rates and commodity prices. In Table 2.8 we provide an institutional comparison of world capital markets including the markets for derivatives.

*Table 2.8: World capital markets: an institutional comparison*

| Country | Controls | Price limits | Transaction tax | Official specialist | Automated quotation | Forward trading | Options trading | Futures trading |
|---|---|---|---|---|---|---|---|---|
| Australia | None | No | Yes | No | Yes | No | Yes | Yes |
| Austria | None | Yes | Yes | Yes | No | No | No | No |
| Belgium | None | Yes | Yes | No | No | Yes | No | No |
| Canada | None | No | No | Yes | Yes | No | Yes | Yes |
| Chile | Mild | Yes | Yes | No | No | No | No | No |
| Colombia | Moderate | Yes | Yes | No | No | No | No | No |
| Denmark | None | No | Yes | No | No | No | No | No |
| Finland | None | No | No | No | No | No | No | No |
| France | None | Yes | Yes | Yes | Yes | Yes | Yes | Yes |
| Germany | None | No | Yes | Yes | No | No | Yes | No |
| Hong Kong | None | No | Yes | No | Yes | No | No | Yes |
| India | Moderate | Yes | Yes | No | No | No | No | No |
| Indonesia | Moderate | Yes | Yes | No | No | No | No | No |
| Ireland | Moderate | No | Yes | No | Yes | No | No | No |
| Italy | None | Yes | Yes | No | No | Yes | No | No |
| Japan | Moderate | Yes | Yes | Yes | Yes | No | No | No |
| Korea | Moderate | Yes | Yes | No | Yes | No | No | No |
| Luxembourg | None | No | No | No | No | Yes | No | No |
| Malaysia | Moderate | No | Yes | No | Yes | No | No | No |
| Mexico | Mild | Yes | No | No | No | Yes | No | No |
| N. Zealand | None | No | No | No | No | No | No | Yes |
| Netherlands | None | Yes | Yes | Yes | No | No | Yes | No |
| Norway | None | No | Yes | No | No | No | No | No |
| Pakistan | Moderate | Yes | Yes | No | No | No | No | No |
| Philippines | Moderate | Yes | Yes | No | No | No | No | No |
| Singapore | None | No | Yes | No | Yes | No | No | No |
| South Africa | None | No | Yes | No | Yes | No | Yes | No |
| Spain | Mild | Yes | Yes | No | No | No | No | No |
| Sweden | None | No | Yes | No | Yes | No | Yes | Yes |
| Switzerland | None | Yes | Yes | No | Yes | Yes | Yes | Yes |
| Taiwan | None | Yes | Yes | No | No | No | No | No |

| Country | Controls | Price limits | Transaction tax | Official specialist | Automated quotation | Forward trading | Options trading | Futures trading |
|---|---|---|---|---|---|---|---|---|
| Thailand | Moderate | Yes | Yes | No | No | No | No | No |
| Turkey | Mild | Yes | No | No | No | No | No | No |
| UK | None | No | Yes | No | Yes | No | Yes | Yes |
| USA | None | No | No | Yes | Yes | No | Yes | Yes |

*Sources*: Akdogan (1992a, 1992b); Kim (1993); Roll (1988); *International Financial Statistics* (various issues).

*Futures contracts*

The most actively traded futures contracts on organized exchanges are interest rate futures in the US Treasury bonds, three-month Eurodollar deposits, yen government bonds, French government bonds, German government bonds, and three-month pound-sterling Treasury bills. Currency futures on the Deutschmark, Japanese yen, Swiss franc, pound-sterling are also widely traded all over the world. Futures on stock market indices such as the Standard & Poor's (S&P) 500 index, S&P 100 index and the (Tokyo) Nikkei 225 stock average have also become popular hedging instruments to reduce exposure to risk.

A futures contract is a legally binding agreement. Unlike forward contracts, futures are traded in organized exchanges such as the Chicago Board of Trade (CBOT) and the Chicago Mercantile Exchange (CME); that is, futures are publicly available. Commodity futures originated at the CBOT in the 1860s. Until 1972 no exchange permitted financial futures trading. In that year, CME first introduced financial futures contracts; many followed later. In the early 1980s derivative exchanges developed futures (also options) contracts on equity indexes. The volume in index futures, as well as financial futures volumes in general, grew steadily during the 1980s. This growth has gained a new momentum in the 1990s.

Futures contracts are fairly standard and homogeneous in quantity, quality, location and delivery time. They are enforceable and include procedures to cover default by either party. Futures are usually offset before they mature; indeed, few futures contracts ever mature (forwards always end in actual spot delivery). Futures are usually used by hedgers and speculators; the environment of these contracts is fairly liquid. Entries and exits are easy. Futures contracts require margin deposits and have brokerage fees, forwards do not have margin requirements. They may have certain legal fees, yet they seldom involve third parties.

In all futures markets, clearing houses exist and their performance is extremely important for the functioning of the markets. Clearing houses clear the positions of long and short traders operating in futures markets, hence they always have zero net position. When prices rise, appropriate transfers are made from the short traders' accounts to the relevant accounts of the long position holders, or vice versa. The clearing houses basically perform the following duties:

(a) matching and reconciliation of all futures transactions;
(b) assuring the financial integrity of transactions;
(c) providing the mechanism for delivery;
(d) performing a banking function by settling monetary differences.

*Trading in futures contracts* In the United States, where futures are traded heavily, all public hedgers and speculators are required to have an account with a Futures Commission Merchant (FCM). A FCM is a certified firm or person soliciting outside orders and registered with the Commodity Futures Trading Commission (CFTC) and/or the National Futures Association (NFA). With each and every new trade, traders must deposit money called initial margin with their account executives. This margin serves as a security deposit. The margin for a public trader in the US is about 10 per cent of the contract's entire value. After depositing the initial margin, traders must always maintain a minimum amount, called the maintenance margin level. This margin varies among contracts. It is roughly between the three-fourths and four-fifths of initial margin.

Let us explain a typical trading in a futures market with the help of an example. Let two traders enter the financial futures markets, one long and the other short a 5000 unit (share) contract at $3.00 per share. Let the initial margin be $2000. Suppose that the price increases. If the (daily) settlement price of the instrument rises, as shown in Table 2.9, money is added to the long trader's account and taken out of the short position holder's account.

*Table 2.9: The flow of money between traders' accounts ($)*

| | | Trader A (Long) | | Trader B (Short) | |
|---|---|---|---|---|---|
| Day | Price | Cumulat. profits | Equity in account | Cumulat. profits | Equity in account |
| 1 | 3.00 | 000 | 2000 | 000 | 2000 |
| 2 | 3.02 | +100 | 2100 | –100 | 1900 |
| 3 | 3.03 | +150 | 2150 | –150 | 1850 |
| 4 | 2.97 | –200 | 1800 | +200 | 2200 |

Apparently, money flows from the short to the long. Note that the long is better off when prices rise. As prices keep rising proper transfers are made between accounts, as given in Table 2.9. Now assume that on day 4 the price suddenly falls $0.07, and the clearing house transfers $350 from the account of the long trader to the account of the short. All the relevant changes in accounts and cumulative profits are shown in Table 2.9.

*Margin call* Follow the same set-up in this example but consider now the following price changes. At the beginning a trader buys a 5000 share contract at $3.00 per share, as previously. Let the maintenance margin level now be $1750.

*Table 2.10: Margin call ($)*

| Day | Price | Profits | Capital | Equity |
|---|---|---|---|---|
| 1 | 3.00 | 000 | 2000 | 2000 |
| 2 | 3.01 | +50 | 2000 | 2050 |
| 3 | 2.98 | –100 | 2000 | 1900 |
| 4 | 2.93 | –350 | 2000 | 1650 |
| Margin call | | –350 | 2350 | 2000 |

Suppose in the second trading day that the settlement price for the relevant futures is $3.01 (see Table 2.10). The long trader makes $50, bringing the equity position up to $2050. Now assume that the price drops $0.03 to $2.98. The equity position of our trader has become $1900. The next day we observe a further drop of $0.05 in the futures price. The new price is $2.93. This brings the equity position down to $1650. The account executive makes a *margin call*. The customer who wants to maintain the market position must deposit $350, and not $100. The initial margin level must be restored. This case is outlined in Table 2.10.

*Capital withdrawal* The price is $3.00 in the first trading, as in the previous examples, and the initial margin level is $2000. Now suppose that the settlement price jumps from $3.00 to $3.10 (see Table 2.11). The customer's equity position increases in value to $2500. Here, the customer has the right, but not the obligation, to withdraw the surplus of $500. The *capital withdrawal* example is shown in Table 2.11.

*Table: 2.11: Capital withdrawal ($)*

| Day | Price | Profits | Capital | Equity |
|---|---|---|---|---|
| 1 | 3.00 | 000 | 2000 | 2000 |
| 2 | 3.10 | +500 | 2000 | 2500 |
| Capital withdrawal | | +500 | 1500 | 2000 |

*Options contracts*

As with the futures contracts, the most widely used options contracts are those with several key interest rates, convertible currency values and stock market indices. Options contracts which give the right but not the obligation to buy (call option) or sell (put option) the underlying instrument at the pre-specified price (exercise price) before the contract expires have become fairly popular among hedgers in international speculative markets because of the flexibility they provide. The largest US futures and options exchanges are the Chicago Board of Trade (CBOT), the Chicago Mercantile Exchange (CME) and the Chicago Board of Options Exchange (CBOE). The major European derivative exchanges are the London International Financial Futures Exchange (LIFFE), and *Marché à Terme d'Instruments Financiers* (MATIF) in Paris. The Japanese futures and options exchanges include the Osaka Securities Exchange (OSE), the Tokyo International Financial Futures Exchange (TIFFE) and the Tokyo Stock Exchange (TSE).

Many new futures and options exchanges, such as Deutsche Terminbörse (in Germany) and the Belgian Futures and Options Exchange (in Belgium), started operating in the late 1980s and early 1990s. On the other hand, in response to increased competition among derivatives exchanges and the rapid growth in the over-the-counter market for options and futures contracts, a number of established exchanges moved to consolidate operations in 1991. The Chicago Board of Trade and the Chicago Mercantile Exchange are in the process of merging their trading and clearing operations and facilities to end duplication and to lower trading costs. The London International Financial Futures Exchange and the London Traded Options Market (LTOM) merged completely in March 1992 to form the London Derivatives Exchange (LDE). Similarly, the European Options Exchange (EOE) and the Stockholm Options Market (SOM) have plans to co-operate on trading and clearing networks.

*Swaps markets*

Swaps markets have grown remarkably in the last decade. A swaps agreement simply covers the exchange of two different debt obligations or two different currencies. In particular, international banks operate in swaps markets. They are much less organized than options or futures markets. Swaps are custom-tailored to meet the fairly specific needs of the parties. This flexibility allows the counterparties to deal with much longer horizons than can be addressed by exchange-traded instruments, stocks or all derivatives. Only the counterparties in swaps know that the swap has taken place. In a futures pit, on the contrary, traders will be able to discern the activity of particular firms.

There are a number of problems with swaps transactions. First, it is usually hard to find the counterparty to meet particular needs. Second, maturities and cash flows in swaps transactions are difficult elements to agree on. Third, swaps cannot be altered or terminated without the agreement of the parties. Fourth, swaps markets have no guarantors. The most common swaps practices are on interest rates and foreign currency.

*Interest rate swaps* A plain vanilla interest rate swap requires two parties who have different expectations about interest rates. If party A has an initial position in a fixed-rate debt instrument and counterparty B has an initial position in a floating rate obligation, when they wish to swap their positions they must agree on (a) maturity and (b) principal. Assume that the swap covers a four-year period and that it involves annual payments on a $100 thousand principal amount. Party A agrees to pay a fixed rate of 12 per cent to counterparty B. In return, party B agrees to pay a floating rate of LIBOR + 3 per cent to party A. Here, party A pays $12000 each year to party B. Party B in return pays an amount that varies as LIBOR varies. One important aspect of interest rate swaps is that payment times (i.e. a specific date) is set with initial agreement between the two parties. What counts is the LIBOR at the time of each payment.

*Currency swaps* In a plain vanilla currency swap, one party holds a currency and wishes to swap it with another currency. There may be several reasons for wishing to swap currencies. One is a simple commercial one: a party may be willing to swap one currency for another just because it needs one more than the other. A second likely reason is hedging. In interest rate swaps there is actually one type of cash flow taking place between the parties. In currency swaps, however, three different sets of cash flow actually take place. First, there is the initial cash flow based on the current exchange rate between any two currencies. Second, annual interest payments take place during the life of the swap. Finally, repayment of the principal amount takes place when the swap agreement matures. A currency swap is much like depositing different currencies simultaneously.

As an example, assume that party A holds Deutschmarks and desires to exchange them with US dollars. Similarly, party B holds US dollars and wishes to swap them for Deutschmarks.

Assume that the current spot exchange rate is DM2 per dollar. Hence, the mark is worth $0.5. Further, let the US interest rate be 5 per cent and the German interest rate 4 per cent. Party A holds DM20 million and desires to exchange them for dollars. Party B in return would pay $10 million to Party A at the initiation of the swap. If the term of the swap is seven years and the parties agree to make annual interest payments, party B will then pay 4 per cent interest on the DM20 million that it has received from A. This amounts, in our example, to DM800 thousand. Party A, on the other hand, will pay to B an amount based on the dollar interest rate in the US. In our example, this is $500 thousand. In actual practice the parties will make only the net payments. As (a) the interest rate and (b) the exchange rate vary in either country, eventually the annual payments will change. At the end of the seven years the parties will once again exchange the principals.

**The emerging financial system and banking**

As a natural result of the developments summarized above, the 1980s opened another era for international finance and investments. The industry became fairly competitive, and in the 1990s the process gathered momentum. The growth in the 1980s was gradual. The implementation of the Single European Act and later the 1988 Liberalization Act in the European Union did foster the evolution of international investments, along with a desire for a compatible world financial system; yet the Community's Single Market in financial services has been institutionally completed in the 1990s. Not only does the EU need a new financial system but also the entire world realizes that domestic financial systems must be dismantled or radically reorganized.

What is this emerging financial system that everyone has to get ready for? One distinct feature of the emerging environment is its disintermediation from the existing banking systems into securitized money and capital markets all over the world. More importantly, this disintermediation is driven by competition that no other market has seen previously. The markets in the financial environment have answers to all questions, ranging from liquidity to growth.

International risk management today can be conducted using relatively confidently futures, options and the other derivatives available in many organized exchanges. Commercial papers and repurchase agreements have recently become the immediate financing instruments of choice. Money market mutual funds are now efficient ways of taking out the deposit liabilities of the commercial banking system. Furthermore, ownership rights, financial claims and state-contingent obligations are rapidly taking the form of liquid assets. Banks in this new environment of securitization have much less space to play in.[3]

With the possible exception of Germany, virtually all industrialized countries have been exposed to intensive securitization, and it is fairly advanced in the United States, the United Kingdom, France and, to a lesser extent, Japan. Traditional balance sheet transactions have declined relative to off-balance-sheet activities. This has also led to cost-cutting and consolidation in the banking sector. Interest rate and foreign exchange contracts, including options and futures, have grown rapidly, as mentioned previously. Banks are currently acting as counterparties to over $3 billion in currency and interest rate swaps. Financial derivative business has become a major source of fee income for international banking institutions. Similarly, numerous bank-led financial conglomerates have started to use their branch networks to move into financially sophisticated new service areas including insurance.

*Table 2.12: Indicators of the relative importance of banks in the financial activities of corporations and households in Germany, Japan and the United States (%)*

| | Bank deposits as a proportion of corporate financial assets | Bank deposits as a proportion of household financial assets | Bank loans as a proportion of corporate liabilities |
|---|---|---|---|
| Germany | | | |
| 1980 | 57.7 | 60.5 | 63.1 |
| 1985 | 51.1 | 54.5 | 60.9 |
| 1990 | 43.8 | 48.9 | 61.3 |
| Japan | | | |
| 1980 | 78.9 | 64.4 | 67.4 |
| 1985 | 77.8 | 58.5 | 67.4 |
| 1990 | 46.5 | 53.2 | 58.8 |
| United States | | | |
| 1980 | 17.8 | 23.1 | 33.0 |
| 1985 | 21.5 | 23.4 | 29.2 |
| 1990 | 18.8 | 21.3 | 25.4 |

*Source*: International Monetary Fund, *International Capital Markets: Developments, Prospects, and Policy Issues*, Washington, D.C.: IMF, 1992.

The declining relative importance of banking business in the three largest economies is readily seen from their aggregate portfolios, reported in Table 2.12. The share of business and household financial assets held in the form of bank deposits declined substantially in the 1980s in Japan and Germany. Simultaneously, bank loans as a proportion of corporate liabilities also declined in these countries.

Germany is still far behind the other industrialized countries in securitization. A couple of large universal banks continue to dominate the financial system there. Private securities exchanges in Germany remain illiquid and fragmented. Large German banks have very close ties to the corporate sector of the economy; many have sizeable equity stakes in corporations. Moreover, quite a few of these universal banks operating in Germany have working links with large companies via their membership on corporate boards. The German stock market is fragmented among eight local exchanges. Over 30 per cent of the turnover of German stocks takes place in London; indeed, the UK stock market is almost three times as large as the German one (see Table 2.1). Although the German government bond market is large, instruments such as commercial paper, futures and options are new to Germany. Until 1991 there was no commercial paper programme in the country. The first interest rate futures contract on a German government obligation was placed in Frankfurt only in late 1990.

There lies the problem of differences in financial structure. The German system, or in general the financial system in continental Europe, is different from that in the United States. On the one hand, German banks enjoy the benefits of exercising fairly strict quality control of which potential local and international borrowers may obtain access to the direct Deutschmark debt markets.[4] On the other hand, the US, and to some extent the UK, system offers the alternative of securitization and a lesser role for the banking system. Each has its own strengths and shortcomings. The evidence indicates that the continental European money and capital markets are moving towards a liquid and disintermediated financial structure, although there remains some role for traditional banking practices.

Which structure is likely to prevail is still an open question. Germany plays a dominant role in European integration, hence the continental view of banking will probably remain in place with some modification in terms of liquidity and intermediation. However, the US and UK markets are among the largest in the world and their existence cannot be ignored. The future of financial integration in the European Union will have answers to some of the questions raised here. As a matter of fact, some form of institutional harmonization must take place not only within the Union but also between the Union and the North America, the Pacific Rim and the rest of the world. The next chapter will address European financial integration from an institutional perspective and try to pinpoint the issues concerning the new financial structure discussed here.

## Notes

1. The phrase 'emerging capital markets' is used by the International Finance Corporation in its classification of the LDC capital markets. Although the IFC does not specify what is meant by 'emerging', the classification implies those LDC capital markets that have either removed or eased the barriers against foreign investors over their exchanges. Some of these markets, such as Korea, Taiwan, Mexico, and Brazil, are fairly large, even larger than many European exchanges. Some are small, such as Jordan and Chile. The IFC closely monitors developments in these markets. The Corporation has a comprehensive 'emerging market data base' and publishes regularly their price, return and risk characteristics.
2. In an appendix to this chapter, we provide (time series) graphs of percentage movements in (monthly) share price indices in 26 countries.
3. Even the conventional credit-rating function of the banks has been increasingly performed by internationally recognized financial service firms such as Moody's and Standard & Poor's.
4. The German banking system plays an important role in the allocation of financial funds, especially in domestic debt markets. The corporate sector in Germany has over the years applied for credits (liquidity) to their 'house bank'. Likewise, when they have accumulated liquidity they deposit it there (IMF, 1992).

## Appendix

In this appendix we supply statistical tables and graphs monitoring the behaviour of country share price indices. The share price indices used here are taken from *International Financial Statistics*. The computation period is January 1972–December 1986. All computations are based on percentage movements in price indices. Percentage movements are computed as first differences in logarithms of levels. That is,

$$R_{i,t} = \log P_{i,t} - \log P_{i,t-1} \qquad \text{(A2.1)}$$

where $i$ is country index, $t$ is time index, $P$ is the share price index, and $R_{i,t}$ is the rate of return on (percentage movement in) the price index of country $i$ at time $t$.

*Appendix A2.1: Basic statistics*

*Table A2.1.1 Autocorrelation coefficients of percentage movements in country share price indices (January 1972–December 1986)*

| Country | $\rho_{t-1}$ | $\rho_{t-2}$ | $\rho_{t-3}$ | $\rho_{t-4}$ |
|---|---|---|---|---|
| UK | 0.339 | 0.096 | 0.128 | 0.260 |
| Germany | 0.206 | 0.126 | 0.184 | 0.060 |
| France | 0.059 | –0.124 | –0.037 | 0.132 |
| Netherlands | 0.266 | 0.113 | 0.112 | 0.058 |
| Belgium | –0.044 | 0.060 | 0.054 | 0.015 |
| Denmark | 0.161 | 0.214 | 0.212 | 0.161 |
| Italy | 0.289 | –0.007 | 0.089 | 0.119 |
| Spain | 0.156 | 0.105 | 0.106 | 0.124 |
| Switzerland | 0.185 | –0.080 | 0.037 | 0.255 |
| Austria | 0.205 | 0.172 | 0.247 | 0.118 |
| Norway | 0.105 | 0.010 | 0.174 | 0.022 |
| Sweden | 0.161 | 0.031 | 0.229 | 0.135 |
| Ireland | 0.077 | 0.075 | 0.180 | 0.135 |
| Japan | 0.421 | 0.313 | 0.211 | 0.224 |
| Canada | –0.052 | 0.003 | 0.144 | 0.038 |
| Australia | 0.264 | –0.046 | 0.047 | 0.085 |
| USA | 0.407 | 0.056 | –0.083 | –0.049 |
| Finland | 0.370 | 0.119 | 0.116 | 0.078 |
| India | 0.444 | 0.208 | 0.137 | 0.133 |
| New Zealand | 0.143 | 0.040 | –0.077 | –0.033 |
| Pakistan | 0.296 | 0.006 | 0.025 | –0.070 |
| South Africa | 0.215 | 0.003 | 0.025 | 0.112 |
| Venezuela | 0.180 | 0.214 | 0.128 | 0.138 |
| Peru | 0.010 | 0.077 | 0.070 | –0.046 |
| Philippines | 0.094 | –0.062 | 0.025 | –0.016 |
| Colombia | 0.228 | 0.046 | 0.163 | 0.082 |

*Table A2.1.2* *Cross-correlation coefficients of percentage movements in country share price indices (period: January 1972–December 1986 monthly)*

| | UK | Germany | France | Netherlands | Belgium | Denmark | Italy | Spain | Switzerland | Austria | Norway | Sweden |
|---|---|---|---|---|---|---|---|---|---|---|---|---|
| UK | 1.000 | 0.355 | 0.142 | 0.441 | 0.397 | 0.161 | 0.218 | 0.108 | 0.390 | 0.047 | 0.198 | 0.142 |
| Germany | 0.355 | 1.000 | 0.174 | 0.659 | 0.334 | 0.183 | 0.195 | 0.272 | 0.484 | –0.030 | 0.130 | 0.119 |
| France | 0.142 | 0.174 | 1.000 | 0.272 | 0.294 | 0.180 | 0.146 | 0.156 | 0.271 | 0.000 | 0.171 | 0.199 |
| Netherlands | 0.441 | 0.659 | 0.272 | 1.000 | 0.456 | 0.239 | 0.296 | 0.280 | 0.563 | 0.046 | 0.320 | 0.265 |
| Belgium | 0.397 | 0.334 | 0.294 | 0.456 | 1.000 | –0.028 | 0.377 | 0.166 | 0.458 | 0.042 | 0.373 | 0.078 |
| Denmark | 0.161 | 0.183 | 0.180 | 0.239 | –0.028 | 1.000 | 0.117 | 0.128 | 0.193 | 0.004 | 0.118 | 0.264 |
| Italy | 0.218 | 0.195 | 0.146 | 0.296 | 0.377 | 0.117 | 1.000 | 0.270 | 0.289 | –0.018 | 0.222 | 0.211 |
| Spain | 0.108 | 0.272 | 0.156 | 0.280 | 0.166 | 0.128 | 0.270 | 1.000 | 0.148 | –0.045 | 0.088 | 0.252 |
| Switzerland | 0.390 | 0.484 | 0.271 | 0.563 | 0.458 | 0.193 | 0.289 | 0.148 | 1.000 | 0.068 | 0.358 | 0.205 |
| Austria | 0.047 | –0.030 | 0.000 | 0.046 | 0.042 | 0.004 | –0.018 | –0.045 | 0.068 | 1.000 | 0.143 | 0.042 |
| Norway | 0.198 | 0.130 | 0.171 | 0.320 | 0.373 | 0.118 | 0.222 | 0.088 | 0.356 | 0.143 | 1.000 | 0.148 |
| Sweden | 0.142 | 0.119 | 0.199 | 0.265 | 0.078 | 0.264 | 0.211 | 0.252 | 0.205 | 0.042 | 0.148 | 1.000 |
| Ireland | 0.289 | 0.231 | 0.031 | 0.304 | 0.292 | 0.056 | 0.261 | 0.154 | 0.247 | –0.019 | 0.127 | 0.038 |
| Finland | 0.035 | 0.084 | 0.193 | 0.255 | 0.204 | –0.009 | 0.090 | 0.077 | 0.191 | –0.007 | 0.106 | 0.159 |
| Canada | 0.230 | 0.181 | 0.371 | 0.292 | 0.127 | 0.153 | 0.200 | 0.070 | 0.395 | –0.037 | 0.272 | 0.280 |
| Australia | 0.310 | 0.336 | 0.207 | 0.416 | 0.358 | 0.162 | 0.339 | 0.108 | 0.449 | –0.013 | 0.301 | 0.176 |
| India | 0.104 | 0.109 | 0.016 | 0.166 | –0.033 | 0.060 | 0.157 | 0.083 | 0.161 | 0.029 | 0.045 | –0.038 |
| Japan | 0.308 | 0.343 | 0.156 | 0.502 | 0.324 | 0.314 | 0.230 | 0.219 | 0.332 | –0.070 | 0.133 | 0.168 |
| N. Zealand | 0.213 | 0.240 | 0.151 | 0.425 | 0.257 | 0.211 | 0.398 | 0.219 | 0.200 | –0.028 | 0.174 | 0.174 |
| Pakistan | 0.096 | –0.005 | 0.094 | 0.025 | 0.032 | 0.140 | 0.048 | 0.054 | 0.041 | 0.001 | –0.000 | 0.073 |
| S. Africa | 0.120 | 0.138 | 0.152 | 0.131 | 0.155 | 0.039 | 0.110 | 0.018 | 0.040 | –0.010 | 0.035 | 0.078 |
| USA | 0.396 | 0.351 | 0.277 | 0.532 | 0.382 | 0.173 | 0.292 | 0.201 | 0.507 | 0.013 | 0.307 | 0.267 |
| Venezuela | 0.049 | 0.032 | –0.065 | 0.083 | –0.035 | 0.073 | 0.099 | 0.155 | 0.072 | 0.040 | 0.039 | 0.054 |
| Peru | –0.006 | –0.129 | 0.092 | –0.079 | 0.019 | 0.053 | 0.120 | –0.015 | –0.068 | –0.046 | –0.021 | –0.077 |
| Philippines | 0.115 | 0.213 | 0.126 | 0.255 | 0.262 | –0.019 | 0.178 | 0.254 | 0.113 | –0.059 | 0.217 | 0.094 |
| Colombia | –0.070 | 0.039 | –0.001 | 0.058 | –0.031 | 0.079 | 0.019 | 0.044 | 0.016 | –0.026 | 0.001 | 0.216 |

| Ireland | Finland | Canada | Australia | India | Japan | N. Zealand | Pakistan | S. Africa | USA | Venezuela | Peru | Philippines | Colombia |
|---|---|---|---|---|---|---|---|---|---|---|---|---|---|
| 0.289 | 0.035 | 0.230 | 0.310 | 0.104 | 0.308 | 0.213 | 0.098 | 0.120 | 0.396 | 0.049 | –0.006 | 0.115 | –0.070 |
| 0.231 | 0.084 | 0.181 | 0.336 | 0.109 | 0.343 | 0.240 | –0.005 | 0.138 | 0.351 | 0.032 | –0.129 | 0.213 | 0.039 |
| 0.031 | 0.193 | 0.371 | 0.207 | 0.016 | 0.156 | 0.151 | 0.094 | 0.152 | 0.277 | –0.065 | 0.092 | 0.126 | –0.001 |
| 0.304 | 0.255 | 0.292 | 0.416 | 0.166 | 0.502 | 0.425 | 0.025 | 0.131 | 0.532 | 0.083 | –0.079 | 0.255 | 0.058 |
| 0.292 | 0.204 | 0.127 | 0.358 | –0.033 | 0.324 | 0.257 | 0.032 | 0.155 | 0.382 | –0.035 | 0.019 | 0.262 | –0.031 |
| 0.056 | –0.009 | 0.153 | 0.162 | 0.060 | 0.314 | 0.211 | 0.140 | 0.039 | 0.173 | 0.073 | 0.053 | –0.019 | 0.079 |
| 0.261 | 0.090 | 0.200 | 0.339 | 0.157 | 0.230 | 0.398 | 0.048 | 0.110 | 0.292 | 0.099 | 0.120 | 0.178 | 0.019 |
| 0.154 | 0.077 | 0.070 | 0.108 | 0.083 | 0.219 | 0.219 | 0.054 | 0.018 | 0.201 | 0.155 | –0.015 | 0.254 | 0.044 |
| 0.247 | 0.191 | 0.395 | 0.449 | 0.161 | 0.332 | 0.200 | 0.041 | 0.040 | 0.507 | 0.072 | –0.068 | 0.113 | 0.016 |
| –0.019 | –0.007 | –0.037 | –0.013 | 0.029 | –0.070 | –0.028 | 0.001 | –0.010 | 0.013 | 0.040 | –0.046 | –0.059 | –0.026 |
| 0.127 | 0.106 | 0.272 | 0.301 | 0.045 | 0.133 | 0.174 | –0.000 | 0.035 | 0.307 | 0.039 | –0.021 | 0.217 | –0.001 |
| 0.038 | 0.159 | 0.280 | 0.176 | –0.038 | 0.168 | 0.174 | 0.073 | 0.078 | 0.267 | 0.054 | –0.077 | 0.094 | 0.216 |
| 1.000 | 0.130 | 0.077 | 0.249 | 0.019 | 0.319 | 0.404 | 0.054 | 0.070 | 0.258 | 0.073 | –0.003 | 0.176 | –0.024 |
| 0.130 | 1.000 | 0.120 | –0.069 | –0.003 | 0.044 | 0.167 | –0.019 | –0.010 | 0.091 | 0.018 | 0.001 | 0.068 | 0.002 |
| 0.077 | 0.120 | 1.000 | 0.371 | 0.104 | 0.208 | 0.082 | –0.015 | 0.157 | 0.538 | –0.018 | 0.120 | 0.025 | 0.020 |
| 0.249 | –0.069 | 0.371 | 1.000 | 0.144 | 0.412 | 0.350 | 0.005 | 0.334 | 0.585 | 0.153 | 0.051 | 0.190 | 0.058 |
| 0.019 | –0.003 | 0.104 | 0.144 | 1.000 | 0.096 | 0.196 | 0.049 | 0.055 | 0.153 | 0.024 | –0.023 | 0.090 | 0.078 |
| 0.319 | 0.044 | 0.208 | 0.412 | 0.096 | 1.000 | 0.376 | –0.064 | 0.187 | 0.406 | 0.124 | 0.046 | 0.167 | –0.015 |
| 0.404 | 0.167 | 0.082 | 0.350 | 0.196 | 0.376 | 1.000 | 0.016 | 0.119 | 0.236 | 0.098 | –0.028 | 0.210 | –0.010 |
| 0.054 | –0.019 | –0.015 | 0.005 | 0.049 | 0.064 | 0.016 | 1.000 | 0.085 | 0.046 | 0.013 | 0.034 | 0.071 | –0.031 |
| 0.070 | –0.010 | 0.157 | 0.334 | 0.055 | 0.187 | 0.119 | 0.085 | 1.000 | 0.203 | 0.073 | –0.040 | 0.135 | 0.009 |
| 0.258 | 0.091 | 0.538 | 0.585 | 0.153 | 0.406 | 0.236 | 0.046 | 0.203 | 1.000 | 0.112 | 0.077 | 0.187 | 0.071 |
| 0.073 | 0.018 | –0.018 | 0.153 | 0.024 | 0.124 | 0.098 | 0.013 | 0.073 | 0.112 | 1.000 | –0.141 | 0.167 | –0.084 |
| –0.003 | 0.001 | 0.120 | 0.051 | –0.023 | 0.046 | –0.028 | 0.034 | –0.040 | 0.077 | –0.141 | 1.000 | –0.029 | –0.076 |
| 0.176 | 0.068 | 0.025 | 0.190 | 0.090 | 0.167 | 0.210 | 0.071 | 0.135 | 0.187 | 0.167 | –0.029 | 1.000 | 0.058 |
| –0.024 | 0.002 | 0.020 | 0.058 | 0.078 | –0.015 | –0.010 | –0.031 | 0.009 | 0.071 | –0.084 | –0.076 | 0.058 | 1.000 |

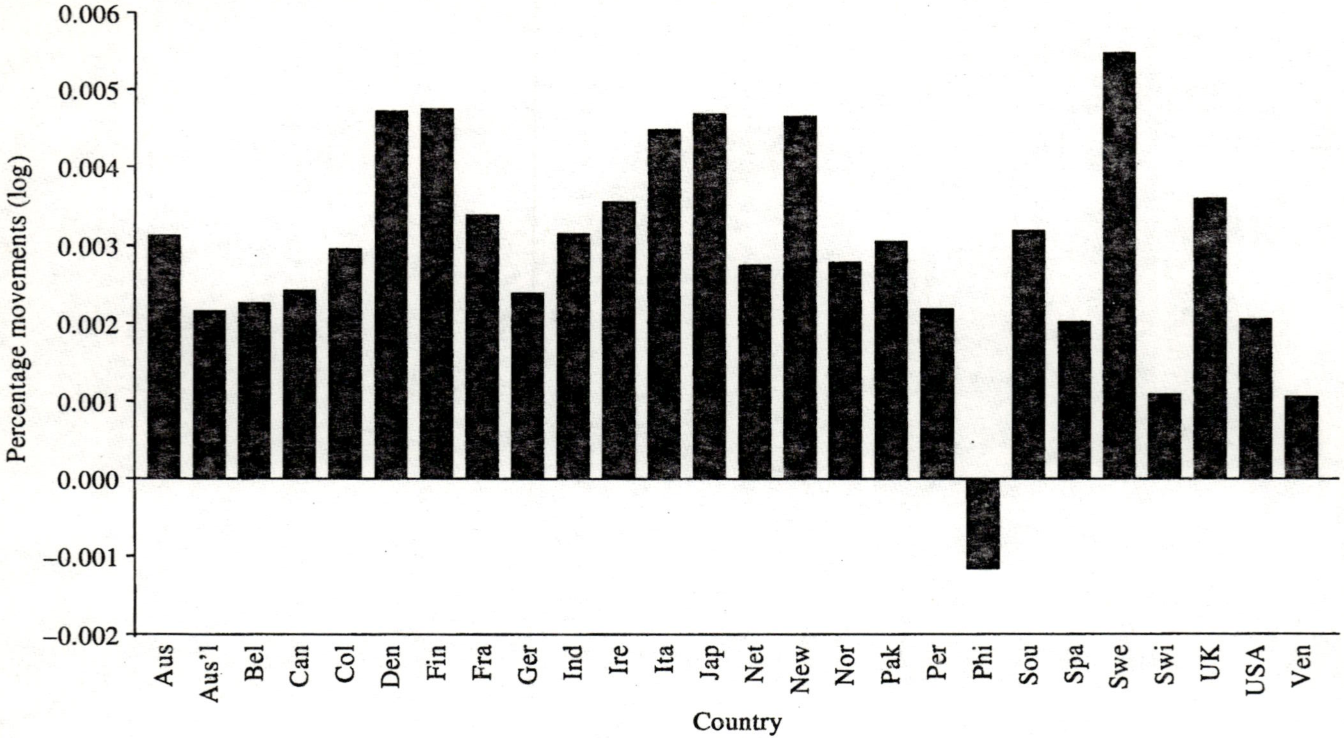


*Figure A2.1.1 Average percentage movements in share prices*

*Appendix A2.2: Time series behaviour of percentage movements in country share price indices*

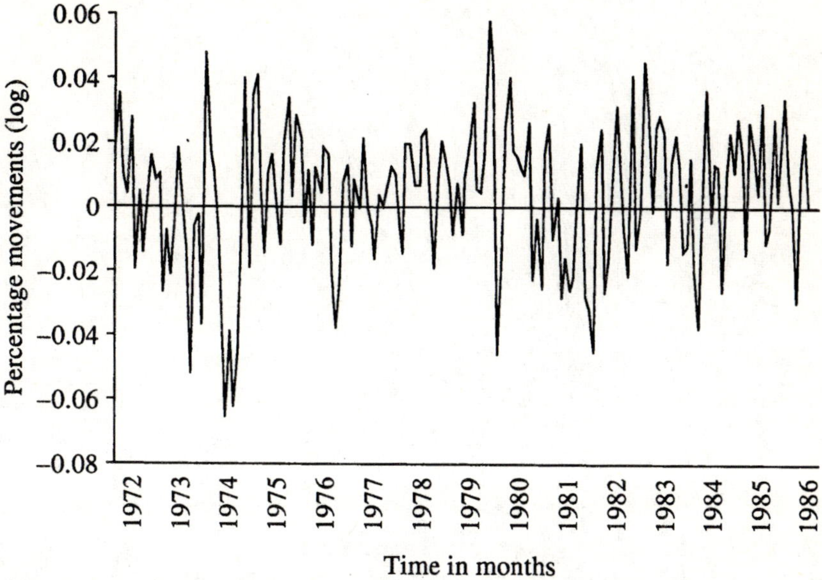


*Figure A2.2.1 Percentage movements in share price index: Australia*

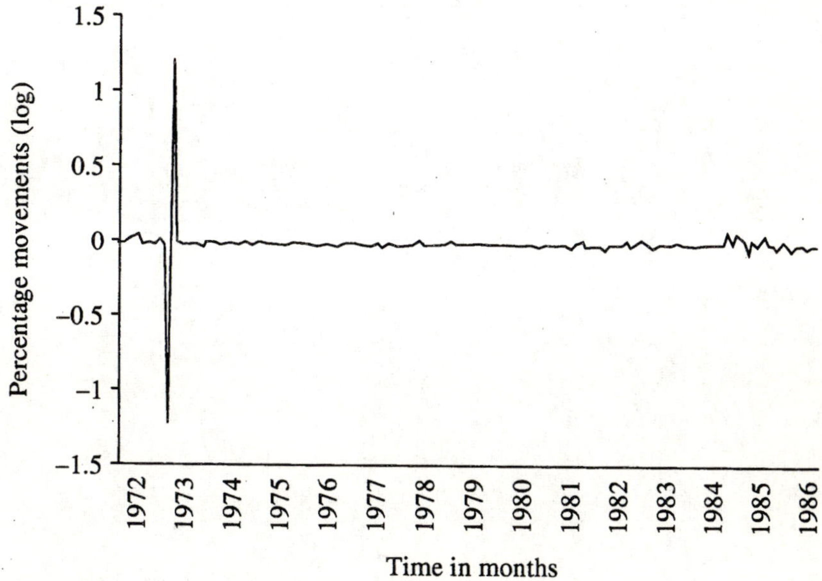


*Figure A2.2.2 Percentage movements in share price index: Austria*

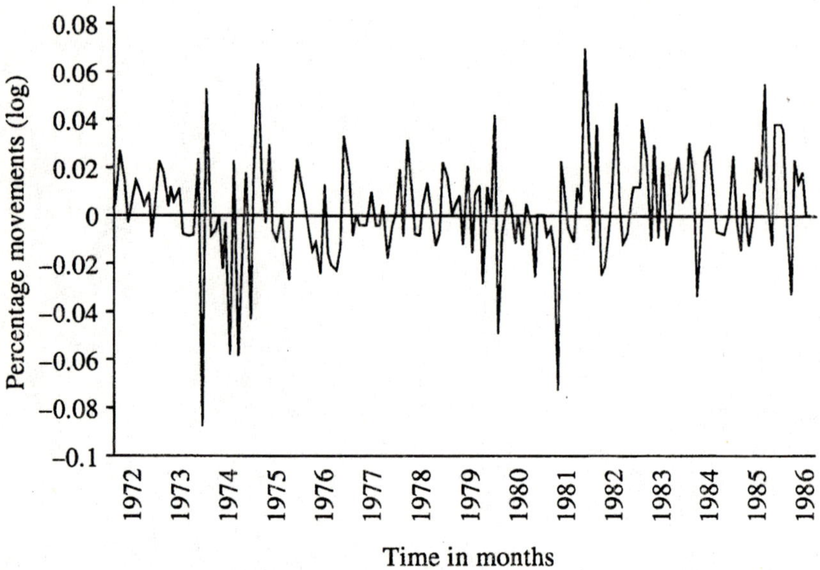


*Figure A2.2.3 Percentage movements in share price index: Belgium*

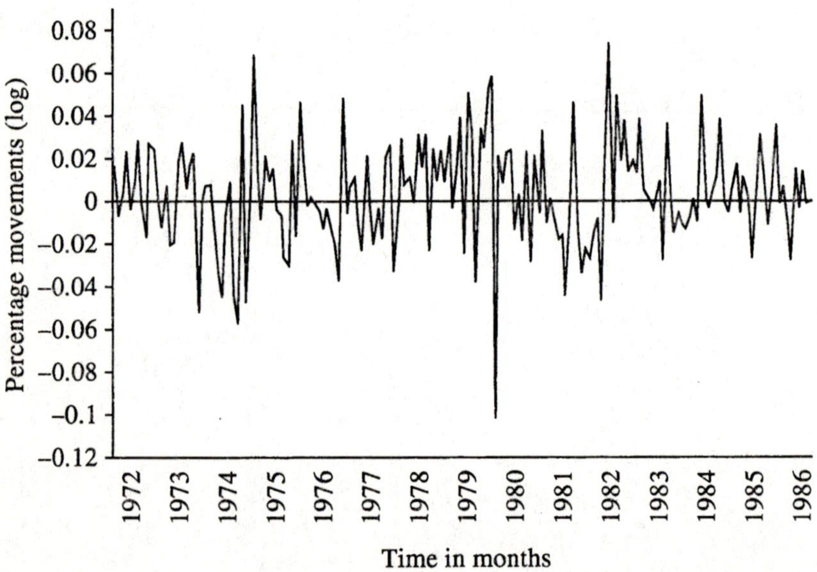


*Figure A2.2.4 Percentage movements in share price index: Canada*

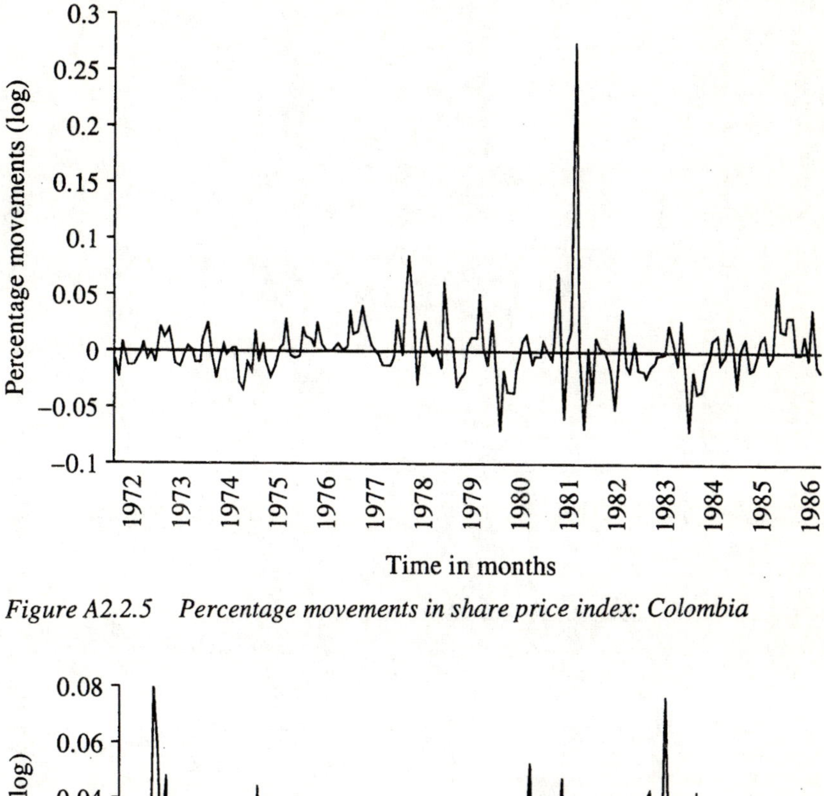


*Figure A2.2.5 Percentage movements in share price index: Colombia*

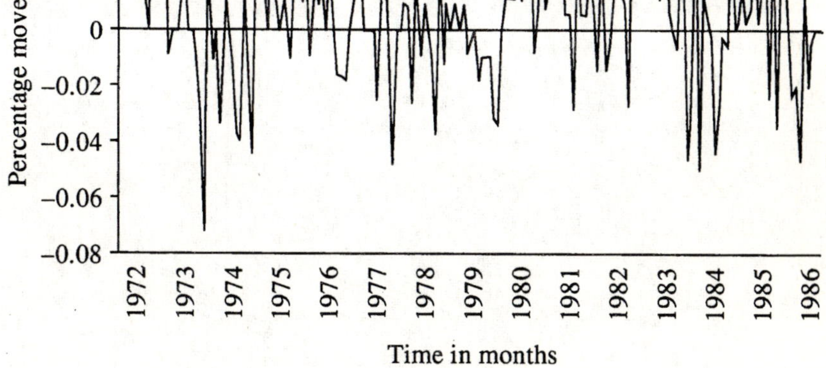


*Figure A2.2.6 Percentage movements in share price index: Denmark*

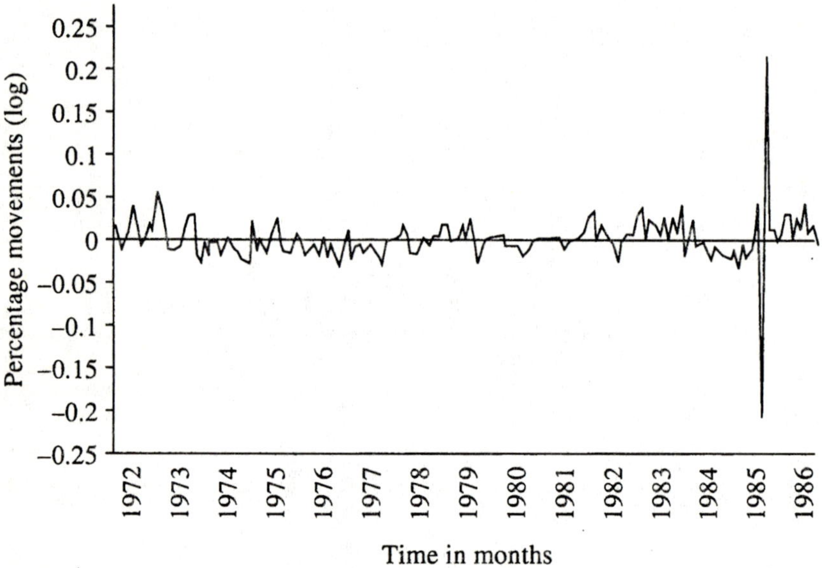


*Figure A2.2.7 Percentage movements in share price index: Finland*

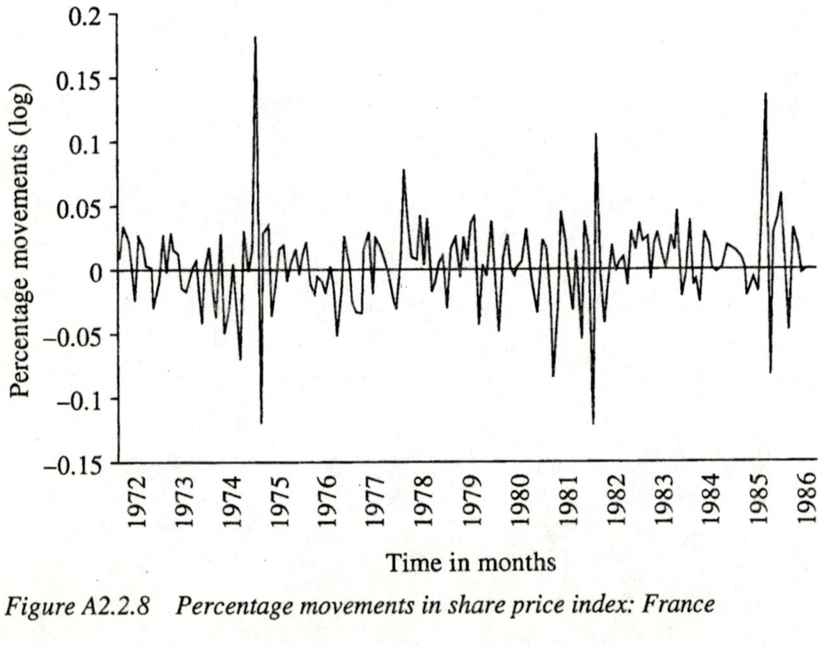


*Figure A2.2.8 Percentage movements in share price index: France*

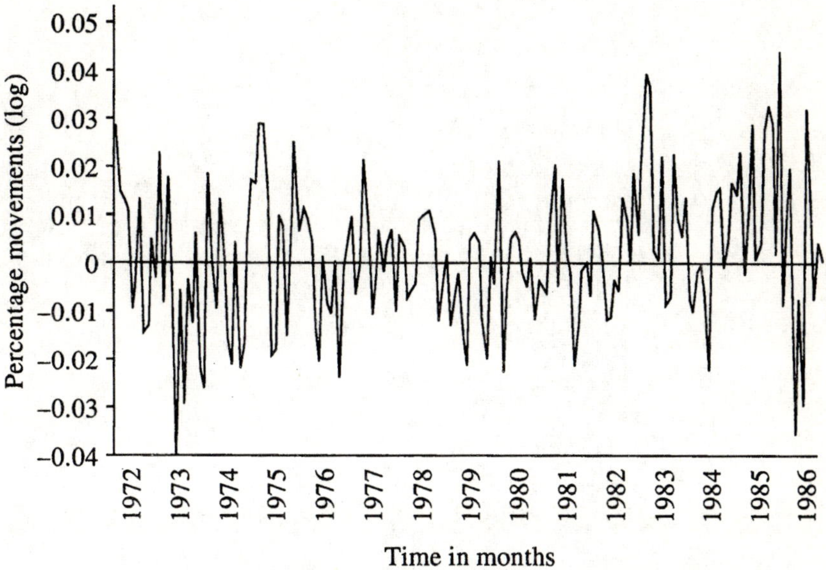


*Figure A2.2.9 Percentage movements in share price index: Germany*

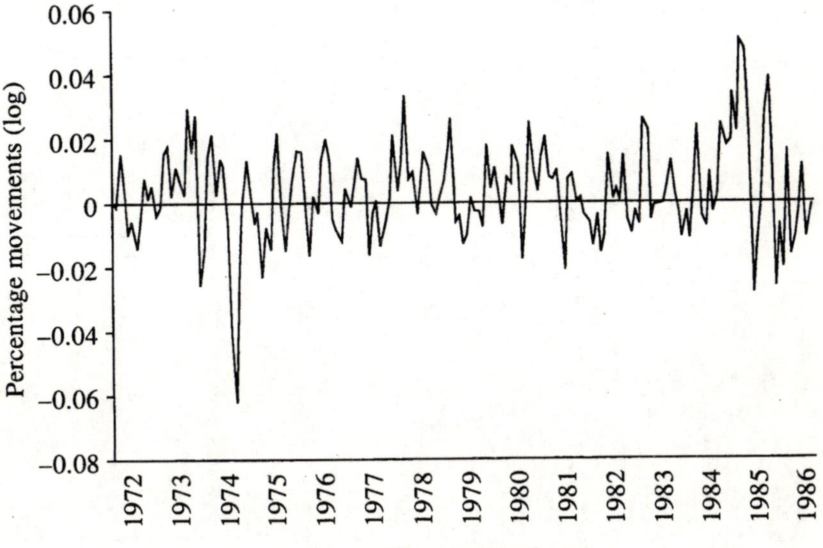


*Figure A2.2.10 Percentage movements in share price index: India*

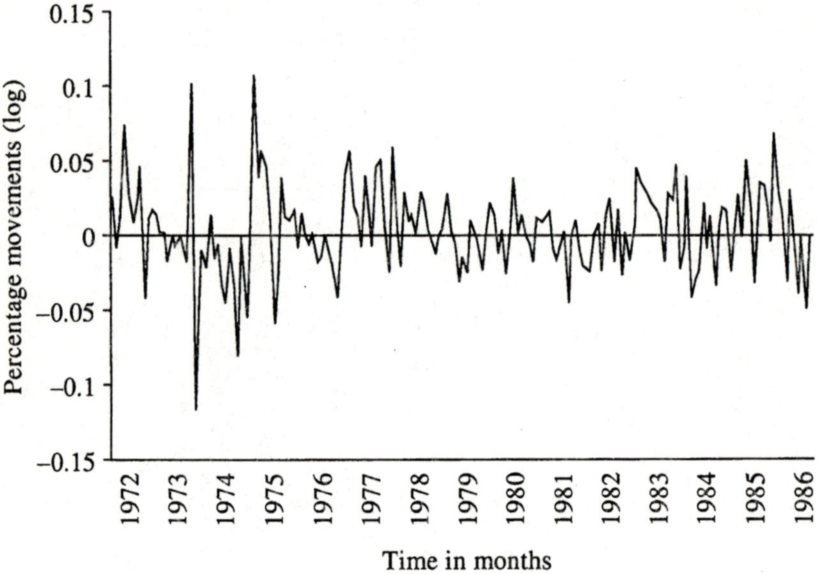


*Figure A2.2.11 Percentage movements in share price index: Ireland*

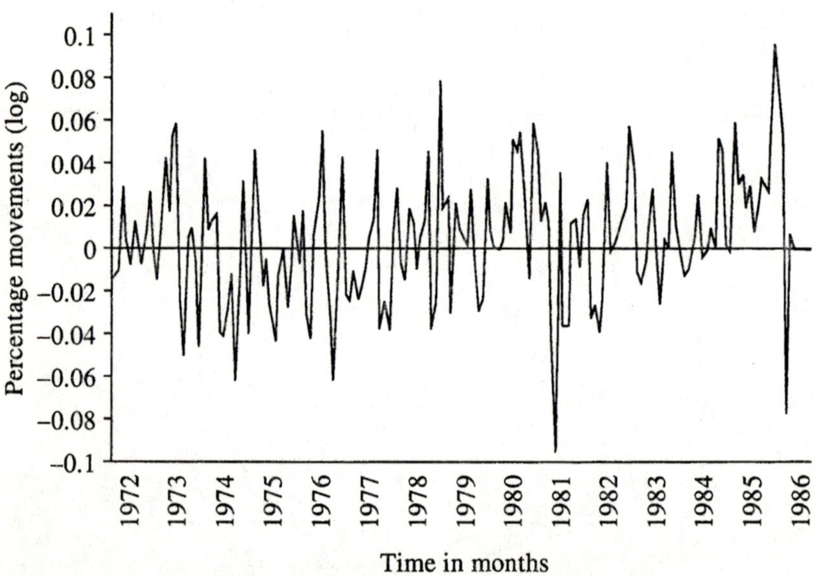


*Figure A2.2.12 Percentage movements in share price index: Italy*

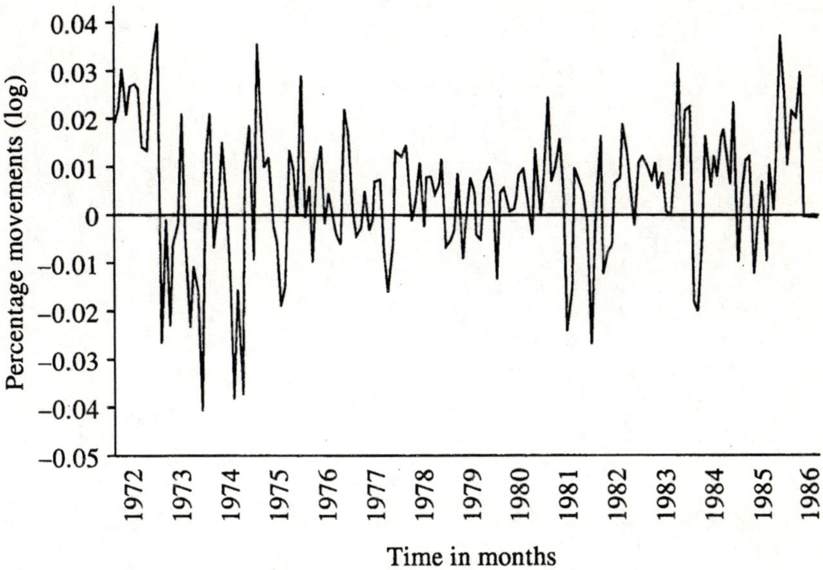


*Figure A2.2.13* *Percentage movements in share price index: Japan*

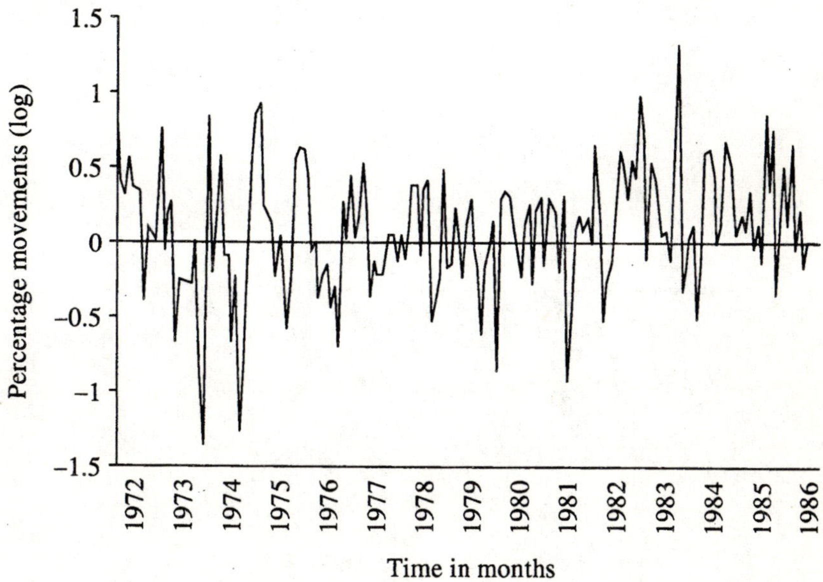


*Figure A2.2.14* *Percentage movements in share price index: The Netherlands*

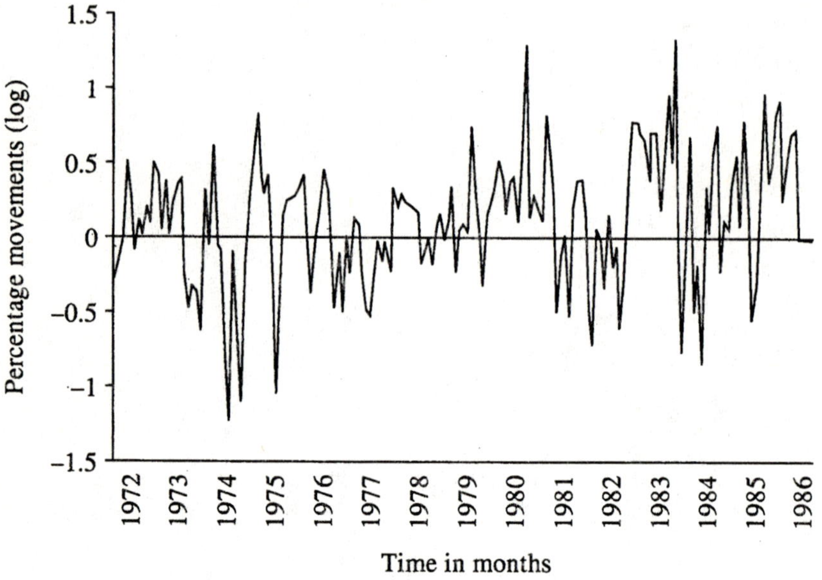


*Figure A2.2.15 Percentage movements in share price index: New Zealand*

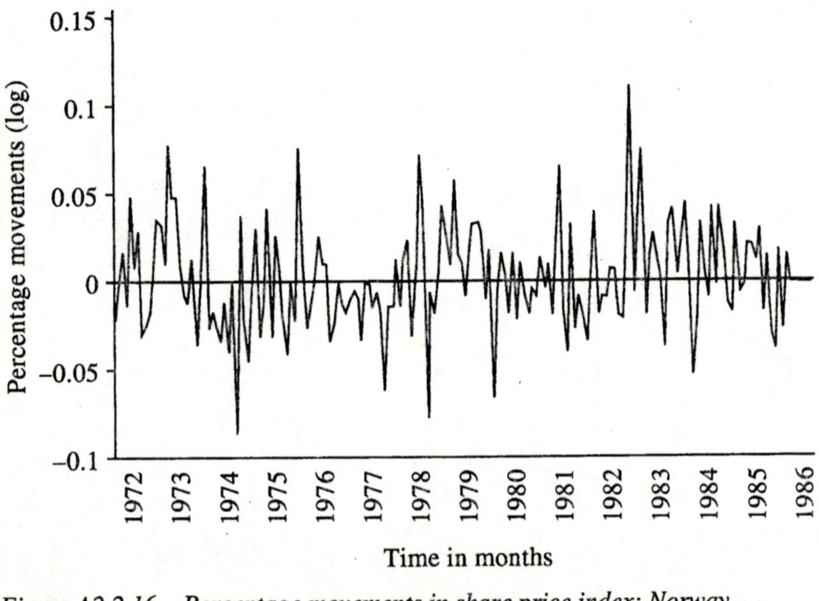


*Figure A2.2.16 Percentage movements in share price index: Norway*

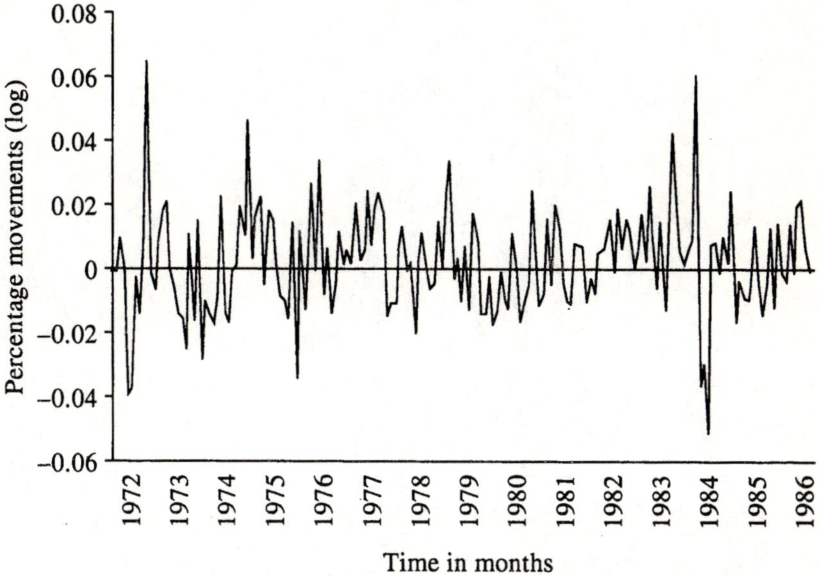


*Figure A2.2.17 Percentage movements in share price index: Pakistan*

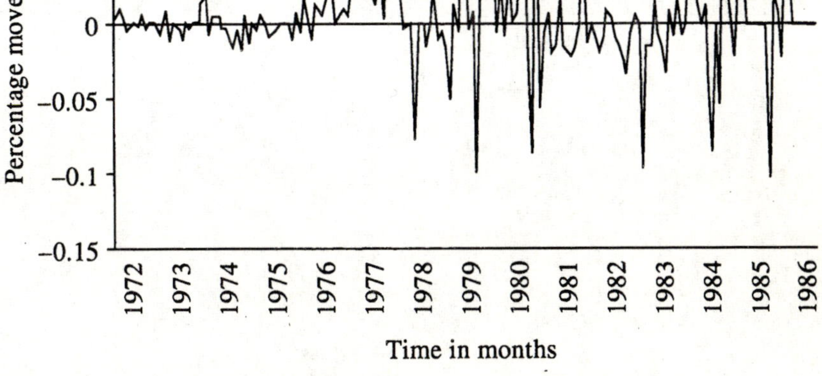


*Figure A2.2.18 Percentage movements in share price index: Peru*

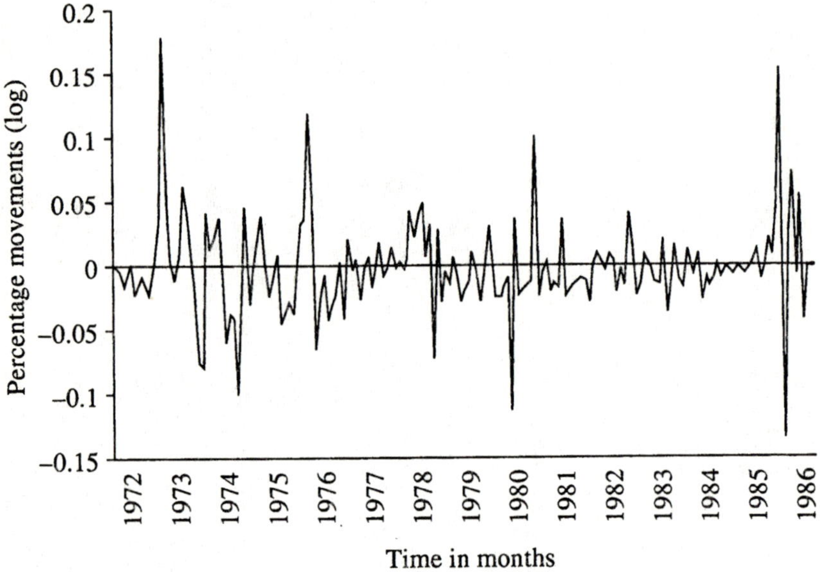


*Figure A2.2.19 Percentage movements in share price index: The Philippines*

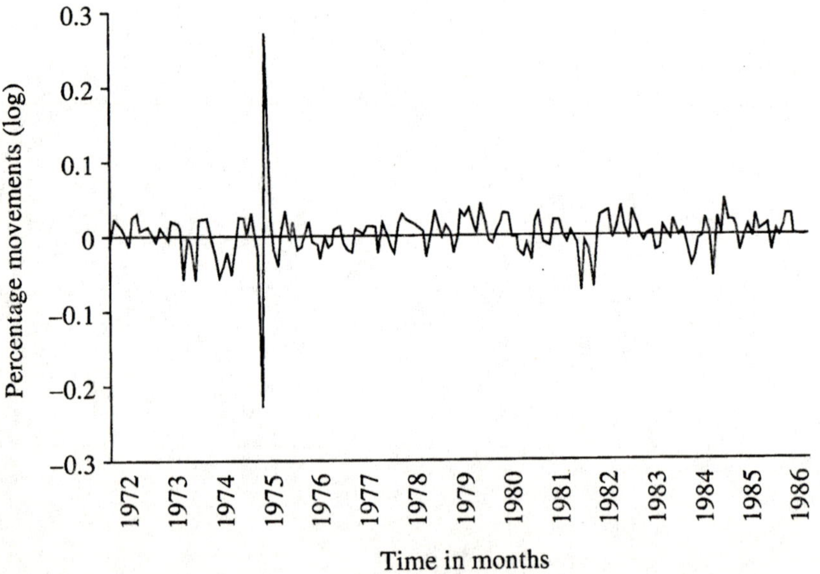


*Figure A2.2.20 Percentage movements in share price index: South Africa*

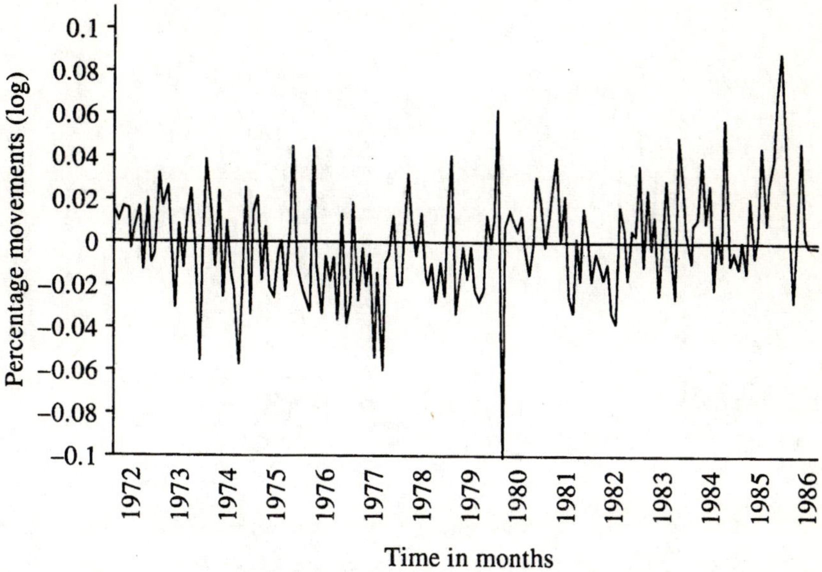


*Figure A2.2.21 Percentage movements in share price index: Spain*

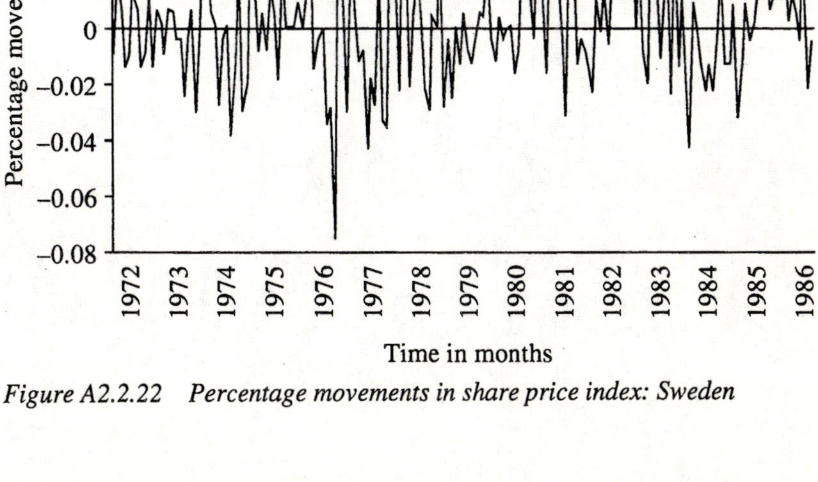


*Figure A2.2.22 Percentage movements in share price index: Sweden*

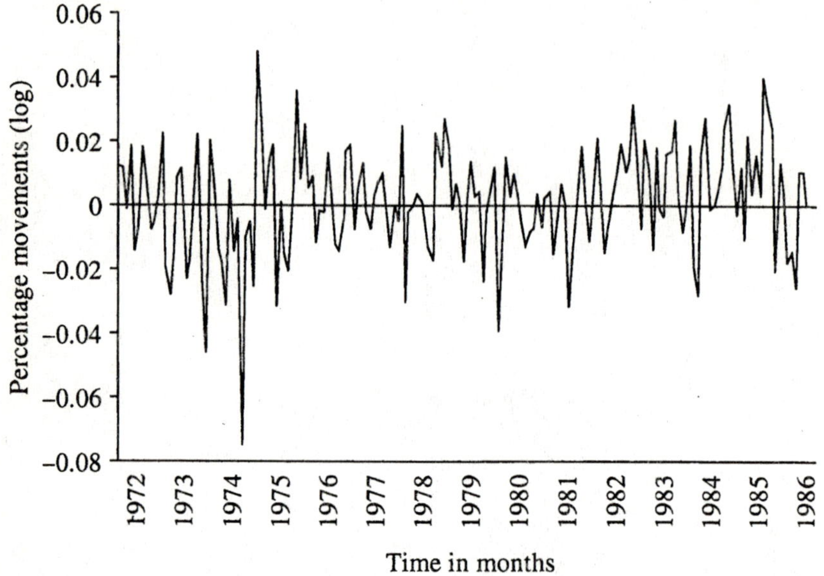


*Figure A2.2.23 Percentage movements in share price index: Switzerland*

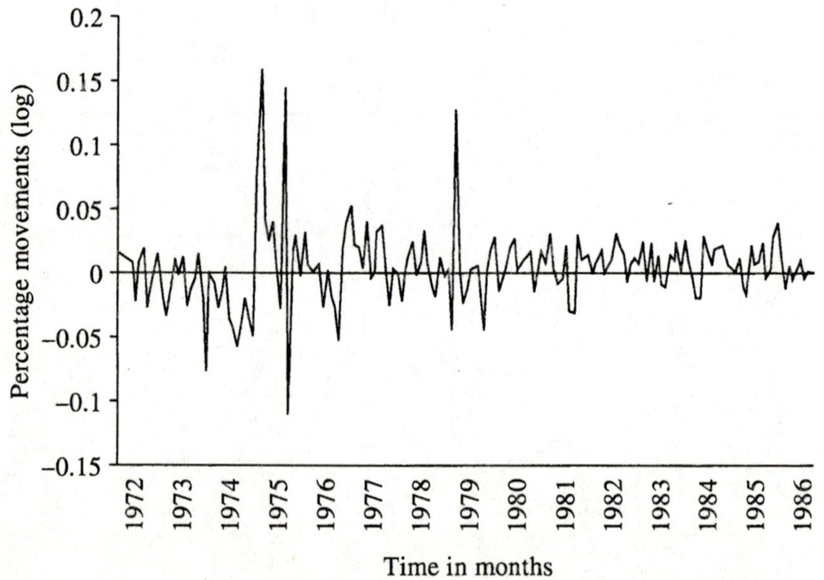


*Figure A2.2.24 Percentage movements in share price index: United Kingdom*

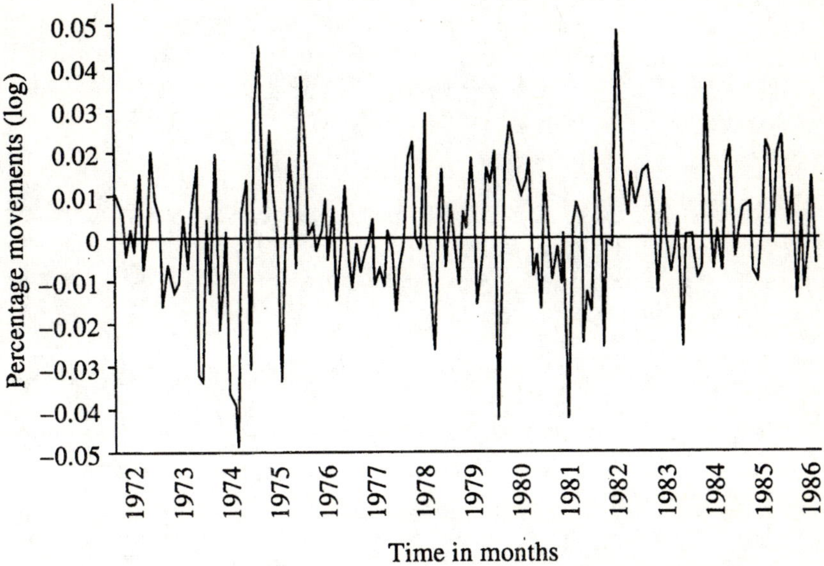


*Figure A2.2.25 Percentage movements in share price index: United States*

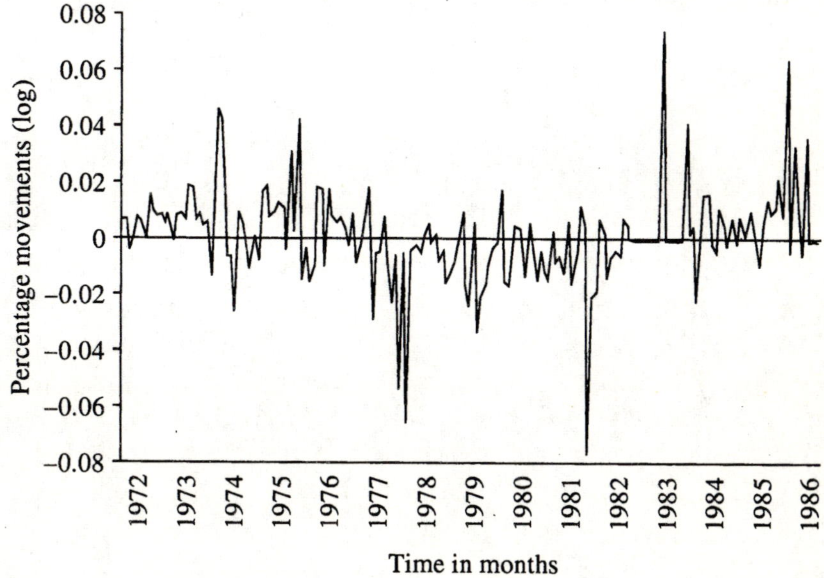


*Figure A2.2.26 Percentage movements in share price index: Venezuela*

*Appendix A2.3: Time series behaviour of percentage movements in regional share price indices*

Here we group countries based on the trading blocs or geographical regions they belong to. Then we establish regional market portfolios (regional share price indices) from country share price indices. The weight of each country in the respective regional share price index is equal. Five regions selected are as follows:

1. European Union (EU): UK, Germany, France, Netherlands, Belgium, Denmark, Italy, Spain, Ireland;
2. European Free Trade Association (EFTA): Switzerland, Sweden, Austria, Norway, Finland;
3. North America: USA, Canada;
4. The Pacific: Japan, Philippines, Australia, New Zealand, India, Pakistan, South Africa;
5. Latin America: Peru, Colombia, Venezuela.

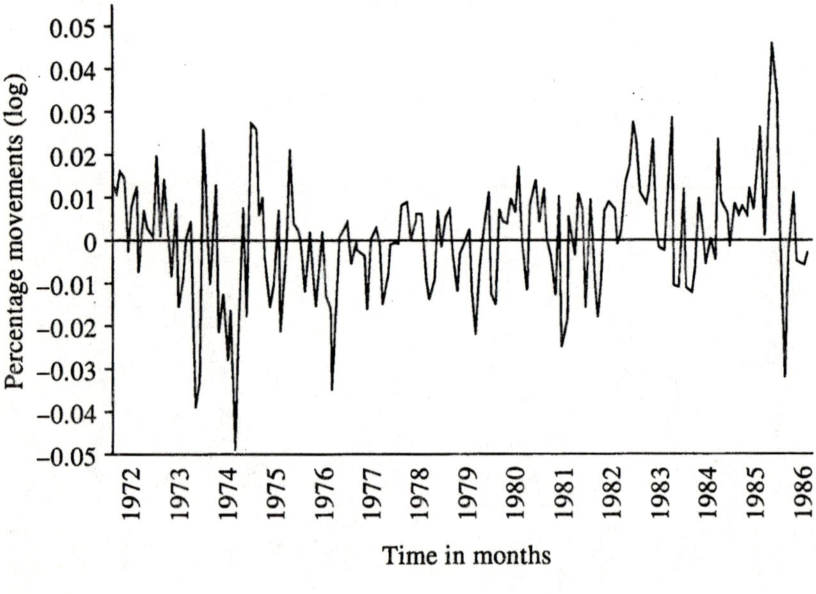


*Figure A2.3.1 Percentage movements in share price index: EC portfolio*

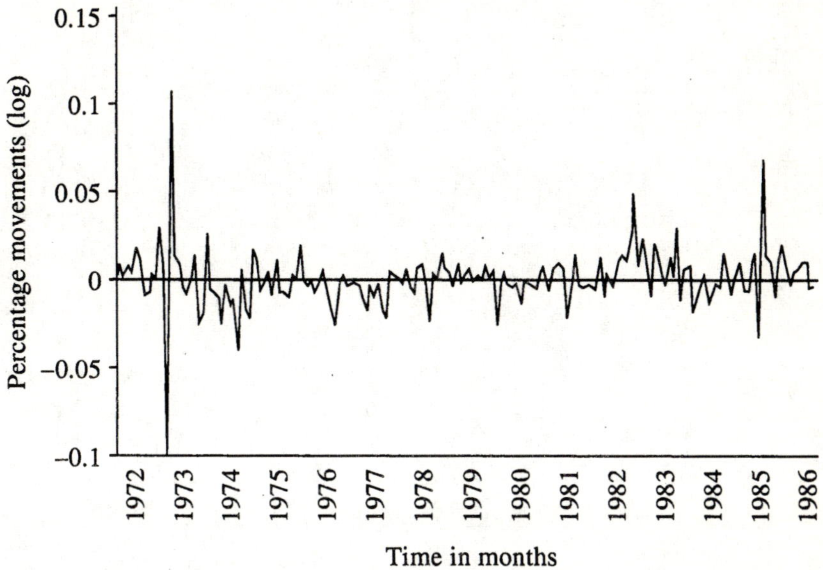


*Figure A2.3.2* *Percentage movements in share price index: EFTA portfolio*

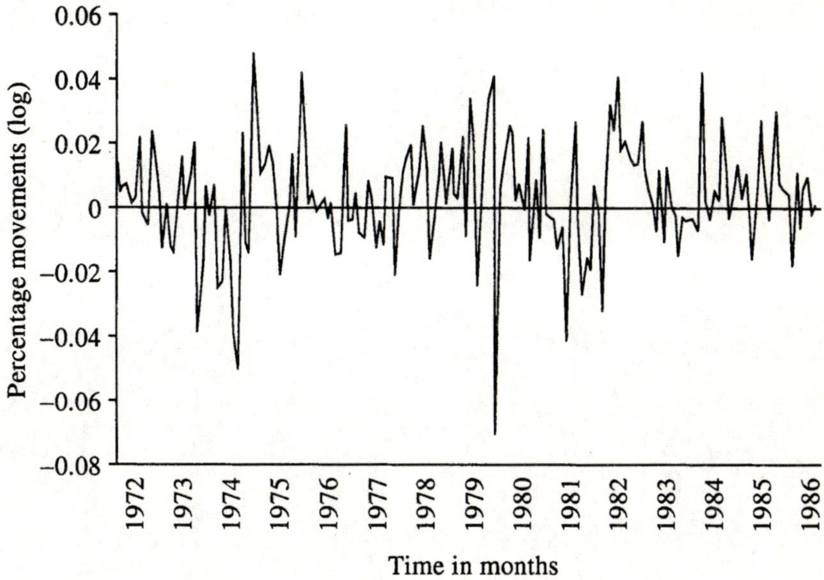


*Figure A2.3.3* *Percentage movements in share price index: North American portfolio*

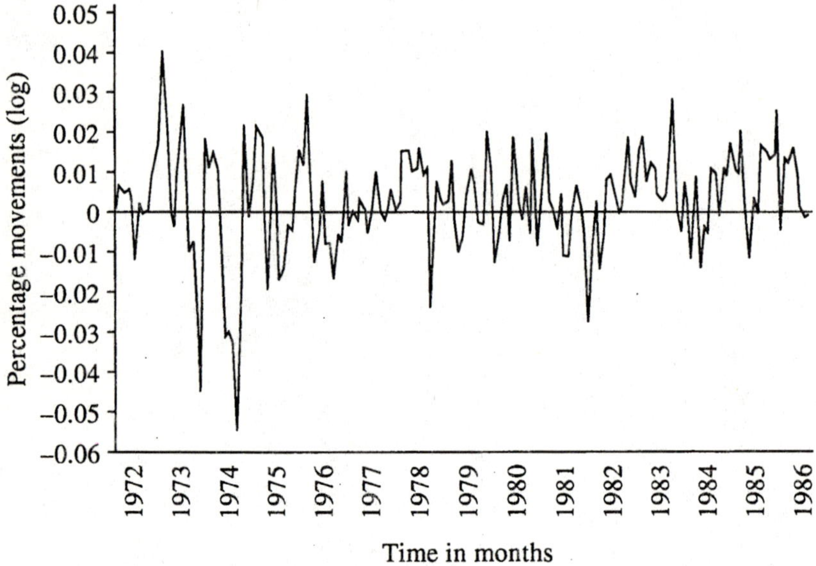


*Figure A2.3.4 Percentage movements in share price index: Pacific portfolio*

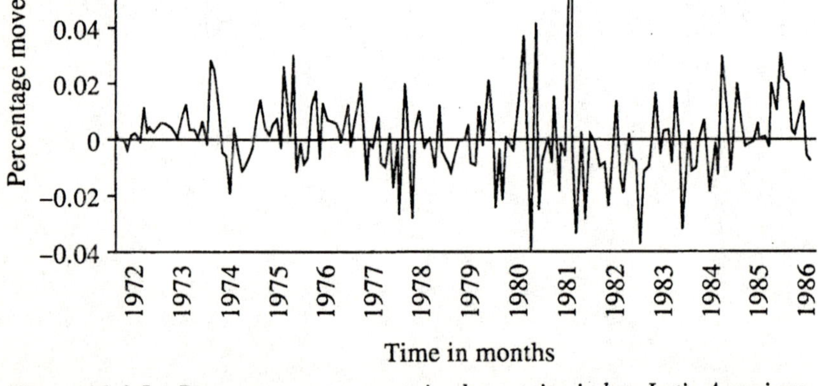


*Figure A2.3.5 Percentage movements in share price index: Latin American portfolio*

# 3 The integration of capital markets: an institutional introduction

## Financial networks

How does fast growth in world capital markets in relation to the increasing tendency toward securitization explain integration? Does it suggest that world markets have become integrated and that there now exists one unified world market for securities? Could one argue *a priori* that world financial markets are more integrated in the 1990s than they were one or two decades ago? These questions cannot be answered without testing the reactions of the markets to institutional developments. Indeed, we shall outline several procedures to test empirically whether the international capital markets are integrated in the following chapters. Here we would like to draw the reader's attention to the prerequisites for market integration.

One of the two vital factors that have made markets practically and institutionally more integrated is the rapid development in telecommunications technology, as we have pointed out in chapter 1 of this book. Investors in different locations can now follow more closely what happens elsewhere in the world than they could in the 1960s or 1970s. Widespread use of computers and the fascinating progress in information management systems have enabled traders of financial instruments to manage their portfolios much more efficiently. On-line data and information availability and the use of high-technology information monitoring systems have enhanced remarkably the opportunities for international portfolio investors.

Traders in the finance sector can buy and sell financial assets, foreign exchange and their derivatives. Highly sophisticated networks of financial trading enable their subscribers to enter their bids and asks and execute their requirements on-line. Traders can buy and sell stocks, bonds, bills, currency, forwards, futures and options on virtually any organized market in the world. Networks such as Reuters and Telerate provide services to their international customers for a fee.[1]

## Financial deregulation

The second major factor that has made world financial markets more integrated is the increasingly unfavourable attitude toward government impediments. The pro-capital-market posture has matured in the past decade: a decade of financial liberalization all over the world. The protectionist ideas of the previous decade disappeared in the 1980s. From 1980 onwards, legal restrictions on ownership of capital, particularly those against foreign capital, have been abolished even in developing countries. Investors, regardless of their country of origin, can now trade in capital assets in most markets in the world without running into much difficulty. In quite a few exchange locations, local and foreign investors have access virtually to the same set of information as a result of the harmonization of accounting disclosure requirements. Transaction taxes have either been removed or have become negligible. Only in a few places do reinvestment conditions against foreigners continue to exist.[2]

Controls of any type would put at risk the integration of international securities markets. Regulation of the listing of securities and accounting disclosure requirements are crucial aspects of any international investment activity. The financial markets cannot improve themselves any further if their integrity is compromised. In a number of instances in the past there have been allegations of insider trading in several countries. Such instances may eventually threaten the future of international investment.

In the 1990s, financial markets in most industrial countries are becoming considerably deregulated. Many developing capital markets have also removed exchange and interest rate controls in order to foster economic development. The process of worldwide deregulation of the finance sector began effectively in the early 1980s. Since then, interest rates, fees and commissions have been to a large extent freely determined by the market forces. Capital and exchange controls against the country of origin of investment have been lifted or eased. No interest rate controls exist in the United States, Germany, Switzerland, the United Kingdom and Italy. Controls against foreign entry were abolished in the UK and Germany in 1979 and 1981 respectively. Foreign entry into the US markets has always been easy. France and Italy had removed their capital controls by 1990. No controls exist in Switzerland, based on the reciprocity principle. Japan eased its international controls between 1980 and 1984.

In the early years of the 1990s, direct government controls on interest rates have disappeared or been reduced to the point of unimportance. Even in Japan, a country where interest rate controls have long been a prominent feature of the financial system, deregulation proceeded quite decisively in 1990 and 1991. The full liberalization of rates on time deposits, scheduled to be completed by August 1993 has not been accomplished. Currently, an advisory council is considering moves to deregulate rates on demand deposits. Several supervisory and regulatory initiatives towards the international banking sector exist. Among them are the international capital adequacy standards for banks (the so-called Basle Accord); the supervision of banks' foreign establishments; permissible banking activities; and deposit insurance schemes. These are specialized topics of interest and cannot be covered in this volume.[3]

In the following sections we shall analyse the European Monetary System (EMS) and its effects on financial integration. The EMS is quite important not only for the EU but also for the rest of the world. The EMS as a system for financial and monetary stability in Europe concerns all who are interested in reducing the risks associated with a system itself. Furthermore, this system is likely to serve as a benchmark for a new world monetary system because it is the only working exchange rate mechanism for convertible currencies.

**Financial regulation and the European Monetary System**

European financial markets have undergone major reforms aiming at fewer capital controls. In this section we shall highlight the important steps taken towards the creation of an economic and monetary union in the European Community from an open-economy macroeconomic standpoint. The first major step towards the creation of a monetary union was the 1969 Hague Summit. The decisions taken at this Summit later became the basis of the 1971 Werner Plan, named after the former Luxembourg prime minister. From this Plan, only an exchange-rate system in which rates fluctuate by up to 2.25 per cent has remained.

Until 1979 no major development of operational importance had taken place. In 1979 the EMS was formed. The 2.25 per cent margin was adopted in principle, with the exception of Italy to whom a 6 per cent margin was granted. The UK did not participate. One of the most important aspects of the EMS was the creation of the European Currency Unit, the ECU. The ECU is a basket of weighted amounts of the member states' currencies, including the UK pound. It serves as a point of reference for many aspects of the EMS.

The main feature of the EMS is the so-called exchange rate mechanism (ERM). Although all twelve members of the EU are technically members of the EMS, only nine of them currently participate in the key agreement to limit exchange rate fluctuations. In the ERM, all possible pairs of currencies are constrained to fluctuate within limited ranges from previously agreed bilateral central rates. The range for most EU states is ±15 per cent. Although the margin for the UK and Spain was initially set at 6 per cent, the UK decided to suspend its membership indefinitely in September 1992. Italy also announced that it would leave the ERM.[4] Belgium and Luxembourg share a single currency.

The central banks of the ERM members have a responsibility to maintain the ranges by currency intervention and, if necessary, certain other policy actions such as interest rate changes. The grid of central rates and contingent intervention limits changes only when a realignment of the central rates of the system takes place.

*The exchange rate mechanism (ERM)*

The ERM defines a divergence benchmark called the parity grid band. Any tension within the system is monitored daily by identifying the pair of currencies for which the market rate diverges most from the agreed central rate. The weakest currency in the ERM is then used as a basis for comparison. Next, the observed divergence of all currencies from their agreed central rate against the weakest currency is plotted on an axis that may vary between 0 (the weakest currency) and 15 for currencies in the narrow band. In principle, currencies in the wide band are not employed as the basis for comparison even when they are the weakest currency in the system.

At the intervention points, the two central banks concerned have theoretically an unlimited obligation to buy the weak currency and sell the strong currency. In practice, however, intervention usually plays a secondary role to interest rate changes and, when necessary, currency realignments. In general, for the central bank of the strong currency the major problem is the possibility that its assets can immediately become dominated by foreign currency claims. For the central bank of the weak currency, on the other hand, the problem is international liquidity, in that it can easily run out of liquid foreign exchange reserves to sell.

For the latter problem, which is common to all soft currency countries, most notably Italy and Spain, the EMS provides credit lines by which each participating central bank makes its own currency available to others. This is what is known as the very short-term financing facility (VSTF) of the EMS. The system makes access to this possibility unlimited only at the intervention points. This facility is not available for longer terms. Fairly strict regulations govern the repayment schedules under the VSTF. Under the Basle–Nyborg agreement, access to the VSFT was increased significantly in September 1987. At present, the duration of drawings under the facility is 3.5 months. The ceiling amount of these drawings can be automatically rolled over for an additional three months. The facility can be made more flexible with the approval of the creditor central bank.

*Monitoring the tensions in the ERM* There are basically two devices by which the daily tensions within the ERM can be monitored closely. The first one is the parity grid band, as mentioned earlier. A benchmark currency is necessary in the ERM in order to see the effectiveness of this monitoring device. The Deutschmark has a long history of being realigned upwards. Tensions that could force interest rate changes, or a possible realignment, can clearly be shown when the parity grid band widens with the benchmark currency, i.e. when the DM rises to the top of the band. The most vulnerable situation that can generate tensions within the parity grid band occurs when the DM is over and above 2 and other currencies are located around the weakest one.

Consider now an alternative situation where the DM is at the bottom of the band, with normally weak 'high-yielding' currencies at the top (either 2.25 or 15 per cent 'above' the DM, depending on the proper range of the member country). Such a situation should be seen as a case of extreme stability in the ERM, possibly with the financial markets confident that there is little chance of a realignment.

*The divergence indicator* (DI) is built to handle the degree of isolation of an ERM currency. One indicator exists for each currency and may vary between −100 (when the currency under consideration is an outlier on the weak side) and +100 (when it is an outlier on the strong side). The critical level of the indicator is ±75. When this level is reached by a currency it should signal that that currency is out of line with its partners. At that point some action on the part of the country whose currency hits the 75 level is necessary: either an interest rate change or intervention is required. In practice, however, the divergence indicator is far less significant than the bilateral rates. Levels over and above 75 are often disregarded for a significantly long period of time.

Technically, the divergence indicator is the ratio, expressed in terms of market premiums associated with a currency's market rate. Specifically, the divergence indicator is the ratio in percentage terms of the adjusted market premium or discount of a currency's market rate against the ECU over its central ECU rate to a currency's maximum divergence spread (MDS):

$$DI = p(100)/MDS \tag{3.1}$$

where $p$ is the premium (discount if it is negative) and is measured as

$$p = [\text{ECU adjusted market} - \text{ECU central}]\,(100)/\text{ECU central} \tag{3.2}$$

This maximum divergence spread is actually the amount by which a currency's market rate against the ECU would differ from its central rate if the currency were 15 per cent off from all other currencies in the system. Since each currency in the ERM has some weight in the ECU, this difference will necessarily be less than 15 per cent. In principle, the greater the weight the smaller the MDS. In the case of the DM for instance, the MDS is smallest at 1.53 per cent.

*The mechanics of realignment in the ERM* When pressures in terms of interest rates or reserve losses become too great, the existing rates make the system vulnerable. That is when central rates are realigned. However, the ERM does not contain a clear-cut formula for realignments. The normal procedure is that the central bank governors of the currencies under most pressure approach the Monetary Committee of the EU. The Committee is expected to make a specific proposal to the central bank governors and finance ministers. An emergency meeting takes place. In practice, realignments occur at weekends.

### *European monetary institutions*

At present, the European Union does not have a central financial institution responsible for overseeing the European Monetary System; instead, there are three essential committees, each of which plays an important role in developing the EMS further.

*Committee of Central Bank Governors* The Committee reviews financial developments and the status of co-ordination among the ERM states. It is also responsible for making proposals to member state governments in all areas related to central banking and monetary policy-making. The Committee meets about ten times each year, usually shortly after the regular G-10 central banks meeting in Basle. The Committee prepared the statutes of the prospective European System of Central Banks (ESCB) that became an epilogue to the Maastricht Treaty. Its annual reports have been published since April 1992.

*Monetary Committee of the European Community* This Committee consists of senior central bank officials and finance ministers of each of the EU countries. Within this Committee, an expert body is formed. This body is charged with overseeing the EMS, providing guidance and advice to the finance ministers and central bank governors. The Committee meets in Brussels once a month.

*ECOFIN (Council of EC Finance and Economics Ministers)* The ECOFIN addresses not only monetary issues concerning the EMS but also other economic problems facing the member states. In this respect it is not a specialized body monitoring monetary issues and disputes. The Council is chaired by the finance minister of the country currently holding the presidency of the EU, which rotates every six months.

As was mentioned above, there are no unambiguous criteria for deciding which of these three institutions is most important. The ECOFIN may be projected to be the most influential body in monetary issues and the future of the EMS because it consists of senior members of EU governments. Yet there is considerable influence on the Committee of central bank governors to ensure the independence and importance of the Bundesbank. Indeed, both Committees have played important roles in selecting the targets for the EMS. For instance, the measures adopted in mid-1987 to strengthen the EMS have come to be known as Basle–Nyborg agreement. Basle is the city where the central bank governors agreed to the proposed changes, and Nyborg is the place where the finance ministers met to discuss the changes.

In 1985 the finance ministers and central bank governors adopted a series of measures to reform the EMS further. The interest rates payable on the ECUs held by member state central banks was made attractive and tied to market rates instead of average discount rates. A different holder status for non-EU central banks and international entities to acquire ECUs was also mentioned at the 1985 meeting of ministers.

A private ECU market next to the official market –with active interbank trade in deposits and loans in ECUs – has grown up gradually. Such transactions became much easier when several banks in the ECU bank association created a settlement system at the Bank for International Settlements (BIS) with the support of the EU Commission in 1986. The ECU is now the fifth most important currency, following the US dollar, the German mark, the Swiss franc and the Japanese yen. It is particularly important in the bond market.

### *The future of the EMS*

*The three-stage Delors Plan* The EC heads of state and government agreed at their summit in June 1988 to have the idea of greater monetary integration *vis-à-vis* greater monetary co-operation examined by a committee chaired by Commission President Jacques Delors. In April 1989 the Delors Committee, consisting of the governors of the twelve central banks and four other experts, completed a major work when it finalized a report on monetary union in the Community. The report highlighted the political, economic and institutional conditions necessary for economic and monetary integration.

More importantly, however, the committee put forward a concrete three-stage plan for the formation of a federally structured independent European System of Central Banks (ESCB). The Delors three-stage plan also included a schedule to reform the existing procedures for co-ordinating economic policy.

*The first phase* of the Delors Plan started on 1 July 1990. The entire plan specifically calls for completion of the monetary union by 1 January 1995, although it sets no predetermined date for the implementation of individual stages.[5] The principal steps of the first stage can be summarized as follows:

(a) removal of physical, technical as well as fiscal barriers in conjunction with the Single European Act;
(b) implementation of structural funds reform and the doubling of their resources;
(c) strengthening of the rules applicable to date regarding economic and fiscal policy co-ordination;
(d) full implementation of the European financial common market;
(e) inclusion of all member states' currencies in the EMS exchange rate mechanism, with the same rules applying to each;
(f) abolition of all existing impediments to the private use of the ECU;
(g) redefinition of the mandate of the Committee of Central Bank Governors with the strengthening of the co-ordination function.

*The second stage* of the Delors Plan includes the following proposals:

(a) review and consolidation of the results of the Single European Act;
(b) enlargement of the resources for structural policies, research as well as infrastructure investments;

(c) extension of the new procedure for the co-ordination of economic policy introduced in stage one, with the adoption of policy guidelines by majority decision;
(d) establishment of the European System of Central Banks (ESCB);
(e) recourse to exchange rate realignments only in exceptional circumstances;
(f) transition from the co-ordination stage of independent monetary policies to a common monetary policy formulated and implemented by the ESCB, with a gradual transfer of decision-making power to a EU institution;
(g) pooling of some part of the exchange reserves for intervention on the currency markets;
(h) narrowing the fluctuation margins within the exchange rate mechanism, depending on the circumstances.

*The final stage* before monetary union includes the following proposals:

(a) irrevocable locking of all exchange rates;
(b) further strengthening of structural regional economic policies when and if necessary;
(c) all rules and procedures of the Union to be made binding, in particular those regarding national budgets and transfers of resources for structural policies, and to be applied by the Council of Ministers, in co-operation with the European Parliament;
(d) new form of representation *vis-à-vis* the assumption that the role of the Union in the process of international policy co-operation will be full;
(e) decisions regarding exchange market intervention in third currencies to be made on the sole responsibility of the ESCB Council;
(f) maintenance of official currency reserves at the ESCB;
(g) transition and changeover to a single currency.

*The European System of Central Banks (ESCB)* The most radical of all institutional changes determined by the Delors Plan is, of course, the establishment of the ESCB. The Bank will be fully autonomous. It will be based on a federal structure because this would best correspond to the political diversity of the EU. The ESCB Council would be composed of the governors of member state central banks and the members of the board, the latter to be appointed by the European Council.

At the final stage, the ESCB will be responsible for formulating and implementing monetary policy as well as managing the Union's exchange rate policy with regard to third currencies. It is also in this final stage that the national central banks are expected to execute operations in accordance with the decisions made by the ESCB Council.

The Delors Committee proposed that the system would be committed to the objective of price stability and that it would support general economic policy set at Union level. Further, the ESCB would also be responsible for the formulation and implementation of monetary policy, exchange rate and reserve management, and the maintenance of a functioning payment system. It would also participate in the co-ordination of the banking supervision policies of the supervisory authorities. At the executive level, the ESCB Council will have policy instruments available. The system could buy and sell government securities on the market as a means of conducting monetary policy. However, it would comply with the provision not to lend to public-sector authorities.

**Macroeconomic aspects of monetary integration in the European Union**

The fixity of exchange rates and currency union seem to be taken as given from the outset as prerequisites for monetary integration. Exchange rates in the European Union have remained much more stable than in the rest of the world. This has brought some level of convergence in the economic policies, particularly the monetary policies, of member states. Further, inflation rates have also converged to some degree. As far as a monetary integration is concerned, however, the problem is not solely one of currency integration or the fixity of exchange rates. After all, monetary integration of some magnitude has already been achieved, and there is every evidence to believe that price and interest rate differentials are in the process of disappearing. Convergence is even more evident for the core EU countries, especially among Germany, France and the Benelux countries.[6]

As long as there is convergence in inflation rates – whether towards the German rate or some other rate, and a relatively fixed exchange rate system continues to exist, one can speak of currency integration. If the exchange rate is fixed, it is of no real importance to have a common currency issued by a common central bank.

However, there is an important element in monetary integration that has recently emerged as a critical decision for the member states. This is the question of monetary policy. Should there be a common monetary policy in the EU? If so, then when should it be implemented? If it is proposed that the monetary policy is independent, then can a member state actually conduct independent monetary policy? What is the range over which a particular central bank is free to act? These questions have consequential macroeconomic implications as far as the future of the EU and the entire European integration programme is concerned.

Europe has now come to a stage where any movement to deepen integration further would jeopardize sovereignty and hence be quite dangerous politically. From now on, further attempts to deepen economic or financial integration will probably have fundamental and irreversible consequences that are not necessarily practical and helpful for monetary integration. At this stage it seems that the monetary decision-makers of the EU states face some important trade-offs as far as macroeconomic policies are concerned.

First of all, in a fixed exchange world in which capital is free to move, monetary policy cannot easily be set independently. The obligations regarding the fixity of exchange rates are likely to reduce the independence of monetary policy in any EU country. Similarly, given an independent monetary policy in a member state and a fixed exchange rate system, capital controls are likely to exist. Finally, if all capital controls are lifted and national governments favour independent monetary policies as opposed to a Union-wide policy, then exchange rates will be flexible to some degree. Thus, if monetary policy is to be independent, there is then a trade-off between the existence and continuity of a fixed exchange rate system within the Union and elimination of all capital controls.

At present, a perfect fixed exchange rate system does not exist. Even the ±2.25 per cent system adopted by the majority of the member states as the essential parameter of the ERM is at stake. The existing margins as of November 1994, though temporary, are ±15 per cent. This seems to provide national governments with even more controllable space in which to move and conduct monetary policies fairly independently. On the other hand, most states have already eliminated capital controls, as we have mentioned previously. EU states that still have some restrictions on capital have been scheduled to remove all controls over their exchanges by 1995. Therefore, it appears impossible to reintroduce capital restrictions individually. If you take as given the non-existence of capital controls, then the trade-off exists between the fixity of exchange rates and the independence of monetary policy.

Monetary policy has also converged. Further, the differences in inflation rates among the member states are modest. Besides, risk premia differentials among the EU capital markets are also modest, based on the results of our international asset-pricing model. Briefly speaking, there is convergence in the financial sector of the Union as a whole with a possible exception of insurance and brokerage. Neither the exchange rates nor the market prices of risk have converged fully, however. All this seems to suggest that there will be less than full convergence in interest rates, exchange rates and risk premia.

Taking into account the rapid developments in computers and telecommunications technology and the deregulation of world financial markets, we ask the following questions. Can the world financial (capital) markets be described as integrated? What is actually meant by the integration of capital markets? We shall summarize in the following chapter some well-known descriptive ways of looking at the issue of capital market integration.

## Notes

1. Fees vary depending on market coverage.
2. In chapter 2 we provided a summary table outlining institutional differences across world capital markets (see Table 2.8).

3. Interested readers can find an excellent overview of recent institutional developments in international banking and supervision practices in World Bank (1992).
4. The future of the ERM does not look promising. As of February 1994 the margin is as high as 15 per cent: this margin became effective in August 1993. The EU finance sector and the central bank governors in the EU want to believe that this is temporary. However, existing economic problems – most notably surging unemployment – seem to press the EU to ease credits. Easy economic and financial policies jeopardize the future of the ERM and the EMS.
5. This specific date is included in a different plan by the European Parliament.
6. On the issue of convergence and price differentials in Europe, see Wieser (1989) and Cecchini (1988).

# 4 Non-asset-pricing models of integration

Taking into account the rapid developments in computers and telecommunications technology and the deregulation of world financial markets, we ask the following questions: Can the world financial (capital) markets be classified as integrated? What is actually meant by the integration of capital markets? Did the institutional developments removing major restrictions against international equity investors create a true integration of capital markets?[1] We shall outline in this chapter some popular descriptive ways of looking into the issue of capital market integration.

This is an introduction to modern asset-pricing theories of financial integration. What we study is not based on asset-pricing theories, however. As we shall see below, these are not statistical tests but may be used to supplement the asset-pricing tests. The first method is based on cross-country interest rate differentials and hence is more relevant for monetary integration. Note here that we do not refer to standard and well-established tests of interest rate parity differentials in the theory of international finance and open-economy macroeconomics. Rather, we monitor the co-movements in simple absolute differentials. The second approach is to monitor the co-movements in stock prices across markets which may be important to detect integration of equity markets.

**Interest rate differentials**

On *a priori* grounds one can maintain that world capital markets have become more integrated by examining the interest rate differentials across markets. The simplest idea behind looking into the differential interest rates is what might be called *interest rate arbitrage*. If arbitrage opportunities exist across interest rates, the financial markets where interest rates are determined can rightly be classified as *segmented*. If, on the other hand, there is convergence in interest rates, one can speak about some degree of integration in world financial markets. This simple approach undermines the well-established parity relations of international finance, namely *interest rate parity differentials*.[2]

Interest rate differentials imply two different types of financial integration depending on the terms of funds traded. Short-term interest rate movements and their differentials across world markets carry important information about the magnitude of monetary integration or the integration of currency markets. It is further important for liquidity considerations since short-term funds are traded basically for reasons associated with immediate financing needs. On the other hand, long-term interest rate differentials are related to growth funds and not the liquidity considerations. Hence, differentials in long-term interest rates across international markets should be associated with what one might call the *integration of (long-term) bond markets*.

*Table 4.1: Long-term and short-term interest rate differentials between the United States and other major countries, 1987–90[a] (% per annum)*

| | Japan | Germany | France | UK |
|---|---|---|---|---|
| Long-term interest rates[b] | | | | |
| 1987 | 2.40 | 1.16 | –1.54 | –2.58 |
| First quarter | | | | |
| Second quarter | 4.22 | 2.51 | –0.58 | –0.62 |
| Third quarter | 2.91 | 2.38 | –0.95 | –1.00 |
| Fourth quarter | 3.92 | 2.52 | –1.10 | –0.54 |
| 1988 | | | | |
| First quarter | 4.12 | 2.08 | –0.99 | –1.07 |
| Second quarter | 4.26 | 2.41 | –0.21 | –0.46 |
| Third quarter | 3.58 | 2.37 | 0.05 | –0.85 |
| Fourth quarter | 4.25 | 2.52 | 0.28 | –0.94 |
| 1989 | | | | |
| First quarter | 4.25 | 2.34 | 0.38 | –0.65 |
| Second quarter | 3.51 | 1.79 | – | –1.53 |
| Third quarter | 3.10 | 1.17 | –0.42 | –1.98 |
| Fourth quarter | 2.56 | 0.53 | –1.12 | –2.74 |
| 1990 | | | | |
| First quarter | 1.72 | 0.09 | –1.39 | –3.12 |
| Second quarter | 2.07 | –0.06 | –1.00 | –3.65 |
| Third quarter | 1.23 | –0.17 | –1.39 | –3.17 |
| Fourth quarter | 1.29 | –0.59 | –1.81 | –2.79 |
| Short–term interest rates[c] | | | | |
| 1987 | | | | |
| First quarter | 1.86 | 1.90 | –2.28 | –4.59 |
| Second quarter | 2.93 | 3.03 | –1.31 | –2.34 |
| Third quarter | 2.88 | 3.02 | –0.98 | –2.86 |
| Fourth quarter | 3.18 | 3.54 | –0.87 | –1.58 |
| 1988 | | | | |
| First quarter | 2.42 | 3.35 | –1.23 | –2.29 |
| Second quarter | 3.04 | 3.66 | –0.53 | –1.18 |
| Third quarter | 3.43 | 3.31 | 0.52 | –3.16 |
| Fourth quarter | 4.34 | 3.70 | 0.64 | –3.69 |
| 1989 | | | | |
| First quarter | 5.06 | 3.38 | 0.63 | –3.46 |
| Second quarter | 4.68 | 2.79 | 0.74 | –3.90 |
| Third quarter | 3.32 | 1.59 | –0.42 | –5.20 |
| Fourth quarter | 2.04 | 0.33 | –1.95 | –6.63 |
| 1990 | | | | |
| First quarter | 1.19 | –0.04 | –2.69 | –6.91 |
| Second quarter | 1.01 | 0.07 | –1.67 | –6.78 |
| Third quarter | 0.17 | –0.30 | –2.09 | –6.90 |
| Fourth quarter | –0.26 | –0.88 | –2.08 | –5.91 |

*Notes:*

[a] The differentials shown should be treated as indicative because they conceal intercountry differences in the maturity structure of long-term rates. For instance, the US long-term rate is on ten-year federal government bonds, while the German rate is the average on government bonds with maturities over three years.

[b] The long-term interest rates are averages of daily or weekly observations of yields on government bonds specified as follows: France–long-term (7–10 years) government bond yield; Federal Republic of Germany–yield on government bonds with maturities of 9–10 years; Japan–over-the-counter sales yield of 10-year government bonds, with longest residual maturity; United Kingdom–yield on medium-dated (10 year) government stock; United States–yield on 10-year treasury bonds.

[c] The short-term interest rates are as follows: France–three-month interbank deposit rate; Federal Republic of Germany–three-month interbank deposit rate; Japan–three-month certificate of deposit rate; United Kingdom–three-month interbank deposit rate; United States–federal funds rate and three-month certificate of deposit rate.

*Source*: 1991. International Monetary Fund.

Table 4.1 displays both the short-term and long-term interest rate differentials between US markets and the other major capital markets of the world. The quarterly data provided there cover the period between 1987 and 1990. Interest rate differentials between the American and Japanese capital markets have decreased remarkably. The long-term interest rate differentials between these two markets has decreased from over 4 per cent in the fourth quarter of 1987 to 1.29 per cent in the same period of 1990. The short-term interest rate differentials between the two has decreased from over 3 per cent in the fourth quarter of 1987 to a figure far below 1 per cent in the same quarter of 1990. As a matter of fact, an examination of the differentials between US rates and Japanese rates in all four quarters of 1990 shows a consistent movement toward interest rate equalization. This tendency can be taken as an indication that currency markets in the US and Japan have become more integrated.

As Table 4.1 further indicates, the interest rate differentials between US rates and those in Germany are quite similar to those between US and Japanese rates. Fairly small differentials seem to exist between US and German interest rates. In the first half of 1990, both the short-term and the long-term interest rates in the US and Germany were virtually the same. In the second half, the differentials – both the long-term and the short-term are still lower than 1 per cent.

To a lesser degree, interest rate differentials between US and French markets have become smaller. Yet the differentials in the case of France – both in the short term and the long term – are in the range of 2 per cent, a much higher difference than those between the US and Japan and between the US and Germany. The interest rate differentials between the US and the UK were apparently high. This is due to the high interest rate policy adopted in the UK during the past several years.

**Co-movements in stock prices**

The interest rate differential *per se* does not capture the developments in markets where equity capital is traded. Therefore, the behaviour of stock prices must be looked at. An intuitive way of examining the issue of integration is to monitor stock market volatilities. Normally, the pairwise correlation coefficients in (a) stock prices, and/or (b) standard deviations of stock prices across world capital markets can be observed. Table 4.2 shows stock market volatility as measured by the standard deviations of changes in stock price indices, a more sensitive measure than stock prices or simple deviations. It is clear from an inspection of the table that there are high degrees of correlation between world capital markets. If the argument that co-movements in stock prices suggest that integration is valid then the contents of Table 4.2 provide evidence favouring integration.

*Table 4.2: Volatility of major stock prices: First quarter 1987–fourth quarter 1990*[a]

| | US | Japan | UK | Germany | France | Italy | Canada |
|---|---|---|---|---|---|---|---|
| 1987 | | | | | | | |
| First quarter | 0.93 | 0.86 | 1.70 | 1.58 | 0.88 | 0.84 | 1.43 |
| Second quarter | 1.12 | 1.30 | 2.07 | 1.47 | 1.07 | 0.88 | 0.66 |
| Third quarter | 0.90 | 1.12 | 3.16 | 0.87 | 0.84 | 1.21 | 0.57 |
| Fourth quarter | 3.65 | 2.83 | 7.31 | 2.97 | 2.43 | 1.99 | 2.69 |
| 1988 | | | | | | | |
| First quarter | 1.43 | 0.99 | 2.91 | 1.86 | 1.53 | 1.65 | 0.84 |
| Second quarter | 1.16 | 0.62 | 1.20 | 1.04 | 1.24 | 1.05 | 0.63 |
| Third quarter | 0.87 | 0.78 | 1.73 | 0.88 | 0.79 | 0.69 | 0.46 |
| Fourth quarter | 0.76 | 0.57 | 1.22 | 0.82 | 0.65 | 0.76 | 0.59 |
| 1989 | | | | | | | |
| First quarter | 0.74 | 0.62 | 1.90 | 0.88 | 1.03 | 0.75 | 0.56 |
| Second quarter | 0.73 | 0.57 | 0.71 | 0.71 | 0.71 | 0.49 | 0.44 |
| Third quarter | 0.68 | 0.45 | 0.82 | 0.82 | 0.47 | 0.73 | 0.39 |
| Fourth quarter | 1.09 | 0.57 | 2.27 | 2.27 | 1.16 | 1.36 | 0.67 |
| 1990 | | | | | | | |
| First quarter | 0.89 | 1.58 | 1.41 | 1.38 | 0.94 | 0.73 | 0.53 |
| Second quarter | 0.77 | 1.58 | 1.88 | 1.33 | 0.80 | 0.54 | 0.70 |
| Third quarter | 1.20 | 2.24 | 2.44 | 1.71 | 1.67 | 1.48 | 0.54 |
| Fourth quarter | 1.10 | 2.59 | 1.30 | 1.62 | 1.07 | 1.30 | 0.57 |

*Note:* [a] For the United States, the stock market index used is Standard & Poor's 500; for Japan, Nikkei 225; for the United Kingdom, the Financial Times Ordinary; for France, CAC General; for Germany, Frankfurt Commerzbank; for Italy, Banca Commerciale; for Canada, Toronto Stock Exchange Composite. Volatility is defined as the standard deviation of the daily proportionate changes in stock market indices over the period indicated.

*Source*: 1991. International Monetary Fund.

The ways described so far to verify whether the world capital markets are integrated are considered to be fairly intuitive. There is no guarantee that world markets are integrated when stock prices are correlated. We need theoretically more convincing tests to examine the issue of integration. This book will cover the modern testing procedures dealing with integration versus the segmentation of capital markets.

A theoretical examination of the concept and the empirical testing procedures will be contemplated in detail later when we introduce the capital asset-pricing models of integration. The idea behind integration can be summarized in a single word: LOOP, that is the law of one price. Hence, what is meant by the integration of capital markets is simply non-existence of differential risk premia for similar or identical financial instruments traded in different locations. Alternatively, capital markets are said to be integrated if the risk associated with similar or identical assets traded on different exchanges carries the same price.

A stricter version of this definition suggests that capital markets are integrated if assets have perfectly correlated rates of return – meaning that identical assets have identical risk premiums, regardless of the location in which they are traded. That is, if risk carries the same price across, for instance, the EU capital markets, then the EU equity markets can be classified as being integrated. A complete integration of capital markets implies the absence of arbitrage opportunities; that is, as markets become integrated arbitrage profits should tend to disappear. Therefore, risk premia differentials suggest some level of segmentation in capital markets, and sources of risk premia differentials should shed some light into the causes of segmentation.

The extent of integration, however, is not so obvious. Of course, one straightforward way of measuring the degree of integration in international capital markets is to look for evidence of barriers against foreign investors. In a financially integrated global market, financial assets traded in different markets, but with identical risk content, will have identical expected returns. Arbitrage will ensure that the risk carries the same price for similar financial instruments registered with different security exchanges. Alternatively, existence of risk premia differentials for identical (strict definition) or similar (loose definition) securities across capital markets implies some degree of segmentation in international capital markets.

**Why is integration desirable?**

This section addresses the social or welfare-related aspects of integration. What can we say, if anything, about the normative side of integration? Why is financial integration particularly desirable; or is it desirable at all? Theoretically, the integration of capital markets is ideal and hence preferable to the presence of segmentation, although there are reservations concerning the feasibility of full-scale integration (Dornbusch, 1988). If we were to take integration as a trade phenomenon, we should simply look at the difference between trade creation and trade diversion.

Three arguments can be advanced for the desirability of (international) capital market integration. One is the efficiency argument which comes from the pure economic theory of trade, and the other two are the risk diversification and capital budgeting arguments, both of which are initiated by the modern theory of finance.

*The argument of economic efficiency*

Based on the competitive auction-pricing model, reducing all kinds of barriers to capital movements leads to a more efficient allocation of the world's resources. The standard economic theory favouring free markets applies to financial capital as well as to labour and goods and services. The underlying assumption is that competitive markets will function and financial capital will seek higher returns to investment, moving from one place where capital is relatively abundant to another where capital is scarce – of course, assuming that there is no barrier.

Indeed, that competition works to clear the markets in an auction-pricing model is better understood and accepted in the context of financial markets than in the product markets or the labour market. Capital asset prices move much more rapidly than do product prices or wages. Moreover, capital markets especially those in the developed parts of the world, are well-organized exchange places equipped with high-technology communications and monitoring systems which can technically respond to rapid changes in asset prices *vis-à-vis* excess demand and supply, and monitor continuously ongoing prices for agents both on and off the floor. This characteristic of capital markets enables the auction-pricing mechanism to function more effectively to clear the markets by eliminating any excess demand or supply that might exist.

*The argument of risk diversification*

The issue whether capital assets are priced according to their local systematic risk content as opposed to the international systematic risk source(s) is of great importance to investors and corporations. It is important to individual investors because of the opportunities in international risk diversification, which are far greater than those in any local risk diversification.

In the past 25–30 years most non-US stocks and bonds have generally outperformed US securities. From the point of view of a US investor, international diversification has been rewarded for those, of course, who have diversified internationally. The explanation of possible gains from international portfolio diversification is related to the indication that international portfolios are likely to exhibit risk-adjusted returns above domestic portfolios since the domestic systematic risk is diversifiable, at least partially.[3] In a segmented market, investors can only diversify the idiosyncratic portion of their total risk. The second part of their risk, the systematic risk, cannot be diversified domestically. However, even systematic risk becomes unsystematic and diversifiable in a world of integrated capital markets.

In passing, one notable characteristic of international diversification associated with market segmentation should be underlined. Segmentation does not necessarily imply that foreigners are not allowed to invest in a particular market. If segmentation is the result of a market imperfection other than direct capital controls against the country of origin of the investor, international diversification is still possible. More importantly, imperfections in international capital markets may allow foreign investors profit opportunities in addition to the gains expected from diversification.

If markets are integrated, one single capital market will exist since the location of exchange places will become unimportant. Then arbitrage will ensure continuously that the market is in equilibrium. However, if markets are segmented arbitrage opportunities will always exist and there will always be some better diversification alternative that will bring higher expected returns to the portfolio.

*The capital budgeting argument*

On the other hand, corporate financial strategies will differ remarkably depending on whether world capital markets are integrated. Domestic firms will face different optimal hedging decisions and encounter different optimal foreign-borrowing versus optimal home-borrowing decisions. Whether the capital assets are priced according to their local risk contents implies different criteria for corporate capital budgeting decisions. If a company has no choice but to raise its capital in a segmented local capital market, it will probably experience a higher cost of capital than a firm with access to world capital markets. Typically, the required rate of return on the common stock of a firm with no exposure to international capital markets hence restricted by its segmented domestic market would be higher than the rate required by investors resident in other capital markets in the world.

We can classify firms making capital budgeting decisions based on their exposure to international capital. Normally, the marginal cost of capital of a firm that employs only domestically available capital is greater than that of a firm using international sources as well. Benefits associated with the integration of capital markets – or the costs of having segmented capital markets – can be summarized as follows.

Three possible cases can be ranked: as follows. Let $MCC_d$, be the marginal cost of capital when capital use is domestic only, $MCC_w$ the marginal cost of capital when international sources are used and, $MCC_i$ marginal cost of capital in an integrated model for securities. The following inequalities among these marginal costs should hold:

$$MCC_d > MCC_w > MCC_i$$

Recently it has been argued that firms will react and take measures to cope with the disadvantages of segmentation. That segmentation creates incentives for firms to adopt countermeasures is suggested by Alexander et *al.* (1988) who argue that segmentation of capital markets will encourage firms to dual-list their stocks on foreign capital markets. They also show that, under segmentation in capital markets, international listing of a security accompanies a reduction in its expected return by affecting the stock price significantly.

## Notes

1. By 'true integration', we mean *market* integration. Markets react to certain developments in such a way that one can speak of a unified world market for securities. As we emphasized in Chapter 3, institutional developments can relax the legal environment for portfolio investors and build the conditions necessary for integration. Yet markets may still be segmented due to certain other factors unrelated to legal restraints imposed by the governments of the national states. We shall discuss several types of direct and indirect barriers over world capital markets, both institutionally and empirically, and their roles in international capital market integration in Chapters 8, 9 and 10.
2. Financial market forces govern international interest rate linkages. The theory of international finance defines two interest parity conditions based on investing in assets denominated in different currencies. The first one is the so-called *covered interest parity condition*. The covered condition establishes a rigid link between international interest rate differentials and forward premia. As long as the covered international differential is different from zero, there will exist incentives for the movements of financial funds from one country to another since arbitrage profits can be made from such an undertaking. Equilibrium in this context is defined as a situation where there are no arbitrage profit opportunities to be made from the movement of financial funds across world markets. This, then, implies that the covered interest differential, *CD*, is zero. In the absence of taxes and transaction costs, the forward premium, $f$, can be expressed in the form of interest rate differential as follows:

$$f \equiv [(F - e)/e] = i - i^*$$

where $F$ is the forward exchange rate, $e$ is the spot exchange rate, and $i$ and $i^*$ are local and foreign interest rates respectively. The interest rate parity differential is simply a restatement of the low of one price.

Contrary to covered investments where currency forwards cover the exchange rate risk which would otherwise be present, uncovered positions involve taking an open position in foreign currencies. Uncovered investments are exposed to the possible effects of exchange rate movements on their returns. The *uncovered interest rate parity condition* is simply the differential between the ongoing interest rates of two countries. Hence, it can be expressed as

$$d = i - i^*.$$

3. Jorion and Schwartz (1986) define integration as 'a situation where investors earn the same risk-adjusted expected return on similar financial instruments in different national markets'.

# PART II

# THE FINANCIAL THEORY OF INTEGRATION

# 5 Asset-pricing models

## The capital market theory

*Systematic and unsystematic risk*

Investors derive their satisfaction associated with buying and selling financial assets from a subjective expected utility function such as the one described below:

$$E(U) = f[E(R), \sigma(R)] \tag{5.1}$$

where $E(R)$ is the expected return, and $\sigma(R)$ is the standard deviation of return. The second moment of the probability distribution of returns, the second argument of the expected utility expression given above, measures the total risk of investment *vis-à-vis* the total variability.

However, when investors select securities, they are not particularly concerned about the size of $\sigma(R)$ because part of the total risk can be diversified away by holding a portfolio of several different financial assets. This part of total risk which can be diversified is called *unsystematic risk*. The remaining portion of total risk, i.e. the *systematic risk*, cannot easily be diversified because it is caused by factors which simultaneously affect the prices of all marketable securities. Investors normally bid up the prices of assets with low systematic risk. Financial assets with relatively high systematic risks, on the other hand, will encounter low demand and market prices that are low relative to assets' income.

*The characteristic line*

The measures of systematic and unsystematic risk are obtained by using what is known as the *characteristic line* of individual securities. A typical characteristic line for some security $i$ is given below.

$$R_{it} = a_i + b_i R_{mt} + e_{it} \tag{5.2}$$

where $a_i$ and $b_i$ = the simple regression intercept and slope statistics, respectively, and $e_t$ = the stochastic error term around the regression line which occurs at date $t$.

The characteristic line given by equation (5.2) represents the nature of systematic and unsystematic risks. Further, it shows the relationship between some instrument $i$ and the market. There are as many characteristic lines as the number of marketable securities. Each characteristic line is called a *market model* for one security.

The estimate of the $b$ coefficient in the characteristic line is of practical importance. The estimator of $b_i$ is called the *beta coefficient*; it measures the slope of the characteristic line. The $a_i$ is the *alpha coefficient* for security $i$, and it is the intercept term of the characteristic line. The alpha and beta statistics are defined as follows:

$$a_i = E(R_i) - b_i E(R_m) \tag{5.3}$$

$$b_i = \text{cov}(R_i, R_m)/\text{var}(R_m) \tag{5.4}$$

where $\text{cov}(R_i, R_m)$ stands for the covariance of returns of the $i$th asset with the market; and it is defined as follows:

$$\text{cov}(R_i, R_m) = (1/T)\sum_{t=I}^{T}[(R_i - E(R_i)(R_m - E(R_m)] = \rho_{im}\sigma(R_i)\sigma R(_m) \tag{5.5}$$

where $\rho_{im}$ is the correlation coefficient between the rate of return to the security $i$ and the market rate of return.

Using the standard ordinary least squares method one can partition the total risk associated with investing in the security $i$, i.e. $\sigma(R_i)$. This is nothing other than the variance of rate of return to this security. From the equation of the characteristic line, the total risk of the ith asset is partitioned as:

$$\text{var}(R_i) = b_i^2 \text{var}(R_m) + \text{var}(e)$$

or:

$$\sigma^2(R_i) = b_i^2\sigma^2(R_m) + \sigma^2(e) \tag{5.6}$$

where the first element of the right-hand side of this equation is the systematic risk and the second part is the unsystematic risk. The latter, which can be diversified by the appropriate choice of instruments in a portfolio, is measured by the residual variance. Using equation (5.6), the fraction of risk that can be eliminated by diversification and the fraction that cannot be abolished as easily can be easily identified. Statistically, the fraction of systematic risk in total risk is nothing other than the determination coefficient of the simple regression expressed in (5.2), and the fraction of unsystematic risk is 1 minus the determination coefficient.

A security with high systematic risk, that is a high beta, will be subject to price declines until the expected return it offers to investors is high enough to compensate for the assumed undiversifiable risk in the market. This level of security price is the *equilibrium price*, and the expected return is the *equilibrium rate of return* for that particular class of risk. This idea of equilibrium is known as the *capital asset-pricing model* (CAPM) or the *security market line* (SML), as it is also called. The CAPM is a linear relationship where the expected return to the *i*th asset is a simple linear function of that asset's sensitivity to the market portfolio; that is, its systematic risk coefficient beta. We shall now express the basics of the capital market theory and the capital asset-pricing model.

*Assumptions of capital market theory*

The theory of capital markets is based on the underlying assumptions of Markowitz portfolio analysis.[1] The following assumptions are necessary to generate the capital market theory:

(a) All investors in capital markets are Markowitz risk diversifiers whose portfolios' locations in a mean-variance plane lie along the *efficient frontier*.[2]
(b) investors can lend and borrow at the same riskless rate;
(c) investors perceive the probability distributions of rates of return to all financial assets identically. That is, all have *homogeneous expectations* or probabilistic beliefs about the future events;
(d) all investors have 'one-period' time horizons;
(e) all investors are price-takers: their individual efforts to buy or sell will not affect the market price;
(f) capital markets are frictionless: that is, no taxes and transaction costs exist when investors trade in securities;
(g) investments are completely divisible and perfectly liquid: that is, frictional sales are possible;
(h) the capital markets are in equilibrium: that is, relevant prices adjust instantaneously when there is any excess demand or supply to clear the markets.[3]

**The capital asset-pricing model**

We have already stated that the underlying idea of Markowitz risk diversification is to find financial assets with low positive or negative covariances. Naturally, demand in the market will be high for those instruments with low positive or negative covariance of returns with the market portfolio. By the same token, tradeable assets with high covariance to the market portfolio, which apparently implies high systematic risk and high beta, will experience low demand in the market. A perfectly competitive asset market will function. That is, the prices of financial assets with high systematic risk will fall, and market prices of securities with low systematic risk will be bid up by investors.[4]

*The capital market line*

According to assumptions 1 and 3, all investors have the same beliefs regarding means, variances and covariances. Hence, everyone will select the market portfolio $M$ when finding the optimal mix of risky securities and riskless assets (see Figure 5.1). The set of assets selected will consist of those portfolios made up of the riskless asset $R_f$ and the risky portfolio $M$. This set is actually a straight line passing through $R_f$ and $M$, called the *capital market line* (CML) . Note that, in the absence of riskless borrowing and ending the efficient frontier will be the curve mentioned in the note 3.

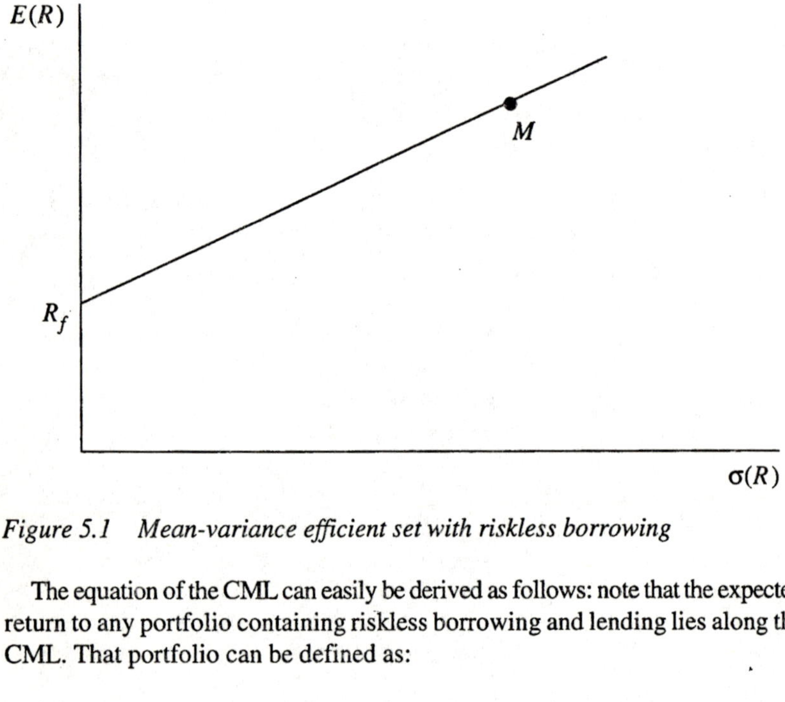


*Figure 5.1 Mean-variance efficient set with riskless borrowing*

The equation of the CML can easily be derived as follows: note that the expected return to any portfolio containing riskless borrowing and lending lies along the CML. That portfolio can be defined as:

$$E(R_p) = wR_f + (1 - w)E\,(R_m) \tag{5.7}$$

where $E(R_p)$ is the fraction invested in the riskless asset. The standard deviation of this portfolio $p$ on the CML is defined by:

$$\sigma(R_p) = (1 - w)\sigma\,(R_m) \tag{5.8}$$

Solving simultaneously $E(R_p)$ and $\sigma(R_p)$ for the fraction $w$, we obtain the following equation for the CML:

$$E(R_p) = R_f + \{[E(R_m) - R_f]/\sigma(R_m)\}/\sigma(R_m) \quad (5.9)$$

Note here that the slope of the CML, $[E(R_m) - R_f]/\sigma(R_m)$, is the marketwide *risk premium* per unit of risk assumed by the investors since it is common to all securities. Given the risk of an efficient portfolio measured by $\sigma(R_p)$, investors expect to receive an additional $[E(R_m) - R_f]/\sigma(R_m)$ units of return over and above the risk-free rate of return for every unit of $\sigma(R_p)$ in an efficient portfolio. This risk premium is also called *market price of risk* for an efficient portfolio. Note that we have assumed the existence of homogeneous expectations about the statistical moments and cross-moments and that no transaction costs exist.

*The security market line or CAPM*

We have previously mentioned that the security market line (SML) is the *equilibrium relationship* between expected returns and risks measured as return variances. Equilibrium rates of return move inversely with the price of the security. Thus, assets having a high covariance with the market will have relatively low prices and high expected return. Similarly, securities with low or negative covariances will experience high prices and hence low equilibrium expected rates of return. This capital market equilibrium relationship is depicted in Figure 5.2. Below are the formal expressions of the CAPM in terms of (a) covariance, and (b) the beta coefficient.[5]

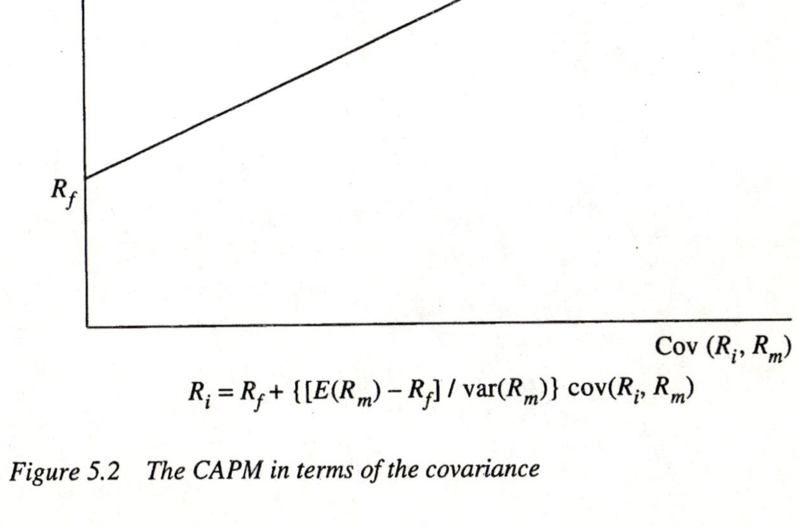


$$R_i = R_f + \{[E(R_m) - R_f] / \text{var}(R_m)\} \text{ cov}(R_i, R_m)$$

*Figure 5.2 The CAPM in terms of the covariance*

*The CAPM in terms of the covariance*

$$E(R_i) = R_f + [E(R_m) - R_f] \operatorname{cov}(R_i, R_m)/\sigma^2(R_m) \qquad (5.10)$$

where $E(R_i)$ = the equilibrium expected rate of return to the *i*th asset; $[E(R_m) - R_f]$ = the slope of CAPM which measures the *market price of systematic risk*; $R_f$ = the risk-free rate of return available in the market; and $\operatorname{cov}(R_i, R_m)$ = the *i*th asset's covariance of rates of return with the market portfolio.

One can see that in the form represented by equation (5.10) the market risk premium per unit of risk is the same as that observed above in the CML. However, unlike the CML, the risk of a security is not its standard deviation but rather its individual contribution to the risk of the market portfolio, which is equal to $\operatorname{cov}(R_i, R_m) / \sigma(R_m)$.

*The CAPM in terms of the beta* Equation (5.10) is rewritten as:

$$E(R_i) = R_f + [E(R_m) - R_f]\beta_i \qquad (5.11)$$

where $\beta_i$ = the *i*th security's beta measured as the ratio of $\operatorname{cov}(R_i, R_m)$ to the $\sigma^2(R_m)$. The CAPM in terms of beta is shown in Figure 5.3.

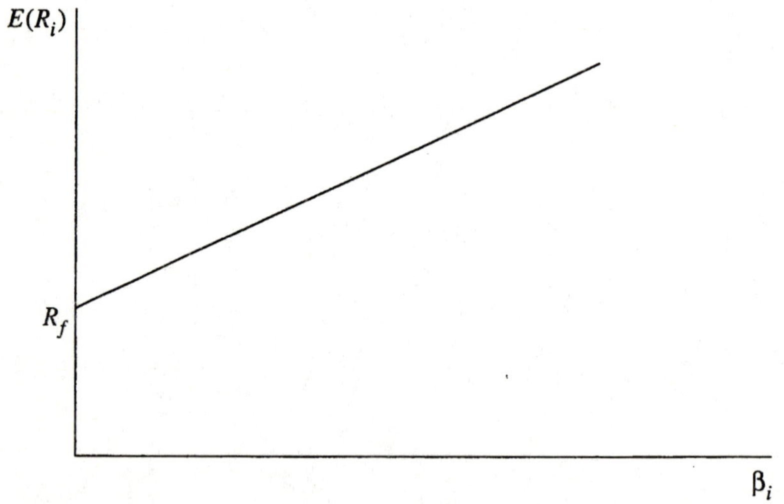


$$E(R_i) = R_f + [E(R_m) - R_f]\,\beta_i$$

*Figure 5.3 The CAPM in terms of the beta coefficient*

**Extensions of CAPM and empirical tests**

The CAPM is a simple linear relation between the excess rate of return to an individual asset or portfolio and the excess rate of return on the benchmark market portfolio. Hence, testing the CAPM should be straightforward. Yet it is not. The opponents of CAPM argue that (a) the relation may not be linear; (b) there might exist factors other than beta needed to explain expected returns; and (c) $R_f$ is not the appropriate riskless rate of return.

Many of the extensions of the standard Sharpe–Lintner model, however, support the simple linear relation of CAPM. There have been numerous empirical tests since Sharpe (1964). The following pages study the extensions of CAPM and important contributions since Sharpe (1964).

*Lintner's work*

Lintner's (1965) model is the same as that of Sharpe (1964), and leads to the same conclusion as Sharpe. Lintner's later (1969) version focuses on rates of return in real terms. This version also shows that the existence of heterogeneous expectations does not critically alter the standard version of the CAPM, except that expected returns and covariances are expressed as complex weighted averages of investor expectations. If investors do have heterogeneous expectations, then the CAPM will be non-testable since the market portfolio is not necessarily efficient.

*Mossin's general equilibrium approach*

Mossin (1966) characterizes a general equilibrium approach to capital asset-pricing. There is no essential difference between Mossin (1966) and the original Sharpe model. Indeed, Mossin's general equilibrium approach implies the existence of the market line. He further relates the concept of the price of risk to the slope of this line.

*Brennan's inclusion of tax effects*

Brennan (1970) explores the effects of taxation on capital asset-pricing. In fact, Brennan's is the only paper in which the equilibrium model in a world with personal as well as corporate taxes is investigated. He looks into the effect of differential tax rates on dividends and capital gains. His model includes a second parameter that causes expected return to depend on dividend yield in addition to systematic risk. The following expected return equation summarizes what Brennan has implied by the capital market equilibrium model with taxes:

$$E(R_k) = \lambda_1 R_f + \lambda_2 \beta_k + \lambda_3 DIV_k \tag{5.12}$$

where $DIV_k$ = the dividend yield on asset $k$.

*Zero-beta CAPM*

Black's (1972) version of CAPM focuses on the absence of riskless asset. In this version of CAPM, the risk-free rate is replaced by a portfolio of risky assets that is uncorrelated to the market portfolio. This uncorrelated portfolio is called zero-beta CAPM since a zero covariance implies zero beta.

*Continuous-time CAPM*

Merton (1973) incorporates investors' concern with future investment opportunities into Sharpe's original model. Merton derives a version of CAPM that assumes that trading takes place continuously over time. The paper also assumes that asset returns are distributed lognormally. Note that, if the risk-free rate of return is nonstochastic over time, the equilibrium rates of return must satisfy

$$E(R_i) = R_f + [E(R_m) - R_f]\beta_i$$

This is the continuous-time analogy to the CAPM and it holds regardless of individual preferences, the distribution of individuals' wealth or their time horizon. In fact, the equation is exactly the same as (5.11). The differences between the two are that in the later equation instantaneous rates of return replaces rates of return over discrete time intervals; and the distribution of returns is normal in (5.11) and lognormal in the other.

Note, however, that investors are exposed to a different type of risk if the risk-free rate is stochastic. This risk is associated with unfavourable shifts in the opportunity set of investors. In this case, Merton (1973) shows that investors will hold portfolios selected from three investment funds: the risk-free asset, the benchmark market portfolio, and another portfolio chosen so that its returns are perfectly negatively correlated with the riskless asset. This model exhibits what is called three-fund separation. The third fund here is necessary to hedge against unanticipated changes in the *stochastic* risk-free rate in the future. The required rate of return on some asset $k$ is

$$E(R_k) = R_f + \lambda_1 [E(R_m) - R_f] + \lambda_2[E(R_p) - R_f] \qquad (5.13)$$

where:

$R_p$ = the rate of return on a portfolio that is perfectly negatively correlated to the riskless asset,
$\lambda_1$ = $(\beta_{km} - \beta_{kp}\beta_{pm}) / (1 - \rho^2_{pm})$
$\lambda_2$ = $(\beta_{kp} - \beta_{km}\beta_{pm}) / (1 - \rho^2_{pm})$
$\rho_{pm}$ = the correlation coefficient between the market portfolio and the selected portfolio $p$
$\beta_{ij}$ = $\text{cov}(R_i, R_j)/\sigma^2(R_j)$.

The $\lambda_2$ will be positive for low beta assets and negative for high beta assets (Merton, 1973). In another paper, Merton (1987) studies market segmentation and conditions for capital market equilibrium under incomplete information.

*Fama–MacBeth approach*

Fama and MacBeth (1973) provide one of the best-known and -applied testing procedures for CAPM. In their procedure, normal or expected returns are predicted according to a cross-sectional relationship whose coefficients are estimated by regressing average portfolio returns on average portfolio betas to ensure that the estimators reflect the nature of the equilibrium relationship between risk and return relationship. That is, given the beta coefficient estimated using the market model (CAPM) for the *i*th security, the expected (normal) returns are calculated employing a cross-sectional relationship. Fama and MacBeth (1973) test four different implications of asset-pricing theories *à la* Sharpe–Lintner. These are:

(a) there is a linear relationship between risk and expected return on an investment portfolio;
(b) the covariance risk is the only type of risk awarded by the market;
(c) there is a positive relation between risk and expected return on an investment portfolio;
(d) the intercept term of the linear regression line is different from the risk-free rate (the higher the risk, the higher is the expected return).

They first estimate the following regression to find the betas:

$$R_i = \alpha_i + \beta_i R_m + e_i \tag{5.14}$$

This is a time-series regression in which Fama and MacBeth estimate the beta of some security (portfolio) *i*. This is the first step of the so-called *Fama–MacBeth two-step procedure*. After running the regression in (5.14) and obtaining the estimates of beta using the standard ordinary least squares (OLS) procedure, Fama and MacBeth estimate the mean returns cross-sectionally against the betas using the following regression:

$$\bar{R}_i = \gamma_{0t} + \gamma_{1t}\beta_i + \gamma_{2t}\beta_i^2 + \gamma_{3t}SE_i + \varepsilon_{it} \tag{5.15}$$

where $\bar{R}_i$ = average rate of return on asset *i*, and $SE_i$ = standard error of the rate of return on asset *i*.

The hypotheses tested are:

(a) linearity: $E(\gamma_{2t}) = 0$;
(b) no systematic effects on non-beta (non-covariance) risk: $E(\gamma_{3t}) = 0$;
(c) positive expected return-risk trade-off: $E(\gamma_{1t}) = 0$.

Fama and MacBeth overall fail to reject the hypothesis that average returns on New York Stock Exchange common stocks reflect the attempts of risk-averse investors to hold efficient portfolios.

*Other extensions and tests of CAPM*

There are several extensions built on the Sharpe–Lintner–Mossin CAPMs. Among the influential tests of CAPM are Black, *et al.* (1972) and Blume and Friend (1973). Rubinstein (1974) explores alternative utility functions that are more general than those assumed by the standard model. Kraus and Litzenberger (1976) take into account the statistical third moments of return distributions. Levy (1978) incorporates transaction costs present in capital market investment decisions into equilibrium. Sharpe (1991) modifies the model to reflect the role of negative holdings. He essentially assumes that investors are unable to take negative positions in assets.

## Notes

1. There is a close link between the Markowitz portfolio theory and the capital market theory that we address here. Named after its originator, Harry M. Markowitz, *Markowitz risk diversification* can be defined as the process of portfolio selection where assets that have less than perfectly positively correlated returns are combined in order to reduce portfolio risk without giving up any portfolio returns (Markowitz, 1959). It can even decrease the risk below the systematic level.

   The benefits of low correlation coefficients in portfolio risk diversification can best be seen by the following formula for portfolio risk:

$$\sigma^2\left(R_p\right) = \sum_{i=1}^{n}\sum_{j=1}^{n} w_i w_j \sigma_{ij}$$

   where $\sigma^2(R_p)$ = variance of the portfolio's rate of return, and $\sigma_{ij} = \text{cov}(R_i, R_j)$, the covariance between the rate of return to the *i*th security and the rate of return to the *j*th security. It denotes variance when $i = j$. Note, however, that the covariance can be expressed in terms of a simple correlation coefficient, $\rho_{ij}$, since $\sigma_{ij} = (\sigma_i)(\sigma_j)(\rho_{ij})$. If the correlation coefficient is zero, say in a two-asset world, then substantial reductions in risk can be obtained. However, risk reduction benefits can become greater as the assets become more and more uncorrelated, in which case $\rho_{ij}$ is negative.
2. If the risk and return characteristics of all marketable securities traded on all available security exchanges were plotted in risk-return space, they all would be dominated by portfolios. The scalloped, quarter-moon-shaped geometric locus of all attainable portfolios is known as the *efficient frontier*. Portfolios, obtained either through the Markowitz risk diversification method or some other diversification technique, will always dominate individual assets because of the risk-reducing advantages that the portfolios offer. Markowitz diversification, however, will generate portfolios that are more efficient than ordinarily diversified portfolios. Assumptions underlying the Markowitz portfolio analysis are:

(a) the statistical moments of the rate of return to any security or portfolio adequately summarize the outcome from the investment;
(b) Investors can visualize the probability distribution of the rate of return to any instrument.
(c) Investors willingly base their decisions on the first two moments of the rate of return, namely the expected return and the variance .
(d) Given the class of risk, investors always prefer a higher rate of return to a lower one. That is, $\delta U[R, \sigma(R)]/\delta E(R) > 0$, where $U = f\{E(R), \sigma(R)\}$. Conversely, given expected returns, investors always prefer less risk. That is, $\delta U/\delta\sigma(R) < 0$.

3. A formal definition of equilibrium appears in the appendix to this chapter.
4. See the appendix for a definition of competitive equilibrium.
5. Mathematical derivation of CAPM can be found in any graduate textbook on finance or investments. See, for instance, Fama and Miller (1972). The original works on CAPM are due Sharpe (1964); Lintner (1965); and Mossin (1966).

## Appendix: The concept of equilibrium

Equilibrium is a vector of prices whereby markets clear (instantaneously or sequentially). That is:

$$\exists\, P = \{P_{1't,}\, P_{2,t,}\, \ldots, P_{m,t}\} \in \Re^n \ni z\,(D_t) = z\,(S_t) = 0\ \forall\, t \qquad \text{(A5.1)}$$

$$P \gg 0 \qquad \text{(A5.2)}$$

where $P_t$ is $(1 \times m)$ vector of prices, and $z(D)$, and $z(S)$ are excess demand and supply respectively.

*Definition A5.1: A formal definition of equilibrium*

Let the index set of all individuals be denoted by $\wp = \{1,2,\ldots,I\}$ and the generic element of $\wp$ by $i$. Let ${}^iP$ be the set of prices on which $i$'s demand correspondence, ${}^i\xi$, is non-empty valued.

$$P = \bigcap_{\wp} {}^iP \qquad \text{(A5.3)}$$

where $P$ is the set of prices on which everyone's excess demand correspondence is well-defined. The $P$ of (A5.3) is the same as those of (A5.1) and (A5.2). Then the *aggregate excess demand correspondence* $\Psi: P \rightarrow \Re^n$, defined as:

$$\Psi(p) = \sum{}_{\wp}^{i}\xi(p) - \left(\sum_{\wp} {}^i\omega^1, 0\right) \qquad \text{(A5.4)}$$

where $\Sigma^i\xi_j(p) - \Sigma^i\omega_j^1$ is demand in excess of supply for a *currently deliverable* security $j$. The *aggregate excess demand* for a futures contract, $j$, is $\Sigma^i\xi j(p)$, the sum of offers to buy such contracts minus the offers to sell them.

An *equilibrium* is a tuple such that

$$\sum_{\wp} {}^{i}z^{*} = \left( \sum_{\wp} {}^{i}\omega^{1}, 0 \right). \tag{A5.5}$$

Such an equilibrium is attainable if $P$ is non-empty (i.e. condition (A5.2) is satisfied).

*Definition A5.2: Competitive equilibrium*
An equilibrium is said to be competitive if the following statements hold simultaneously:

*Assumption A5.2.1* Prices adjust fully to clear the markets. If there is excess demand (supply) the adjustment is upward (downward).

*Assumption A5.2.2* All agents face the same price system.

*Assumption A5.2.3* All contracts are made at the beginning of all dates, and there exists a sequence of spot markets, one for each date.

*Assumption A5.2.4* Markets open and close once and for all at each date, and no incentives exist to reopen the markets within the same date; hence, sequential trading is not allowed.

*Assumption A5.2.5* There are enough institutions which enable the economic units to transfer wealth freely over time.

*Definition A5.3: Temporary equilibrium*
Equilibrium is still competitive. However, sequential trading is ruled in. Adjustments are made only by price movements, a usual postulate in any competitive equilibrium. Exchange takes place sequentially over time.

*Definition A5.4: Temporary equilibrium with quantity rationing*
Unlike competitive equilibrium, prices cannot fully adjust. They are temporarily fixed and adjustments are made by quantity rationing.

*A representative agent's problem*
Let now ${}^{i}S_t$ be the set of all possible signals that an agent may receive by the date $t$. Assume further that this ${}_{i}S_t$ is a separable metric space. Then an agent's

problem is to choose an action $a_t \in A_t$, given the signals up to date $t$, and all the agent's previous decisions (actions).

An action $a_t$ is basically a commitment to exchange something either currently available or available in some foreseeable future. Hence $a_t$ may involve:

(a) a commitment to exchange currently available securities;
(b) a commitment to exchange specified quantities of securities to be delivered at later dates (*forward contracts*); or
(c) a commitment to exchange the forward contracts entailing the delivery or the receipt, at specified dates, of a particular security to hold securities of various maturity dates.

# 6 International asset-pricing and the financial theory of integration

## International risk diversification

The benefits associated with international risk diversification is well documented in the literature. The opportunities to be exploited in world capital markets are almost unlimited. Hence, investors who diversify internationally expand the opportunity set along which they can select the optimum investment portfolio. Internationally well-diversified portfolios dominate domestically diversified portfolios (Ibbotson *et al.*, 1982; Levy and Sarnat, 1970).

The benefits from international diversification are closely related to the degree of segmentation of capital markets. If integration of the world markets is complete, then advantageous arbitrage opportunities may not exist. Yet this does not imply that investors do not gain when they invest internationally. They can diversify part of the locally systematic risk as well as the idiosyncratic risk. Put differently, systematic risk can be diversified away via selecting the investment portfolio from internationally traded securities along with the domestically traded ones. Hence, an internationally diversified portfolio would still be preferable.

However, as world markets become more integrated, arbitrage across markets becomes more difficult. If capital markets are perfectly integrated, which implies that there exists a unified world market for securities, costless arbitrage opportunities disappear. Investors benefit only from being offered a greater number of securities whereby they can reduce their risk exposure. On the other hand, if world markets are segmented, then costless arbitrage opportunities remain in place to be exploited. The gains from international diversification are potentially greater in a world of segmented capital markets than the diversification benefits in an integrated world market. Potential diversification gains under segmentation has two components. First, there is the benefit associated with having a larger investment opportunity set. Second, there are the benefits from international arbitrage which is absent under integration.

Varying benefits from international risk diversification, depending on the degree of segmentation, make the issue of capital market integration critical. It is important for investors who want to diversify internationally to know whether the world capital markets are integrated. In some cases, potential losses associated with selecting a portfolio when a more efficient (in the mean-variance sense) one exists could be colossal. In this chapter we shall discuss the issue of international capital market integration using several techniques suggested in the literature. The following section addresses what we call non-asset-pricing theories of integration.

**Non-asset-pricing models of integration**

We shall briefly examine what we call non-asset-pricing models of capital market integration before concentrating on international asset-pricing models. These procedures propose some *ad hoc* way of measuring integration. They are not based on the existence of an equilibrium relation in capital markets. Although they are descriptive and lack analytical support, they are routinely used by practitioners as well as academicians in the field of finance. We shall mention two of such methods commonly employed in the literature. The following paragraphs give a brief descriptive account of those models that are not based on asset-pricing relations.

*Correlation coefficients*

Before the modern international asset-pricing models were adopted, numerous previous works had focused on the difference between segmentation and integration solely on the basis of simple correlation coefficients. By calculating correlation coefficients across equity returns in the stock exchanges of various countries, some have linked capital market integration to the magnitude of these coefficients. High positive correlation coefficients in stock market price indices are taken to suggest the existence of possible capital market integration. These procedures monitor time series behaviour of prices and interest rates.

For instance, Ibbotson, *et al.* (1982) find high degrees of correlation within various groups of countries. They show that Germany, Switzerland and the Netherlands exhibited a great deal of co-movement as did the United States, Canada, Australia, Hong Kong and Singapore. They further argued that these co-movements of returns should be a signal for capital market integration.[1]

Correlation coefficients across the world capital markets are increasingly high at times of sharp decline in stock prices. It is interesting to note that all simple correlation coefficients of total percentage market movements for major stock price indices are negative during the month of October 1987. Roll (1988) reports that October 1987 was the only month when all markets moved in the same direction. Yet both before and after that crash the correlations were positive but moderate in size, and rarely above 0.5. In Chapter 1, we reported cross-correlation coefficients in world capital markets.

*Interest rate parity*

Another approach that is not based on capital asset-pricing models is to test the validity of interest rate parity and link such tests to the tests for market integrations. Aliber (1973), Marston (1976) and Roll and Solnik (1977) are among those who adopted interest rate validity tests. The underlying argument behind these interest rate parity papers is the assumption that there exist perfect capital markets and that this assumption is sufficient to set forward an interest rate parity relation. Since perfect capital markets should imply capital market integration, there arises a link between the tests of interest rate parity and the test of integration of international capital markets. Therefore, if the parity differentials disappear one can speak of integration.

There is one major problem in adopting this method: its important weakness is a lack of generality. It is questionable to conclude that security markets are integrated when the parity relation holds, because the interest rate parity differential is only a measure of money market segmentation. If interest rate parity differentials disappear or tend to disappear, this implies monetary integration and not necessarily the integration of capital markets, a major part of which is made up of equities.

**The capital asset-pricing model of integration**

The question whether there exists a unified world market for securities necessitates a model in which we can define risk. The standard approach to defining risk utilizes a pricing model for capital assets. As we have shown in the previous chapter, the capital asset pricing model (CAPM) measures the price per unit of risk assumed by investors who trade in securities in a given market. That the market is international is important for the purposes of integration for the reasons that we have mentioned above and those we shall outline below.

Although the academic literature that has focused on the issue of integration versus segmentation in the context of international capital markets is relatively small, interest in the topic has arisen recently because of the growing interest in political integration. Basically two rival asset-pricing models are inquired for testing the hypothesis given above to furnish a satisfactory answer to the question whether capital markets are internationally integrated. One is a model which defines risk domestically, and the other one is a model where risk is defined in an international context. The former assumes that the sources of risk are local whereas the latter takes risk as determined by international forces.

If the former pricing model is correct, then assets are said to priced domestically by national factor(s). If, on the other hand, the latter is relevant, the pricing structure of capital assets cannot be explained solely by a purely domestic factor (or factors), and international sources are important for pricing purposes. Obviously, an asset-pricing model where common sources of risk are assumed to be international postulates in a strict sense that there is one integrated world capital market.

*The literature*

A rich body of literature on capital market integration has adopted modern asset-pricing models, and tests have been made to determine whether capital assets are priced in an integrated world market as opposed to a number of segmented local (national) markets. Specifically, the literature has tested the hypothesis that assets are priced according to their local systematic risk source(s) against the null hypothesis of no relationship or the hypothesis that assets are priced in an integrated model against the null hypothesis of no relationship. However, the issue of capital market segmentation versus integration is still unsettled. If there were no barriers to international investment then, theoretically, all capital assets in all countries would be priced according to a model of an integrated international capital market.

Theory also postulates that, if capital controls remained in place, a segmented market model would be more appropriate for asset-pricing purposes than an integrated global market model. Numerous previous works – with the possible exception of Stehle (1977) – focused on the presence or absence of segmentation in capital markets with no reference to the sources of segmentation. Most have failed to accept that world capital markets are integrated (see, for instance, Solnik, 1974a, 1977; Adler and Dumas, 1975, 1983; Ibbotson *et al.*, 1982).

Some recent studies have argued, however, that a widespread rejection of capital market integration should not suggest that there are no empirical questions left unanswered; they have given special emphasis to the sources of segmentation in capital markets. Basically three different sources, all of which can be put under the heading of market imperfections, have been recognized:

(a) market imperfections in the form of direct barriers to investment, such as government impediments and capital controls (Stulz, 1981a, 1981b; Errunza and Losq, 1985; Gultekin *et al.* 1990);
(b) market imperfections associated with the lack of ability of a group of investors (Jorion and Schwartz, 1986); and finally
(c) implications of exchange rate risk on international asset-pricing (Solnik, 1974a, 1977).

Market imperfections as sources of segmentation in capital markets will be studied in the following chapter.

*International CAPM* The mean-variance CAPMs predict that the world market portfolio will be mean-variance efficient under the hypothesis that capital asset markets are internationally integrated. Provided that the individual measures an asset's risk by the covariance of its real return with the real return on his portfolio, the capital market structure of international stock prices is believed to be approximated by a single index market model, as is that of domestic prices.

An international market portfolio is simply a basket of securities selected from the various capital markets of the world. A composite world index, on the other hand, is a weighted average of either the domestic market indices or individual portfolios established locally from all over the world. In practice, the former is more common. If the weights are equal, then the portfolio is called equally weighted (EWP). More often, though, the weights are unequal and based on market capitalizations. Portfolios set with capitalization weights are known as value weighted portfolios (VWP). In either case, the focus is on whether the single index is priced by the data.

If the international index or some other benchmark international market portfolio is priced, this could be a signal for integration, since it postulates that the international factor, a world index of returns, is an important determinant for equity return variations. Therefore, one might conclude that the international pricing of capital assets is the correct model. If, however, the international model is insignificant and the composite index is not priced, this can imply that domestic factors are still important for pricing purposes and that the segmentation is the right model.

*Early models and work of Solnik* The international extension of CAPM was first studied by Solnik (1974a, 1974b) who tested whether the standard Sharpe (1964) and Lintner (1965) model holds internationally. His test is actually a joint test. The hypothesis that the Sharpe–Lintner model is internationally valid also amounts to a test of international capital market integration. A rejection of such an hypothesis implies that (a) some world market portfolio is not mean-variance efficient, and that (b) world capital markets are segmented (or they can be classified as such).

Solnik derived a single-index model and further investigated whether a domestic factor can solely capture the behaviour of security prices. What is meant by the behaviour of security prices here is not only their time-series performance but also, by virtue of the entire class of empirical capital asset-pricing models in the Sharpe–Lintner tradition, their cross-sectional behaviour (Black *et al.*, 1972; Fama and MacBeth, 1973).

Cross-sectional behaviour is captured in the behaviour of expected returns to securities. In this context, an international version of the capital asset-pricing model *per se* should explain both time-series and cross-sectional variations in stock returns *vis-à-vis* some world market portfolio if integration has indeed taken place. The following is the international version of a single-index model that is in essence similar to that of Solnik (1974a):

$$E(R_i) = \beta_{iw} E(R_w) \tag{6.1}$$

where $R_i$ is the excess rate of return on asset $i$ calculated as the difference between the actual rate of return and some riskless rate of return $R_f$; $R_w$ is the excess rate of return from some benchmark world portfolio; and $\beta_{iw}$ is the beta of the $i$th security or portfolio with respect to the world market portfolio. A zero intercept in this return-generating process corresponds to the Sharpe–Lintner version and a non-zero intercept implies a version of the Black model. The *i*th security's beta *vis-à-vis* the international market portfolio in (6.1) is given by

$$\beta_{iw} = E(R_i, R_w)/E(R_w^2) \tag{6.2}$$

where $E(R_i, R_w)$ can be measured by the covariance between the security's (or a particular portfolio's) rate of return and the rate of return to some well-diversified world market portfolio. $E(R_w^2)$ is measured by the variance of the return to the world market portfolio in a regression where the excess rate of return to the *i*th security is run against the rate of return to the market portfolio.

Similarly, a domestic capital asset-pricing model, that is the standard Sharpe–Lintner model, implies that the following relation between the excess expected return to some security or portfolio $i, E(R_i)$ and the excess expected return to the domestic market portfolio, $E(R_d)$ which is assumed to be domestically well-diversified holds:

$$E(R_i) = [E(R_i, R_d)/E(R_d^2)]\ E(R_d) \tag{6.3}$$

The question raised here is whether a single world index model would give a reasonable description of international asset prices. If the argument is valid, then the parameters of the two regressions, one that regresses returns on a domestic market index (portfolio), and the other that regresses returns on an international market index (portfolio) should answer the question of integration or segmentation.[2] To be safe econometrically, the returns must be orthogonalized to some domestic portfolio and to the international one. That part of return on the domestic portfolio that is uncorrelated to the world portfolio should be taken as an explanatory variable along with the rate of return on the world market portfolio in a regression that attempts to explain the time-series behaviour of portfolio or individual security returns (Stehle, 1977).

Note that the capital asset-pricing model does not preclude the possibility that the time-series regression will result in significant risk premia estimates. Rather, it requires that portfolio returns have their sensitivity coefficients (i.e. the betas) determine the behaviour of the excess expected returns. This amounts to testing whether the security or portfolio betas are statistically significant. If they are, it can be concluded that, using the standard finance vocabulary, the risk is priced.

If the international sources of uncertainty embodied in some selected benchmark world market portfolio are priced according to the capital asset-pricing model at hand, such as that given by (6.1), then the capital markets may be classified as integrated. To summarize, it might be suggested that the world capital markets are said to be integrated if the international factor (i.e. some benchmark portfolio established internationally) is priced, or that markets are segmented if a purely national factor is priced. Adopting the model outlined here, many of the empirical works in the literature fail to reject the hypothesis that world markets are integrated.

In one of the early works comparing the international and domestic versions of the CAPM, Stehle (1977), whose model is based empirically on the Fama–MacBeth cross-sectional, time-series approach, cannot reject the hypothesis of segmentation, nor can he reject the integration hypothesis. Stehle adopts a multi-period capital market equilibrium model based on logarithmic utility functions. He proceeds to test whether risk premia on US stocks during the period 1956–75 were determined as if the US market were segmented from the rest of the world or were integrated fully. It turns out that the data do not provide any support for the domestic model. Yet he cannot accept the validity of the international model either.

Given the multivariate probability distributions of a domestic market and an international index, Stehle regresses the domestic market index against the world index to isolate the purely domestic one by projection. The regression using the incorrect measure of risk will have a residual that is not independently distributed from the independent variable. As a result of this, the ordinary least square estimates will be inconsistent.

What follows from Stehle's work is, therefore, that it is necessary to identify those parts of the total rate of return variations representing a diversifiable risk in a segmented but not in an international market, or vice versa. Stehle's model of integration that is based upon the orthogonalization of the domestic market portfolio from the world portfolio has been widely adopted by recent studies in the literature.

*Recent applications of international CAPM* Having employed standard single-factor asset-pricing models, recent literature in international asset-pricing and capital market segmentation have concentrated on testing whether or not international capital market integration exists. These works have in general adopted an international single asset-pricing model in the Sharpe–Lintner tradition based on the standard assumption that the return on any security is a linear function of the return on the domestic market index. In the international context, the domestic market index translates into an international market portfolio or a composite world index. Following the work of Solnik, the literature has theoretically and empirically dealt with the issue. Here we shall provide a brief review of the literature adopting several international versions of the Sharpe–Lintner capital asset-pricing model.

Having examined the issue of market segmentation for the Canadian stock market, Jorion and Schwartz (1986) reject integration in a relatively recent study. Their test supports a strong degree of segmentation between Canadian markets and the global North American market. A 'mild' market integration, that is partial integration in some degree, is only supported for the interlisted stocks.

Mild integration would be the case if there were capital controls against the country of origin of investment in one market but the restrictions were absent in the other(s). Jorion and Schwartz suggest that their rejection of the joint hypothesis of integration of the North American equity market combined with the CAPM is due to their adoption of the maximum-likelihood technique, more powerful than the traditional Fama–MacBeth two-pass approach.

In two other recent studies, Alexander *et al.* (1988) provide evidence of high covariances between a sample of Canadian and US securities. Their results are inconsistent with those of Jorion and Schwartz. They show that international listing of securities accompanies a reduction in the expected return on the stock. They further draw a parallel between the insignificant decline in the alpha-adjusted average returns of Canadian securities and an integrated market between US and Canadian markets. Their work seems to suggest that the stock prices, when they are introduced to international listing, are set in a relatively more integrated market than in the pre-interlisting period.

*Empirical models of Errunza and Losq* Errunza and Losq (1985), applying a model originally developed by Stulz (1981a and 1981b) find evidence to support the mild segmentation hypothesis in their work which includes a large number of world capital markets. Their work, unlike that of many others, is based on the assumption that the only market imperfection is 'the assumed inability of a class of investors to trade in a subset of securities' (Errunza and Losq, 1985). They suggest that the securities inaccessible to some investors display super risk premiums that are proportional to the conditional market risk, a new concept of risk which means conditional covariance between the return on a security specific and the return on the market portfolio.

Errunza and Losq break down the market into segments in terms of restrictions against foreign investors. It is then appropriate to investigate which segment has earned the excess premia. The proper classification here, they suggest, is the one where the division of securities is based on how accessible they are for foreign investors; the set of accessible securities is then observed to see if they exhibit excess premia.

Using the work of Errunza and Losq (1985) we shall outline the approach. Consider the following model, according to which only the securities that are free of capital controls are priced:

$$E(R_i - R_f) = \delta V \mathrm{cov}\,[R_i, R_m] \qquad (6.4)$$

where $R_i$ is the return to a security accessible by all investors, $R_f$, and $R_m$ are the riskless rate and market rate of return respectively, $\delta$ is the absolute risk-aversion coefficient for the aggregate population of investors, and $V$ stands for the market value of the world portfolio. The securities that are priced according to equation (6.4) do not earn super risk premiums.

On the other hand, the securities that are under formal capital controls are priced according to a return-generating model similar to the following:

$$E(R_j - R_f) - \delta V \text{cov}[R_j, R_m] = \delta' V' \text{cov}[R_j, R'] \quad (6.5)$$

where $R_j$ is the rate of return to a security inaccessible to all investors, $R'$ is the rate of return to the portfolio of such securities, $\delta'$ is the difference in risk aversion between the investors free of control and the investors who do not have the access to a group of securities, $V'$ is the market value of the portfolio consisting of inaccessible securities, and cov$[R_j, R']$ is the 'conditional market risk' of security $j$ which is the conditional covariance between its return and the rate of return on the market portfolio of inaccessible securities.

What equations (6.4) and (6.5) suggest is that securities that are accessible to both domestic and foreign investors are priced as though the two markets were completely integrated. On the other hand, securities access to which is denied some investors (such as domestically traded securities) earn super risk premia. This should shed some light on the issue of the receiver of the premia.[3]

Following the work by Errunza and Losq, one can in a similar way classify securities on the basis of dual-listing. The interlisted securities should have different characteristics, in that dual (or in general international) listing of securities accompanies a reduction in their expected returns if the market is segmented.

*Consumption-based CAPMs* In addition to the standard versions of CAPM, versions based on consumption have been proposed to test for integration. Consumption-based CAPMs were originally proposed by Lucas (1978). These models measure an asset's risk as the covariance of its real return with the growth in consumption (see, for instance, Wheatley, 1988). Consumption-based capital asset-pricing models test the equality of the marginal rate of substitution across countries. In an empirical work, Obsteld (1986) fails to reject the hypothesis of integration. Wheatley (1988), using a discrete-time version of the consumption-based asset-pricing model, cannot provide enough evidence against the joint hypothesis that equity markets are integrated internationally and that the asset-pricing model holds.

Wheatley, who defines risk as the covariance of an asset's real return with the growth in real consumption, provides several tests of international capital market integration. All his tests are based on a simple consumption asset-pricing model that attempts to predict that there is an asset-pricing line for each country, which relates an individual's expected real return on each asset to the covariance of this return with the growth in the individual's real consumption. His tests provide very little evidence against the joint hypothesis that the stock markets are internationally integrated and that the particular asset-pricing model holds.

*The conditional version of international CAPM* The CAPMs assume that the market portfolio is mean-variance efficient and that observations on a benchmark return for a single beta model are *a priori* available. It is typically assumed in CAPM applications that observations on a vector of returns, including the return on the aggregate market portfolio, are normally distributed with probability distributions independent and identical over time. To deal with this problem, a conditional version of CAPM has been suggested.

Extending the work of Roll (1977), Hansen and Hodrick (1980, 1983) demonstrate that, once the expectation operators preceding excess returns are conditional upon an information set which is a subset of the investors' information set, the benchmark return lies on the conditional mean-variance frontier. What follows is that a benchmark return is on the conditional mean-variance frontier if any other return that has the same conditional mean as the benchmark also has a conditional variance that is at least as large as that of the benchmark (Hansen and Hodrick, 1983).

Conditional versions of CAPM in an international context have been tested by Harvey (1991), who tests whether conditional CAPMs are consistent with the behaviour of returns in 17 selected countries and measures the conditional risk. He provides evidence on the conditional mean-variance efficiency of the benchmark portfolio.

### *Critiques of international CAPM*

*On assumptions* Although the single-index models are widely used in the literature, this should not suggest that they are trouble-free. The most important problem is the problem of *ex ante* efficiency, which is common not only to the international versions of CAPMs but also to the domestic ones. The CAPMs assume that the market portfolio is mean-variance efficient and that observations on a benchmark return for a single beta model are *a priori* available. It is typically assumed in CAPM applications that observations on a vector of returns, including the return on the aggregate market portfolio, are normally distributed, with probability distributions independent and identical over time.

To deal with this problem, a conditional version of CAPM has been suggested. Extending the work of Roll (1977), Hansen and Richard (1983) demonstrate that, once the expectation operators preceding excess returns are conditioned upon an information set which is a subset of the investors' information set, the benchmark return lies on the conditional mean-variance frontier. Any other return that has the same conditional mean as the benchmark also has a conditional variance that is at least as large as that of the benchmark (Hansen and Hodrick, 1983).

Critics argue that, when it comes to international pricing, the validity of a single-factor return-generating model is still an open question. Solnik warns about the complexities of an international single-factor model, such as the non-existence of a universal risk-free asset and the presence of exchange rate risk. In addition, the single-index models in the standard Sharpe–Lintner tradition have encountered several other empirical problems. One such problem lies in the difficulty in assuming a universal logarithmic utility function or no correlation between exchange rates and stock returns and domestic consumption deflators, and/or the assumption of purchasing power parity. He assumes that all securities are affected by the international factor through their national index. Although Solnik discovers that the international regression for country indices supports international pricing of risk, he concludes that this is unrealistic and that two stocks with the same country risk could have different sensitivity to international developments for several other reasons (Solnik, 1974a).

One other drawback of an international single-index CAPM is its apparent inability to decompose risk. Sources of systematic risk are assumed to be embodied in a single international market index. Hence, it has been argued that a pricing model in which systematic risk, international or domestic, can be decomposed into several different sources that are orthogonal among themselves should be preferred to a single-index CAPM.

*On identifying the sources of segmentation* All or some of the assumptions are inherent in single-index capital asset-pricing models. Recent models, such as versions of the arbitrage pricing theory argue that single-index models cannot capture the structure of international asset prices. Equally importantly, single-index international CAPMs are criticized for their weakness in addressing the sources of capital market segmentation. In a world where institutional integration has taken place gradually, what creates segmentation is very important.

It has then been argued that an asset-pricing framework which can correctly identify the sources of segmentation would be preferred. One counterargument to this is that, because of the variety and complexity of market imperfections caused either by deliberate actions on the part of national governments or by ignorance, it is quite hard or even impossible to write down a general model that can capture the behaviour of international asset prices (Gultekin *et al.*, 1990).

*On results* Most studies that adopt international versions of standard capital asset-pricing models and compare a domestic market to an international benchmark market have concluded that world markets are neither integrated nor segmented (Errunza and Losq, 1985; Alexander et *al.* 1988). This conclusion essentially suggests that domestic factors still play a major role in international asset-pricing although regional trading blocs and bilateral free trade agreements as well as customs unions have come to dominate world trade and financial markets.

In spite of its critics, there is consensus in the literature that when and if a single-index model is appropriate and a mean-variance efficient market portfolio exists, it is probably the best model. Hence, if assumptions are not violated radically, international CAPM is the right way of dealing with the issue of international pricing as well as the integration of world capital markets.

## Notes

1. Contrary to this argument are the findings of most recent studies that adopt asset-pricing models. Among these, Errunza and Losq (1985) find evidence supporting what they call 'mildly segmented' world capital markets. Similarly, Jorion and Schwartz (1986) reject the hypothesis of integration between the Canadian and the US capital markets. For an account of the inappropriateness of the covariance matrix of returns, see Adler and Dumas (1975 and 1983) who argue that the matrix does not give information on the presence or absence of capital market integration. See also Solnik (1977).
2. The two-step procedure underlined here is due to Fama and MacBeth (1973).
3. Equations (6.4) and (6.5) assume that there is 'mild' segmentation. In the event of integration, all securities should be priced according to a single model and the questions relate to excess expected returns or 'super' risk premia, since securities are accessible to all investors.

# 7 The arbitrage pricing theory of integration

## Introduction

As critics of the standard single-index CAPMs have emphasized, it is questionable whether a single global world index would properly describe the international structure of capital assets. That is, the results of two-cross sectional regressions that employ one of the two alternative systematic risk measures as the single independent variable cannot answer whether capital markets are segmented or integrated. Returns are likely to be affected by several other independent and international factors in addition to the national risk content. Thus, return should follow a multifactor linear generating process wherein the domestic market index may be one of the factors.

Two major multifactor return generating processes have been adopted in the literature. One is the standard multi-beta CAPM where all factors represent some form of portfolio of assets. The essence of this model is no different from the single-index CAPM. The other is the Roll–Ross arbitrage pricing theory where the factors that determine the variations in asset returns are not necessarily portfolios of the original securities.

This chapter is devoted to the international arbitrage pricing theory and its application to the issue of integration of capital markets. We shall first outline the underlying approach of some standard arbitrage pricing models. Next, we look into the international dimensions of the Roll–Ross arbitrage pricing models with applications to the theory of integration.

## What is arbitrage pricing theory?

The arbitrage pricing theory (APT) was first formulated by Ross (1976) and advanced in Roll and Ross (1980). It offers a testable alternative to the capital asset-pricing model. Unlike CAPM which predicts that security rates of return are linearly related to a single common factor, the rate of return on the market portfolio, the APT is intuitively the same as CAPM but is much more general.

The return-generating stochastic process under the assumption of APT is a linear multifactor regression where several ($k$) number of factors make up the systematic risk. Hence, APT decomposes systematic risk. Consider the following multifactor return-generating model similar to those adopted widely in the literature:

$$R_{it} = E(R_i) + \sum_{k=1}^{K} b_{ik}\delta_{kt} + \epsilon_{it} \quad i = 1,..N$$

with

$$E(\delta_{kt}) = E(\epsilon_{it} \mid \delta_{kt}) = 0 \text{ for all } i \text{ and } k \qquad (7.1)$$

where: $R_{it}$ ≡ return on security $i$ between time $t$–1 and $t$ for any finite $i$
$E(R_i)$ ≡ expected return on security $i$
$\delta_{kt}$ ≡ The $k$th common factor, i.e. source of systematic risk between time $t$–1 and $t$
$b_{ik}$ ≡ the $k$th common factor sensitivity of the return on security $i$, also called factor loading
$\epsilon_{ik}$ ≡ the idiosyncratic unsystematic risk or the residual risk of the return on the $i$th security between time $t$–1 and time $t$. It is assumed to have zero mean and finite variance and to be sufficiently independent for a law of large numbers to apply.

The return on an arbitrage portfolio:

$$E(R_i) \approx q_0 + b_{i1}q_1 + b_{i2}q_2 + \ldots + b_{ik}q_k \qquad (7..2)$$

where: $q_0$ ≡ expected return on the zero-beta (risk free) asset
$q_k$ ≡ the risk premium on the $k$th common factor, $k = 1, \ldots, K$.

Some important characteristics of APT are worth mentioning, because they do not appear in standard CAPMs. The arbitrage portfolio such as the one described by the equation (7.1) is assumed to be well diversified in the sense that the residual risk is negligible. This portfolio based on the arbitrage condition of capital assets is nearly riskless. That is, it has a zero capital investment, hence zero return. The APT makes no assumptions concerning the empirical probability distribution of asset returns. The market portfolio does not play a special role in APT. It need not be efficient (neither mean-variance nor any other efficiency). The APT results in the relative pricing of any subset of capital assets; therefore, the entire set of assets need not be measured in order to test the theory of asset pricing.

**Empirical tests of arbitrage pricing**

Empirically, the task of a multifactor return-generating APT here is to estimate the risk premia, that is a vector of $q$s, and to test whether the $q$s are priced. Works by Roll and Ross (1980), Reinganum (1983), Chen (1983), Dhrymes *et al.* (1984) have tested the APT using daily returns to equities. The seminal paper by Roll and Ross (1980) employed daily returns data for NYSE and AMEX companies registered with the exchanges on both 3 July 1962, and 31 December 1972. There were over 2600 daily observations for each stock. They selected 1260 securities and divided into groups of 30. Their analysis showed that there are at least three priced factors. The method they adopted is what is known as statistical factor analysis.

After the work of Roll and Ross, factor analysis has been frequently used in the finance literature to extract independent return generators. It is essential that these return generators are orthogonalized to each other. In general, the algorithm of statistical factor analysis searches time-series data of some $T + 1$ periods' security or portfolio rates of return over a cross-section of $N$ different assets.

The analysis statistically extracts those risk factors that systematically affect the returns of capital assets in the sample at hand. There is a simultaneous analysis of all the returns from several $N$ assets over $T + 1$ periods in a matrix, as in (7.3):

$$\begin{bmatrix} R_{1,t}, R_{1,t+1}, \ldots, R_{1,t+T} \\ R_{2,t}, R_{2,t+1}, \ldots, R_{2,t+T} \\ \vdots \\ R_{N,t}, R_{N,t+1}, \ldots, R_{N,t+T} \end{bmatrix} \tag{7.3}$$

From this matrix of returns, factors (explanatory variables) are extracted. The purpose of doing factor analysis is to reduce the $N \times T + 1$ matrix of returns to a smaller matrix that explains most of the variation in returns. The $k$ common factors are extracted. The values of these factors are called factor scores ($\delta_{i,t}$) as shown in (7.4):

$$\begin{bmatrix} \delta_{1,t}, \delta_{1,t+1}, \ldots, \delta_{1,t+T} \\ \delta_{2,t}, \delta_{2,t+1}, \ldots, \delta_{2,t+T} \\ \vdots \\ \delta_{k,t}, \delta_{k,t+1}, \ldots, \delta_{k,t+T} \end{bmatrix} \tag{7.4}$$

Once the factors are extracted, the regression of the return generating process is run. Factor loadings associated with the significant factors are estimated and used in the estimation of the factor risk premia.

**The international arbitrage pricing model of integration**

In an international arbitrage pricing model (IAPT), investors of different countries are assumed to adjust nominal (dollar) returns by a random variable. Some recent works have employed an international version of a multifactor asset-pricing model where equilibrium rates of return are set by arbitrage conditions. Among those who have applied IAPT are Berges (1981), Cho *et al*, (1986), Korajczyk and Viallet (1986), Gultekin *et al.* (1990). International arbitrage pricing theory, unlike the single-index pricing models, attributes the changes in stock returns to more than one factor that are not necessarily portfolio related.

To test for integration or segmentation in capital markets, vectors of risk premia across stock markets are compared to see if the risk premia differentials exist. The definition of capital market integration in the context of arbitrage pricing theory is driven from an arbitrage condition of asset prices. Specifically, if arbitrage ensures that risk carries the same price in, say, two different stock markets in two countries, then it follows that these two markets are integrated. That is, capital markets are said to be integrated if assets with perfectly correlated rates of return have the same price regardless of the location in which they are traded. According to Stulz (1981b) it is only natural to look at the integration of capital markets based on risk premia differentials, for differential risk premia should imply some degree of segmentation.

*A comparison of IAPT and ICAPM*

IAPT differs from the standard CAPM in that differences in consumption tastes and relative price uncertainty are incorporated in arbitrage pricing models. Hence, international arbitrage pricing model is a multiconsumption real CAPM (Solnik, 1983). We shall clarify the advantages and disadvantages associated with employing arbitrage pricing models for the purpose of testing for integration.

*Advantages of IAPT* First of all, APMs are not based on utility though they still require the definition of a riskless portfolio. One important weakness of CAPM does not arise in APT. Both in single-beta and multi-beta CAPMs, explanatory variables must be the portfolio(s) of individual securities. This issue brings about the problems associated with selecting portfolios. Factors in an APM, on the other hand, are not constrained to be the portfolios of the original assets.

One of the advantages of employing the APT in an international capital asset-pricing framework is that it avoids the problem of purchasing power parity deviations, because the pricing and estimation of risk premia in this model are based on an arbitrage condition of nominal returns. More importantly, the conclusion drawn from the domestic CAPM, that a well-identified market portfolio is mean-variance efficient, does not exist internationally because a world market portfolio is not optimal in the sense that investors will hold different portfolios, particularly the 'hedge' ones. Accordingly, the portfolio identification problem present in an international CAPM may be eliminated in an international arbitrage pricing model (Solnik, 1983).

*Disadvantages of IAPT* Arbitrage pricing models when applied to international pricing of capital assets also have disadvantages over CAPM. One disadvantage of an APM is that the factor-analytic approach through which explanatory factors are extracted is a purely statistical technique that can result in factors that in general make no economic sense at all. Another disadvantage of adopting an APT model is that the factor-elimination process and testing are both costly and non-standard. Indeed, this, along with the problem of the correct number of factors, has been the major criticism of the APT.

*The issue of the correct number of factors* Considerable empirical research has been done on the problem of the right number of factors, another issue that is to a large extent related to the use of the factor-analytic approach. Solnik argues that the number of common factors in an international APT must be small compared to the number of assets for the APT to be a viable and useful theory of asset prices.

Solnik proposes a combination of international factors common to specific types of assets such as stocks plus national factors affecting only domestic assets (Solnik, 1983). Others have preferred a prespecified-factor approach wherein systematic risk factors are selected by the researchers' common sense about a particular return-generating process rather than a purely statistical extraction method (see, for a discussion of the prespecified-factors method, Gultekin *et al.*, 1990).

In a similar effort, Ehrhardt (1987) criticizes previous empirical research on APT on the same matter, and argues that the typical significance tests employed to extract the factors are inappropriate when the estimated model residuals for all securities have insignificant means but are not distributed independently. In that case the standard significance tests would indicate incorrectly that more factors are needed. Ehrhardt argues that, when this is the case, the researcher has already extracted enough factors and that the results of the case can then be viewed with a greater degree of confidence. If, on the other hand, the means are significant, this would imply that the estimated model is not a true APM, even when the residuals are independently distributed. Ehrhardt raises the point that the typical tests for factor extraction usually overstate the relevant number of factors and that the standard statistical procedures are insufficient, because they fail to determine when the estimated model satisfies equilibrium conditions.

The APT, in spite of these disadvantages, provides an empirical framework that can be useful, depending on the case. One advantage of an international APT over a CAPM is on exchange rates. Some technical problems posed by currency translation and aggregation in the international CAPM do not arise in the international arbitrage pricing model (Solnik, 1983). This is clearly an advantage of arbitrage pricing.

## Macroeconomic risk diversification and the IAPT

### *Chen's analysis of macroeconomic factors*

Although it is mathematically impossible to employ factor analysis to identify unambiguously the underlying factors that derive asset returns, Chen *et al.* (1983) have managed to correlate several macroeconomic variables as sources of systematic risk with returns on five portfolios that mimic the underlying factor structure. Out of five, four macroeconomic variables were significant. These are:

(a) an index of industrial production;
(b) changes in a default risk premium (they have measured this premium by the differences in promised yields to maturity on AAA versus Baa corporate bonds);
(c) twists in the yield curve as measured by differences in promised yields to maturity on long- and short-term government bonds;
(d) unanticipated rate of inflation.

The economic rationale behind these factors derived by Chen *et al.* seems quite reasonable. They incorporate one major drawback of APMs that have been criticized on the basis of their use of the factor-analytic approach and their lack of economic intuition on the part of the factors extracted.

Extracting the priced sources of risk associated with macroeconomic factors from the unpriced ones, a natural outcome of asset-pricing models is important for international investors who have the change of diversifying away part of the systematic risk in addition to the idiosyncratic risk.

Generally, two conditions must be held for the existence of a premium to be paid for local sources of risk: (a) if the country is small but subject to capital controls, then expected returns to purely domestic assets would carry a premium over and above the risk-free rate and the expected domestic market return would be unusually high; (b) if the market were not small enough, then the local market-specific sources of risk could not be eliminated by international diversification.

*The Bayesian approach to the IAPT*

McElroy and Burmeister (1988) suggest measuring the macroeconomic risk sources as forecast errors from a Bayesian vector autoregression in their model, where equilibrium rates of return are determined based on the assumption that the expected return of an arbitrage portfolio is zero. The empirical methodology they employ is due to Litterman (1986).

We shall outline the underlying characteristics of the model used by McElroy and Burmeister. Let the linear return generating model of k-factors be

$$R_{it} = E_{it} + \sum_{j=1}^{k-1} B_{ijt} F_{jt} + \epsilon_{it} \tag{7.5}$$

where $i = 1,\dots N$ is the index of assets, $t = 1,\dots T$ is the time index $R_{it}$ and $E_{it}$ are the actual and expected rates of return on asset $i$ at time $t$. $B_{ijt}$ stands for the $j$th factor loading of asset $i$ at time $t$, and $F_{jt}$ is the value of the risk factor $j$ estimated as the innovation from the Bayesian VARs. The last term of the expression, $\in_{it}$ is some unobservable risk specific to asset $i$ at time $t$.

Ross (1976) shows that a no-arbitrage condition in a sequential economy meant that the expected return of asset $i$ at time $t$ is approximately given by

$$E_{it} = \delta_{0t} + \sum_{j=1}^{k-1} B_{ijt}\delta_{jt} \tag{7.6}$$

where $\delta_{0t}$ stands for the risk-free rate of interest, and $\delta_{jt}$ is the risk premium associated with assuming one unit of risk from factor $j$. Hence, the equation (7.6) postulates that the expected return to some asset $i$ differs from the risk-free rate of return by an amount depending on the factor loadings and the market prices of the risk factors. Note that $B_{ijt}\delta_{jt}$ is nothing other than asset $i$'s excess expected return over and above the risk-free rate $\delta_{0t}$. Thus, the risk premium associated with facing the particular risk source $j$ is given by $B_{ijt}\delta_{jt}$.

Substituting (7.6) into (7.5) yields

$$R_{it} = \delta_0 + \sum_{j=1}^{k-1} B_{ij}\delta_j + \sum_{j=1}^{k-1} B_{ij}F_{it} + \in_{it} \tag{7.7}$$

The equation (7.7) is a set of $N$ APT equations that will be estimated. The errors in the linear factor model of (7.5) may involve a residual market factor term $\in_{mt}$ as in

$$\in_{it} = \sum_{i=1}^{N} B_{ikt} \in_{mt} + u_{it} \tag{7.8}$$

Here the $\in_{it}$ may be thought of as representing the pervasive sources of macroeconomic risk omitted from the specification of $F_{jt}$. Thus, the $k$th factor will be the $\in_{jt}$.

The conventional procedure of estimating factor sensitivities based on the work of Black, Jensen, and Scholes (1972) differs from the approach of equation (7.5). The traditional method suggests using time series data to estimate the factor loadings first and then cross-sectionally estimating the average returns against these factor sensitivities. McElroy and Burmeister (1988) have advocated to consider the estimating factor loadings and factor prices simultaneously using nonlinear least squares procedures to avoid the error in variables problem which would otherwise occur. This is indeed the second advantage of the McElroy–Burmeister approach. As we have pointed out, the first advantage is associated with the Bayesian methodology which can generate probability distributions of future events that are more reliable than those produced by traditional techniques.

# 8 The role of controls in integration

## Capital controls and the issue of integration

This section deals with the role of market imperfections in the segmentation of capital markets. We shall classify imperfections as those associated with (a) direct barriers or capital controls, and (b) barriers other than government impediments. In addition, exchange rate volatility also generates systematic risk and hence becomes important in equilibrium pricing of internationally traded capital assets. The methods that will be studied here can be applied to any pricing model for capital assets. The key concept on which we shall concentrate is some form of market imperfection present in capital markets.

### *Restrictions on capital and segmentation*

Which type of market imperfection causes segmentation is still an open question. Identifying market imperfections as causes of segmentation in practice is important to different economic agents for varying reasons. It is important to specify the market imperfection to corporations making capital budgeting decisions, to macroeconomic policy-makers who think that they deal correctly with the efficient distribution of existing financial capital among the various sectors in their economies, and finally to the investors facing different risks when they invest in foreign securities traded in world capital markets. We shall now mention the types of imperfections that are likely to cause, and hence be treated as possible sources of, segmentation in equity markets.

It has long been recognized in the economics and finance literature that the barriers to international investment are the real sources of segmentation in equity markets. The belief about the market-distortion effects of restrictions on capital movements is almost unanimous. Departing from this motivation some recent research has pointed out that a widespread rejection of integration should not suggest that there are no empirical questions left unanswered and that future research ought to aim at the specific causes of segmentation in world capital markets.

Gultekin *et al.* (1990), who argue that generalized tests of capital market integration are likely to be uninformative, suggest the use of case-specific studies in which the experiences of one or two countries are examined rather than the status of integration *vis-à-vis* the world capital market as a whole. In their event study, Gultekin *et al.* take the specific case of the Japanese capital market versus its US counterpart, where they focus on the type of market imperfection created by capital controls, i.e. direct barriers to investment.

*Types of market imperfection*

There are, in general, three major sources that create market imperfection in the context of international capital markets, as suggested in the literature of capital asset-pricing. As we have mentioned previously, these sources are direct or legal barriers, indirect barriers, and exchange rate volatility. There is sufficient evidence in the literature of international capital markets to show that legal barriers are in most cases the only source of capital market segmentation.

The common sources of segmentation in world capital markets have been studied in the academic literature by several scholars. We shall summarize the three groups based on the implications of these sources as covered in the literature of international asset-pricing. As we shall see from these groups, models and testing procedures for capital market integration cannot be general, because the type of imperfection varies from one case to another. Hence, as we have suggested earlier, the appropriateness of case studies depends on the type of imperfection assumed to test for integration.

*Direct barriers* The presence of government controls or the legal barriers in general constitutes direct barriers. Legal barriers are anything that explicitly discriminates against the country of origin of the investor. More specifically, we see direct controls in the form of:

(a) restrictions on the ownership of foreign securities;
(b) juridical status differences between foreign and domestic investments;
(c) differential taxation;
(d) other government impediments against the free movement of capital.

The effects of market imperfections in the form of direct barriers to investment on asset-pricing are widely studied in the literature. Direct barriers, or legal restrictions, to international investment is the most studied market imperfection for integration purposes. Numerous capital controls over the markets can be classified as direct or legal barriers.

Mean-variance CAPMs with direct barriers to international investment first appear in Black (1972) and Stulz (1981b). Both authors focus on legal barriers seen in the form of taxes. Black models capital controls as taxes on long positions in foreign (foreign currency denominated) assets – with corresponding subsidies on short positions. Stulz (1981b), however, considers them as taxes on both long and short positions. Assuming (or extracting) that exchange rate risk is either negligible or absent, direct barriers are examined by Black (1974) and Stulz (1981a, 1981b), Jorion and Schwartz (1986) and Gultekin *et al.* (1990).

Gultekin *et al.* (1990), employing an arbitrage pricing model, look into the effects of liberalization in Japan on the integration between the Japanese and

US markets and conclude that the source of segmentation can be traced to legal barriers based on the nationality of the issuing firms, while Jorion and Schwartz (1986) reach the same conclusion with a fairly standard CAPM when they examine the integration of the Canadian stock market with a benchmark North American market.

*Exchange rate volatility* When investors want to trade in foreign capital markets, they face a fundamentally different type of risk associated with exchange rates. International investors buy securities denominated in foreign currencies. Variations in exchange rates will reduce or induce returns to the securities quoted in foreign exchange places. Part of the systematic risk associated with trading in foreign securities is what is called exchange rate risk. This type of risk might make up a sizeable portion of risk when systematic risk is decomposed.

Exchange rate risk will impose an additional burden and hence it is important for the international investor if this risk is priced in the foreign market. On *a priori* grounds, it can be argued that whether the exchange rate risk is offered at a premium, as well as how big it is, is highly related to the exchange rate system in the country where the security is traded. In general, exchange rate risk is expected to be high in a flexible rate system and low in a fixed rate system. As a matter of fact, the exchange rate is almost non-existent if there is complete fixity, in which case investors will always know the ongoing exchange rate. One example of a fixed exchange rate system is the European Exchange Rate Mechanism (ERM), where currencies are allowed to fluctuate only within small margins. The ERM has been explained previously in some detail (see Chapter 3).

Exchange rate risk and its effect on international asset-pricing have been dealt with in the literature (see Solnik, 1974a, 1977). Given that no government impediments to the capital markets exist and that investors are engaged with no particular irrationality whatsoever, some early work on integration adopted capital asset-pricing models when there is differential exchange rate risk.

The well-known study based on the assumption of exchange rate risk is that of Solnik (1974a, 1974b, 1974d, 1977). Solnik postulates that not all investors face the same investment opportunity set because of the presence of different exchange rate risks, depending upon the investor's country of origin.

In a paper that has important insights for measuring exchange rate risk, Hansen and Hodrick (1983) deal with the pricing of exchange rates in a capital asset-pricing framework, where they investigate the risk premium in the forward foreign exchange market. One of the models they adopt is a single-beta latent variable model by which they attempt to measure risk. They find that the risk premia are significant in at least two of the major currencies they have included.

*Indirect barriers* We name those market imperfections other than legal barriers to investment indirect barriers. This type of imperfection is the assumed inability of a group of investors to trade in a foreign capital market. If there exists some irrationality on the part of international investors, then we can speak of the existence of an indirect barrier.

This assumed inability of a class of investors to trade in international capital markets may relate to barriers such as:

(a) the difficulty of obtaining information about foreign securities;
(b) financial reporting differences across national markets;
(c) language barriers;
(d) any other implicit or explicit cost of being a foreigner in a foreign market.

*Pinpointing the sources of segmentation*
There are basically two methods of examining the issue of capital market integration. One is the method of interlisted stocks that looks independently into the integration of those stocks that are dually listed and those that are not. The second method examines the effect of the liberalization of capital markets and distinguishes the pre- and post-liberalization periods. We now outline these two approaches. These two methods can be modified, depending on the markets under consideration. Furthermore, if there is no stock (or very few) interlisted, the first method is inapplicable. The second method, on the other hand, depends on the existence of a regime switch year.

*The method of interlisted stocks* This method is based on how well (or badly) the interlisted stocks in more than one exchange are integrated. Two possible outcomes are:

(a) if market imperfections were caused by indirect barriers (the term is due to Jorion and Schwartz, 1985) and if indirect barriers were the only source of segmentation in capital markets, then we would expect that interlisted stocks are integrated but the purely domestic stocks (those that are not interlisted) are segmented. Based on the classification of Jorion and Schwartz the following indirect barriers are common:

    - difficulty in obtaining information about foreign stocks;
    - differences in the depth and quality of financial reporting due to the differences in accounting disclosure requirements;
    - impediments based on traditional practices, such as reluctance to deal with foreigners, or any indirect cost of doing business abroad.

    One can argue that such indirect barriers in the EU have become less important as the member states open up to trade and finance within the Union.

(b) If, on the other hand both the interlisted and the domestic stocks are segmented, we could then conclude that the effective barriers are of the legal type, such as:

- differential juridical status between domestic and international investments;
- differential tax considerations;
- restrictions on ownership of foreign securities;
- any other governmental barrier linked to the origin of the security.

*The method of regime switches* Since the end of the 1970s, world capital markets have been subject to fewer capital controls almost everywhere. Restrictions on foreign capital have been gradually lifted, even in the third world markets. Therefore, one can look at the pre- and post-liberalization periods in one or two specific markets and compare the risk premia between or among the markets under consideration. One should not necessarily choose the interlisted stocks to test for equity market integration.

The disadvantage of the method is its lack of generality. That is, if markets are segmented for reasons other than controls of national governments, then this method does not help much. Furthermore, there should exist a major liberalization act in order to identify the differential risk premia between the pre- and post-act periods. Given the fact that quite a few national governments have lifted capital controls over their markets, however, this method can explain a good part of market segmentation. Besides, lack of generality seems to be the common problem in all international capital asset-pricing models.

Based on two possible outcomes, we can evaluate the issue of capital market segmentation in this method as follows:

(a) if government impediments to foreign investment are the only source of segmentation, the price of risk in two or more selected capital markets should be different before but not after a specific liberalization act;
(b) if, on the other hand, the risk premia do not differ significantly from their pre-liberalization levels, one can argue that capital restrictions are the real source of lack of integration and that there are other reasons for market segmentations.

## Tests and econometric problems

### *Tests*

We have mentioned repeatedly the standard testing procedure first suggested by Fama and MacBeth (1973). We shall here describe this procedure along with an additional statistical test approach adopted in the literature. Tests normally involve inspecting whether the equality of the vector of risk premia is verified by the sample data, and use cross-sectional regressions of stock returns on the estimated betas (factor loadings in arbitrage pricing applications).

The first approach is the well-known Fama–MacBeth (1973) procedure. In this two-step procedure, normal or expected returns are predicted according to a cross-sectional relationship whose coefficients are estimated by regressing average portfolio returns on average portfolio betas to ensure that the estimators reflect the nature of equilibrium relationship between risk and return relationship. That is, given the beta coefficient estimated using the market model (CAPM) for the *i*th security, the expected (normal) returns are calculated employing a cross-sectional relationship.

The second test suggests an alternative to the Fama–MacBeth approach through the standard use of time-series mean rates of stock (portfolio) returns in each period, assuming that periods are distinguished from one another by major capital market liberalization legislation. Mean rates of both pre- and post-liberalization periods, for instance, are taken as the dependent variables in the cross-sections and estimate the vector of risk premia jointly with a seemingly unrelated regression (SURE). The equality of the risk premia is tested with a standard *t*-test or *F*-test of linear constraint.

*Roll's critique once again*

As Roll (1977) pointed out, the standard capital asset-pricing model is equivalent to the mean-variance efficiency of the market portfolio – or a market index. One major econometric difficulty arises because the market index is unidentifiable. Therefore, investors cannot test whether a preselected portfolio is *ex post* efficient. As long as the market index is unidentifiable only *ex ante* efficiency can be testable. This is, indeed, the most important weakness of the mean-variance efficient capital asset-pricing models.

Most empirical studies of the CAPM use cross-sectional regressions to test the *ex ante* linear relation between the factor loadings (security betas) and expected returns implied by the mean-variance efficiency of the market portfolio. This approach has been criticized (Roll, 1977, among others) for it has a serious empirical problem: the problem of errors in variables; that is, the true values of factor loadings are unknown since the regressors are estimates. To some extent this can be avoided by using portfolio observations or observed market indices instead of security observations. There is a possibility that the security risk characteristics are non-stationary over time. Stehle (1977) argues that empirical tests using security risk characteristics as independent variables must take this non-stationarity into consideration to avoid possible biases.

*Suggested solutions to econometric problems*

The measurement error problem brings about the problem of inconsistency. When the independent variables in a regression are measured with some error, according to a well-known rule of econometrics the regressors, the estimates of the coefficients of independent variables, will be inconsistent. Either OLS should be avoided since the error term is heteroscedastic, or else one of the following ways should be adopted to eliminate inconsistency:

(a) Observations can be grouped. If the groups are formed independently of the measurement errors, the OLS based on the group means will be able to yield consistent parameter estimates. The use of an incorrectly specified functional relationship in general does not affect the efficiency of the grouping method. (See Stehle, 1974, 1977.)

(b) Direct use of instrumental variables. It becomes important whether the exact functional form of the relationship between a particular independent variable and its instrument is known in determining the efficiency of the instrumental variable method. If an incorrectly specified relationship is used, the misuse reduces the efficiency of this method. If, on the other hand, the exact functional form is known, the instrumental variable technique is always more efficient than an OLS-based grouping.

As far as the arbitrage pricing models are concerned, econometric problems do not seem to be serious, except that some factor extraction procedures are purely statistical. This is indeed one of the reasons that makes APT a useful testable alternative to the standard CAPMs, because mean variance efficiency in general does not hold in an international context and some modification in the underlying assumptions of CAPM are necessary.

# PART III

# EMPIRICAL TESTS

# 9 The integration of European capital markets: an institutional review

## An overview of European capital markets

Capital markets in Europe, with the possible exception of the United Kingdom, have been traditionally less important in channelling financial funds. The existence of a well-developed commercial banking system has taken the lead in attracting and distributing funds, thereby decreasing the market values of European equities which constitute only a small portion of the world equity market. Taken separately, the European equity markets are much smaller in aggregate market values than those of Japan and the US, the two giant equity markets in the world.

Despite its small size in market capitalization, the European – and particularly European Union – equity markets on average have outperformed US equities over the past 15 years. Besides, the appreciation of European currencies against the US dollar has attracted the non-European investors – most notably from the US – who want to diversify internationally. However, recent developments in the EU to deepen both political and economic integration have discriminated against non-EU investors. Therefore, large numbers of the US and Japanese equity investors have gradually lost a potential area of diversification and thereby the benefits associated with optimum portfolios that are made up of both domestic and international securities.

This argument is especially valid in a segmented world equity market because, when securities are priced according to their local systematic risk, part of that risk becomes unsystematic and hence diversifiable in a global context. As the share of diversifiable risk increases, optimum hedging decisions are revised. International diversification offers different hedging strategies for equity investors who are willing to trade in foreign securities.

Whether a particular European capital market is segmented from the rest of Europe (or the rest of the world) or can be classified as integrated is unclear empirically. In the light of recent developments towards greater financial integration within the Union, one might argue that the EU equity markets are now more integrated than ever and that European equities are priced in an integrated market and not according to their domestic systematic risk content. Whether the EC capital markets are integrated poses important questions of concern to both European equity investors and companies in the EU that make capital budgeting decisions.

In spite of its importance, there are few studies that deal with the issue of equity market integration. It is true that much has been said and written about the European single market economy; however, there is little research reported in the literature of economics and finance on the topic of financial integration in Europe using capital asset-pricing models. A rich body of studies on European financial integration have either taken European integration as given from the outset (see, for instance, Razin and Sadka 1989, 1990; Micossi, 1988) or they have focused on a wide range of institutional aspects of capital market integration. Others have dealt with the open-economy macroeconomic aspects of European integration, such as the implications of a stand in favour of a fixed exchange rate, that is, of a common currency or common monetary policy in Europe. Yet other works argue that capital market integration is not particularly desirable and have focused on the normative dimension of financial integration (Dornbusch, 1988).

In the following chapter we shall look into the hypothesis that the institutional framework that is expected to prepare the European Union for the single market does not by any means guarantee that the financial markets will act as if there were one EU market. If they do not become one market, that is if the national markets are segmented, then returns on domestic portfolios will be less than those on European portfolios. This means that there would exist a European portfolio superior to domestic portfolios. Alternatively, if the supranational (EU-wide) market portfolio is the mean-variance efficient one, then any other portfolio set locally will not be efficient.

Having described what the following chapter is about, we outline now what the present chapter intends to do. Its primary purpose is to equip the reader with the necessary institutional background concerning the European Union financial markets so that she/he can follow without loss of generality the material that will be presented in the next chapter, where the empirical tests will be carried out.[1] Once we complete the empirical examination of the issue of capital market integration versus segmentation in European capital markets, our principal concern will shift to the sources of segmentation if the tests support the hypothesis that European markets are not integrated. This chapter has two main sections. First, we provide an institutional account of financial integration within the European Community. Second, we study European monetary integration, the integration of European currency markets, for it is in several respects closely related to the reaction of capital markets to developments in the European monetary sector.

## The history of financial integration in the European Union

### *Early years*

The history of the idea of financial integration within the European Union goes back to the early 1960s. The Council of Ministers of the then European Community – with six member states – had adopted two directives setting out initial obligations for the removal of capital controls in member states in 1960 and 1962 respectively. These directives to deregulate capital transactions were associated with a number of basic financial freedoms in the Community such as short-term and medium-term credits, personal capital movements, investments and trade in quoted securities. A third proposal was also submitted by the Commission in 1964. This was intended to remove the remaining discrimination in the legislation of member states regarding stock exchange listing, the issuing and placing of securities, and the acquisition of securities through financial institutions. Nevertheless, this proposition was rejected by the Council of Ministers.

The early years of the 1960s were relatively successful for the future of the Community. The policy actions taken at Community level would have been much more effective, had the international economic circumstances of the late 1960s and the 1970s been more favourable. Two major events caused serious setbacks to the liberalization of capital movements, the underlying objective of the two early proposals of the Community. First, the end of Bretton Woods agreement and the US Treasury's decision to end the dependence of dollar on gold brought about uncertainties for the future of the EC. Second, the oil crises of the 1970s simply forced EC member states to concentrate more on their domestic problems. The impacts of these two external shocks for EC equity markets were that most member states reintroduced controls on capital movements. Also, the three new members of the Community, the United Kingdom, Ireland and Denmark, brought with them strict controls on capital which provoked pessimism about the future of European economic unity.

Starting off with such an undesirable economic climate, there was little in the 1970s that contributed significantly to the financial integration in Europe. An effort was made to harmonize, at least to a minimum degree, the different regulations of the member countries on the admission of securities to stock exchange listing and the information provided to investors. In 1972 the EC Commission, in a proposal for a first directive in this area, stated that the omissions and differences in the information available to the public concerning securities constituted a 'second barrier' to capital movements between the member states which prevented the securities markets benefiting fully from the advantages achieved by the partial removal of currency restrictions. A second consideration was the operation of a single securities market within the EC. Since 1979 the EC Council of Ministers has adopted important directives in this particular area.

The March 1979 directive co-ordinating conditions for the admission of securities to official stock exchange listing was the first stage.[2] This directive covered the conditions required of issuers of securities, including the minimum issue price, the company's period of existence, free negotiability, sufficient distribution and the provision of appropriate information for investors. The purpose of this directive was to encourage member states to provide equivalent protection for investors at Community level. The directive, however, did not provide for co-ordination; it left a great deal of discretion for member states to apply or not to apply. Under this directive, for instance, they could decide – if they wished – not to apply this directive to units issued by collective investment undertakings other than the closed-end type, or to securities issued by a member state or its regional or local authorities.[3]

In addition, there were a small number of Commission recommendations that were adopted, but directives were limited in number in the 1970s. In one such recommendation, the Commission was of the opinion that a European code of conduct should be adopted. It recommended to member states that they should ensure the observation of certain basic principles to further facilitate the process of harmonization through directives by making clear in advance what approach the Commission would be adopting.[4]

*Changing attitudes and the Single European Act*

Unlike the 1970s, the 1980s were promising for the European Community. After the second oil shock in a decade (1979) Europe gradually entered into a new phase, and slow but sustained economic growth in most states was observed. Economic pressures of the early and mid-1970s were to an extent relieved and European issues once again became dominant over domestic problems. First of all, the Community started the decade with the European Monetary System which entered into force in 1979. The EC countries participating in the exchange rate mechanism (ERM) pursued a number of policies that brought about convergence in cost and commodity prices.[5]

In a significant effort, two member states by their own initiative removed all restrictions on capital movements in their national markets. The United Kingdom and Germany eliminated all capital controls in 1979 and 1981 respectively, and although these were more independent national attempts rather than EC-originated tasks, they accelerated the movement towards financial unity in other member states.

One important step toward the liberalization of capital movements was the March 1980 directive co-ordinating the requirements for the drawing up, scrutiny and distribution of the published particulars for admission of securities to official stock exchange listing.[6] The directive specifies items of information that must be published when equities, debt securities, as well as those certificates representing shares, are admitted to stock exchange listing. This directive was followed by a Council Resolution of 15 February 1982 on the directive concerning information to be regularly published by companies whose shares are already admitted to stock exchange listing.[7]

The year 1983 was one of the most consequential in the history of the Community. In this year the European Commission, the executive body of the EC, initiated a new 'European approach' to financial integration in a communication. Since this year, which saw the first initiative, capital controls that existed over the European markets, except in Germany and Britain, have been gradually lifted. In the following year, 1984, it was proposed that exchange controls would also be eliminated in most EC countries by the end of 1988.

The most radical attempt towards a European single market economy, however, came in the second half of the 1980s, a period that was considered to be the most promising for the future of the Community. The so-called Cockfield White Paper, dated 1985 and almost fully adopted by the Commission President Jacques Delors, foreshadowed complete integration. The White Paper constituted the main body of what has come to be known as 'the Single European Act'. With its two directives it implemented for the first time the 'new approach' to completing the internal market in the spirit of the 1983 communication. Specifically, the principle of mutual recognition of the legal provisions of the Community states based on a minimum level of co-ordination of national provisions and control by the country of registration or country of origin was promulgated.

The framework for the approximation of legal provisions so as to achieve approximately equal conditions of competition and effective protection for investors in all EC member states was set out in the Co-ordination Directive. The second directive, the Liberalization Directive, required that member states remove all restrictions on the free marketing of units. The field of application, the admission conditions, the structure of investment funds and their investment policy, the information to be supplied to unit-holders, the general obligations of funds, the observance of the laws of the member state in which the units are marketed, the rights and obligations of the supervisory authorities and the creation of a contract committee are covered by the provisions of the Co-ordination Directive.[8]

The Commission communication of 1983 and the White Paper of 1985 essentially involved four areas of action towards full financial integration: removal of restrictions on capital movements and on the provision of financial services across national borders; a series of regulations to ensure the stable and efficient functioning of capital markets; tax harmonization measures to remove fiscal distortions; and lending–borrowing activity of Community institutions.

The removal of obstacles to capital movements was aimed at in a subsequent directive adopted by the Council of Ministers in 1986. This directive enlarged the categories of capital transactions that are subject to the unconditional liberalization to include equities, bonds and long-term trade credits. The directive further required that member states refrain from introducing new authorization procedures that are more stringent than those existing on the date of entry into force of the directive.

In 1987, a Council directive aimed to abolish indirect taxes on transactions in securities. The argument in favour of abolition was largely motivated by the absence, or minimal presence, of taxes on stock exchange transactions on major financial markets, such as the American and Japanese. In the same year another directive co-ordinated investor protection, the removal of distortions and the combat of fraud.

There was another important EC directive in June 1988 on the liberalization of capital movements. The directive was a clear decision on the full liberalization of capital movements.[9] This 1988 directive was the second phase to abolish all remaining restrictions on capital movements. The particular capital movements that are covered by this directive are monetary transactions, especially short-term transactions, financial credits, operations in current and deposit accounts, accounts opened abroad and transactions in money market instruments.[10]

This important directive stipulated two deadlines for the removal of the remaining controls on capital movements. 1 July 1990 was chosen as the deadline for their removal in France and Italy; both removed these barriers before the deadline. The rest of the member states were asked to remove all remaining restrictions by the end of 1992. But they were unable to meet the deadline. In Greece, Ireland and Portugal there still exist several capital controls. The 1988 directive was important in term of monetary policy-making in the Community. It contained a provision on the responsibility of national authorities in terms of monetary policy measures adopted in the absence of a common European currency.

That France and Italy abolished remaining capital restrictions in January and May 1990, respectively, ahead of the July 1 deadline stipulated in the 1988 directive on the liberalization of capital movements, was a major success. Belgium and Luxembourg ended the dual exchange rate market regime for both current and capital transactions in March 1990. Spain and the United Kingdom finally joined the ERM in June 1989 and October 1990 respectively.

*Remaining obstacles*

There still remain important disagreements among EU states over such issues as stock exchange listings, share trading across borders and capital adequacy. In May 1990 an agreement was reached for a European list to be developed by the end of 1991. Although this has to a large extent been achieved, it is still incomplete. The idea of a European list, originally proposed by France, involves listing Europe's leading companies on all stock exchanges within the Union, allowing investors to trade in shares issued by foreign companies through their own national stock exchange. France initially had wanted to restrict the list to 300 companies, selected largely by the size of the home country's GNP. Later, she agreed to drop these restrictions. The list is to be open-ended and GNP will play no role in the selection of companies to be listed.

Despite the gathering wave of deregulation since the mid-1980s, national exchanges have only recently begun to seek ways and means to break down the remaining barriers between them to make a working environment for investors wishing to trade across borders. The idea of Europe-wide share trading is yet to be worked out. Britain argues that European share markets are fragmented and that they are still unattractive to large investors – especially those from the US and Japan. Officials of the London International Stock Exchange believe that investors want a wholesale market spanning the continent. This belief, of course, undermines national securities markets.

On the other hand, a group led by France and including Belgium, Italy and Spain insist that all securities business should pass through recognized national exchanges in order to give investors the highest level of protection. Therefore, no business should be conducted off-market; but if somehow it is, then investors should give express permission for their dealing to bypass the organized markets. The group also insists that all trades should be disclosed immediately and that trading in a given security should be allowed only on exchanges where that security is officially listed.

The issue of off-market trading appears to be an important dispute among member states. It clearly favours institutions that already have a big market share. The disagreement between the French-led camp and Britain or Germany, who see no need to limit trading in this way, is partially explained by the large share of the business that German and British banks and brokers want to secure. Many of these banks still continue to rely on a substantial amount of business in their domestic markets.

Small competitors and many outsiders suffer from being excluded from much of the trading. This strengthens the position of existing market leaders and results in the internationalization of stock markets through a small number of banks, similar to securities trading in Germany, which is dominated by a handful of large banks. The consensus between the giant and loosely regulated Euromarkets of the UK and the German trading sector, which at present has no formal exchange, seems to outweigh the French-led group.

In spite of all these disputes, there still is widespread optimism in the Union. The single market established in January 1993 is seen as an historical step on all counts. Optimism cannot be taken for granted for the time being since the process of eliminating major obstacles is underway. Furthermore, as we have pointed out in Chapter 3, the ERM margins are extremely high (15 per cent), and this adversely affects developments in the entire finance sector of Europe. In particular, the reactions of currency markets do not suggest that financial integration is underway. There was some degree of convergence in monetary policy as well as inflation rates in the Community in the 1980s (Cecchini, 1988). Financial integration of European currency markets was extraordinary both in terms of speed and of size prior to the European recession of the 1990s. Many politicians and some scholars considered monetary integration irreversible in the late 1980s.

We shall highlight some aspects of monetary integration relevant for equity market integration in the European Union. As our interest lies in the integration of equity markets, the reaction of capital markets is more important for us.

As barriers and many government controls are gradually lifted over the European capital markets a *complete integration* in the *legal sense* has to a large extent taken place. Whether the opening up of capital markets can proceed without further significant monetary integration, such as a truly common monetary policy and/or a common currency with a common central bank, is unclear. Monetary integration seems to come to a point where the results of further integration are both unpredictable and presumably marginal. The trend towards integration has actually become more evident since the Single European Act came into force in 1987.

Whether the Single European Act has been an important step towards the integration of European capital markets will be tested empirically in the following chapter. All the questions that have been raised here have important policy implications for equity market integration. Favourable institutional developments do not necessarily suggest that the EU will enjoy full capital market integration in the practical sense. Without examining empirically the existing level of capital market integration (or segmentation) in the EU, any answers to these questions would fall short of new macroeconomic measures to enhance financial integration. A similar type of uncertainty exists on the part of equity market investors whose decisions will surely be different in an integrated European capital market.

In the next chapter we shall attempt to test for integration, using the data from the equity markets in the European Community. Before introducing the empirical models, we shall first review some of the basic literature addressing the issues relevant to European financial integration.

## Notes

1. The existing monetary system in Europe has been studied in Chapter 3. This chapter supplements Chapter 3.
2. Directive 79/279/EEC.
3. Council Directive of 5 March 1979, Article 1.
4. In a memorandum dated 25 July 1977, the European Commission specified the content of the code. Six general principles were set out. The first principle emphasized the importance of the code as a departure for future directives. The second principle was that information provided to savers must be complete and accurate, since lack of knowledge is a source of imperfection in any market. The third general principle related to equality of treatment for shareholders. 'The fourth, the fifth, and the sixth general principles are more particularly concerned with certain categories of persons the importance of whose role in the realization of the code's objectives is beyond doubt, namely the members of companies' supervisory boards, company directors and company managers (principle 4), financial intermediaries and persons concerned professionally in transactions in securities (principles 5 and 6)' (*Official Journal of the European Communities*, 77/534/EEC, 25 July 1977, pp. L212/38–39).
5. See Cecchini (1988) on the issue of convergence.
6. Directive 80/390/EEC.
7. Directive 82/121/EEC.
8. Obligations such as the ban on borrowing.
9. The Council Directive of June 1988 was intended to implement the Article 67 of the EEC Treaty.
10. Council Directive 88/361/EEC.

# 10 An empirical model and test for European Union integration

## Introduction and literature review

So far we have described the theoretical framework of international asset-pricing models and their relevance to the theory of capital market integration. Nothing of an empirical nature has appeared in the previous chapters and everything we have described has been descriptive. This and the remaining chapters are devoted to the empirical examination of the issue of integration versus segmentation. In this chapter we shall develop a simple capital asset-pricing model to test for integration using a sample of the European capital markets. We shall first give a brief account of the existing literature dealing with the empirical aspects of European financial integration.

Contrary to common belief, there has been little empirical work done on European financial integration. It is true that the academicians, economists and specialists interested in the European internal market economy have studied a variety of issues concerning European integration. As a natural result, much has been written on the prospects for an integrated market for goods and services as well as securities traded within the European Union. From an institutional angle, on the other hand, it is easy to find a substantial amount of work that attempts to evaluate the legal and procedural bases of the internal market.

Nevertheless, there appears to be less interest among scholars and researchers in capital market integration from an empirical viewpoint. There does not exist a sufficient amount of quantitative work on European capital markets under a continental single market economy. The absence of reliable empirical work on the integration of European capital markets makes it difficult to conclude that the EU securities markets are indeed integrated. One reason for this lack – only in the context of European finance – is a peculiarity of European capital markets. That European Union specialists and others do not deal empirically with the capital market integration issue seems to imply that they find it more practical and interesting to capture institutional and procedural insights into the European internal market, or that the existence of a well-developed banking sector in Europe may have given a secondary role to European stock markets in the academic literature.

The only possible exception is the early work of Solnik (1974a, 1977) who in particular attempted to determine the international market structure of asset prices both theoretically and empirically. Solnik's papers, however dated, are among the most influential works addressing the theory of international asset pricing. His main concern was by no means the integration of European capital markets; rather, he looked at American, Japanese and European equity returns to describe an international asset-pricing model. Solnik's pioneer work in 1974 indicated that the domestic beta of a security cannot be taken as the true measure of its risk although his data set of eight European and two non-European (United States and Japan) stock prices covered the time period from 1966 to 1971, a period when European integration was still in its infancy.

A line should be drawn between monetary integration and the integration of capital (equity) markets, particularly in the context of European Union. Although there are few studies that have dealt with the issue of European financial integration *vis-à-vis* European equity markets, there is a rich body of literature that has focused on monetary integration. The method that has been adopted to test for monetary integration is based upon the validity of interest rate parity in European markets. Aliber (1973) and Roll and Solnik (1977) studied the Eurocurrency markets. They overwhelmingly validated the interest rate parity relationship in short-term Eurocurrency markets.[1] Convergence in interest rates, that is the tendency toward equalization in interest rates, does not tell us much in terms of capital market integration. Rather, it should be taken as a sign of money market integration. The issues of monetary integration and convergence in interest rates have been previously examined in detail in Chapters 3 and 4.

There is one recent study that particularly deals with the issue of segmentation of the European equity markets. Beckers *et al.* (1992) study the relevance of some international factors for returns. They intuitively set the common factors important for asset-pricing purposes. The key feature of their work is their use of the sector distribution of portfolios. Surprisingly, they provide evidence that certain European industry effects have become less important and local market factors have become more important in the recent past. They argue that the decreasing importance of sector effects may be partially due to the fact that each company in their sample is uniquely classified in one industry. They also explain their evidence for segmentation by the fact that balance sheet and income statements are not sufficiently harmonized to support a test of the relevance of financial ratios as common company attributes.

**Empirical problems**

In general, the issue of integration of international (or of European) capital markets is elusive empirically. The major difficulty lies in the portfolio identification problem that we have already raised several times. In addition, there are various other difficulties, major and minor, in doing research on the issue of segmentation versus integration, most of which have been raised in the previous sections of this volume. However, two major problems associated with empirical research in this field are worth noting before introducing the model.

First, the theory of international capital asset-pricing is non-standard. The controversy over which pricing model is to be utilized will later be discussed in detail. However, we shall address some key aspects of this controversy now. The present debate in international asset-pricing is due to the varying assumptions on utility functions, market imperfections and sources of price uncertainty. Some theoretical models, for instance, assume that all investors, irrespective of where they live, consume the same good, with different stochastic domestic inflation rates (Grauer *et al.* 1976). Others assume that exchange rates reflect relative price variations in the sense of deviations from purchasing power parity with non-stochastic price changes and different tastes across countries (see Solnik, 1974a). Absence of a consensus in the literature on international capital markets and asset-pricing to the question of integration or segmentation is closely related to the fundamental differences on microeconomic theoretical assumptions.

The second major difficulty lies in the complexity and variety of capital controls. National governments' impediments to capital movements are so complex that generalized tests of capital market integration often fail to be informative. Although regional free trade blocs and bilateral trade agreements have to some degree harmonized several national policies among and between the trading partners, there are practically as many different foreign capital regimes as there are countries. This complication obviously poses a great challenge to the theory of international asset-pricing and the integration of capital markets. The lack of consensus in empirical work in the field could be traced to non-standard theory due to this complexity.

**A capital asset-pricing model**

We shall start with a single-index capital asset-pricing model. This model is employed as the principal empirical tool for several reasons, most of which have been mentioned earlier in the text. First, there are the general benefits common to all CAPM applications. The underlying assumptions of CAPM avoid some important empirical problems that would otherwise arise. Once we use a CAPM and assume that there exists a universal logarithmic utility function for all investors trading in all exchange places, the price level and those questions related to purchasing power parity differentials become irrelevant for optimum portfolio choice purposes.

In other words, that there is exchange rate risk and that there exists purchasing power parity deviations across the markets can be assumed away. Therefore, all equity prices can simply be converted into one (any) currency and the analysis performed in nominal terms. One other reason for employing a single-index CAPM is that we use macro data on stock market prices from which we calculate the returns.

We do not utilize individual security returns. Therefore, we are limited to stock market indices and the portfolios made based on appreciations and depreciations in stock market indices in the European Union markets in the sample. This might create problems associated with small sample size in cross-sectional regressions as far as the tests are concerned. A pricing model such as an APT in particular requires a large individual security data set.

Although we primarily use a single-index capital asset-pricing model, an alternative multi-index pricing model such as an arbitrage pricing model of capital assets, in spite of its empirical advantages, does not seem particularly necessary. All general aspects of empirical single-beta CAPMs make these models appropriate in the context of European Union capital markets.

There are several reasons why a single index CAPM is preferable. First, exchange rate risk within the Union was presumably small during our test period since the ERM margins were relatively small. The margin for most currencies was ±2.25 per cent. The margins were pushed up to 15 per cent later in August 1993. Greece along with Portugal are yet to join the ERM.[2] Our basic argument here is that, in a fixed exchange rate world, there is no particular need for a model such as the APT that can avoid exchange rate arbitrage. Besides, it has been observed that there is convergence in most commodity prices across the community (Cecchini, 1988),

This would suggest that there is little need for the avoidance of purchasing power parity deviations, a significant advantage of the international arbitrage pricing models over standard CAPMs *à la* Sharpe–Lintner. Further, a multi-factor model – either in the framework of the multi-beta CAPM or arbitrage pricing – would not be desirable for a possible high correlation between and among the European Union market factors.

The model adopted here not only serves to test for integration, but also it helps to extract the underlying character of market imperfections. A rich body of earlier papers dealing with the theory of international asset-pricing and international capital movements have shown that different risk premia for similar assets traded in different exchanges are caused by some type of market imperfection and/or government impediments against foreign capital.

However, since market imperfections have been seen in varying forms from one market to another – that is, the type of imperfection peculiar to that market – the theory that links market imperfections to segmentation is not a standard one. Hence, it is important to have an asset-pricing model where the sources of segmentation can be identified, when and if it is the case. The simple capital asset-pricing model that we shall develop here will also be used to pinpoint the sources of segmentation.

*The methodology*

Before conducting any empirical test, we find it both appropriate and necessary to assume that there exists a particular market imperfection in equity markets. A good example of a market imperfection is a specific national government impediment against the free movement of capital from one market to another. We therefore assume the presence of a government's direct capital control over markets and assume away all other market imperfections – whether or not they exist – for the question of integration is an elusive one.[3]

When we suspect that the capital controls over stock markets are the only source of segmentation, the underlying idea is that the (possible) risk premia differentials are caused by national governments' impediments. The reason for focusing on capital controls and assuming away the other two major market imperfections, namely exchange rate risk and investors' irrationality, is not because the recent literature is biased toward the assumption that capital controls are important sources of segmentation in stock markets. Rather, we find it more appropriate to disregard the existence of exchange rate risk and/or irrationality across the EU capital markets because of the particular developments towards financial union that have taken place within the Union.

Further, the assumption of the inability of a group of investors to trade in a class of securities can be assumed away because EU citizens have gradually become accustomed to the idea of being European. A pan-European securities market is in the mind of any EU investor. The problems that arose from language have diminished remarkably. Therefore, most indirect barriers, such as difficulties associated with being a foreigner in a foreign market, language and any other barrier related to the origin of investment, have become less important. We think that neither the inability of a group of investors to trade in foreign securities for reasons other than governments' impediments nor exchange rate risk is to be taken as underlying market imperfections that can cause segmentation in the EU capital markets, although one can never rule out that possibility.

There are, however, a number of problems with the methodology we follow here. First, empirical tests are done with *ex post* data, whereas the underlying theory is *ex ante*. Second, the assumption that investors have logarithmic utility functions may pose danger when the behaviour towards risk is different.[4] Third, the basic model the specifics and several versions of which are given below lacks generality.[5] Yet all these problems are common to most international asset-pricing models and it is quite difficult to establish a standard international model for capital asset-pricing without making some assumption about the utility functions or reversing the difficulty of *ex post* data.

### *Data*

We select a couple of important dates, as far as the liberalization of capital markets is concerned, in the recent past of the EU. These dates should be thought of as times of regime switches. One is 1983, when the new approach to financial integration was initiated; another is the year 1985, when the White Paper was introduced. A final one is 1987, when the White Paper was implemented as the 'Single European Act.'

Although none of these years amounts to a clear regime switch, it may still be expected that asset-pricing will be different before and after each of these dates. That is, it seems reasonable that the pricing of European Community securities will become more international as opposed to domestic as we move from 1983 to 1985, from 1985 to 1987, and finally from 1987 onwards. Thus, a European model of capital asset-pricing is likely to explain the volatility of equity returns better than a domestic model can because institutional integration takes place gradually. This would imply that a European Union composite model, wherein systematic risk is associated with an EU composite market index, is priced after a cut-off year when capital controls against the investors' country of origin are lifted or scheduled to be lifted but not before.

The data on security price indices of the national markets as published by the International Monetary Fund (IMF) are adopted.

Monthly rates of return on local (national) market portfolios are computed as appreciations or depreciations in share price indices. The share price indices, $R_i$ are taken from *International Financial Statistics* (*IFS*), published by the International Monetary Fund (IMF), for the period from June 1978 to January 1992. The EC market index return, $R_{ec}$, is computed as a value-weighted average of national market returns. The weights are the shares of local markets in total EC market capitalization. The value weighted average is calculated as follows:

$$R_{ect,s} = \sum_{i=1}^{k} w_{i,s} R_{it,s} \tag{10.1}$$

where $i = 1,2,..k$ is the local market index (in our sample $k = 8$, namely the markets of the United Kingdom, Germany, France, Netherlands, Belgium, Denmark, Italy and Spain), and $w_{i,s}$ stand for the proportions of the member state equity market capitalizations in total EC market (composite) capitalization at sub period $s =$ 1,2,3. We partition the data into three sub-periods, each of which is divided from one another by a major EC Commission directive on liberalizing capital movements within the Community. That is, $s = 1$ for the sub-period before the 1983 EC Commission directive; $s = 2$ for the sub-period between the 1983 directive and the Single European Act (SEA); and finally $s = 3$ for the post-SEA period.

Market capitalizations adopted to obtain the assigned weights are given in Table 10.1 (see also Table 10.2). The market values are taken as the average values for each EC member state of the entire sample period from 1978/6 to 1992/1. The other EC members, namely Ireland, Portugal, Luxembourg and Greece, are excluded from the sample for lack of sufficient data. The risk-free rate used to obtain the excess returns is one-month Treasury bill rate in the UK. The data on this rate are gathered from the Morgan Guaranty Trust Company of New York.

*Table 10.1: Market values of European equities at end 1980 (US$bn)*

| Countries | US$bn | % Europe index | % EC index |
|---|---|---|---|
| Belgium | 10.0 | 0.022 | 0.025 |
| Denmark | 4.0 | 0.009 | 0.010 |
| France | 53.0 | 0.116 | 0.135 |
| Germany | 71.0 | 0.155 | 0.180 |
| Netherlands | 25.0 | 0.055 | 0.064 |
| Italy | 25.0 | 0.055 | 0.064 |
| Spain | 16.3 | 0.036 | 0.041 |
| United Kingdom | 190.0 | 0.415 | 0.481 |
| **EC total** | **394.3** | **0.863** | **1.000** |
| Austria | 1.9 | 0.004 | |
| Norway | 2.6 | 0.006 | |
| Sweden | 12.2 | 0.027 | |
| Switzerland | 46.0 | 0.100 | |
| **EFTA total** | **62.7** | **0.137** | |
| **EC + EFTA** | **457.0** | **1.000** | |

*Source*: *Financial Analysts Journal*, several issues, and author's own calculations.

*Table 10.2: Market value of EC capital markets in sample as % of total EC market capitalization as of 1980*

| Market | % of EC market value |
|---|---|
| UK | 48.1 |
| Germany | 18.0 |
| France | 13.5 |
| Netherlands | 6.4 |
| Belgium | 2.5 |
| Denmark | 1.0 |
| Italy | 6.4 |
| Spain | 4.1 |
| **Total EC** | **100.0** |

*Problem specification*

A European Union-wide market portfolio should be mean-variance efficient if the EU capital markets are integrated. If EU investors have the same opportunity set, then an EU version of the standard single-index Sharpe–Lintner asset-pricing model should hold. We therefore test jointly that the EU-wide CAPM holds and that the markets are not segmented. We assume that the following statements are true:[6]

*Assumption 1:* The EU capital markets are perfect and frictionless;
*Assumption 2:* The expected utility of each European investor, irrespective of the country of origin, can be represented as a function of the expected value and the variance of the returns on the investment portfolio;
*Assumption 3:* Each EU investor can freely trade at the same riskless rate;
*Assumption 4:* The returns are assumed to be normally distributed.

Under these assumptions a European model for securities should be mean-variance efficient and the systematic risk *vis-à-vis* the EU index should be priced. A purely EU CAPM implies:

$$E(R_{i,s}) = \gamma_{0ts} + \gamma_{1,s}\beta_{i,s} \tag{10.2}$$

where $R_{i,s}$ is the excess return, that is the actual return minus the risk-free rate, to the *i*th market's portfolio at period *s*, and $\beta_{i,s}$ is the *i*th local market's beta at the same period.

Adopting the international CAPM given by (10.2), we devise an empirical test as follows.[7] Given the probability distribution of the rate of return to local and European market portfolio, the stochastic return generating process is formulated as:

$$R_{it,s} = \alpha_{i,s} + \beta_{i,s}R_{ect,s} + U_{it,s} \tag{10. 3}$$

where: $R_{it,s}$ ≡ the nominal excess rate of return on market *i*'s portfolio as observed at sub-period *s*.
$R_{ect,s}$ ≡ the nominal excess rate of return to the world market index at sub-period *s*.
$U_{it,s}$ ≡ the residual term associated with the idiosyncratic risk at sub-period *s*.

All returns are expressed in a common currency. Standard assumptions about the distribution of the error term follow. That is:

$E(U_{i,s}) = 0$,
$E(U_{i,s}, U_{j,s}) = 0$ when $i \neq j$,
$E(U_{i,s}, U_{j,s}) = \sigma_{U,s}{}^2$ when $i=j$, and
$E(U_{i,s}, R_{ec,s}) = 0$ for the relevant range of $i$ and $j$.

According to equations (10.2) and (10.3), the systematic risk relative to the composite EU portfolio should have explanatory power for the pricing of portfolios if integration is the correct model.

The time-series regression of equation (10.3) estimates the market portfolio sensitivity coefficients, i.e. the betas. Following Fama and MacBeth (1973), we estimate the risk premia cross-sectionally by the regression

$$\text{Mean}(R_{i,s}) = \mu_0 + \mu_{1,s}\beta_{i,s} + V_{i,s} \tag{10.4}$$

where mean($R_{i,s}$) is the average excess rate of return in the $i$th (national) market at sub-period $s$ and it is the empirical counterpart of $E(R_{i,s})$, and $\mu_{1,s}$ is price associated with assuming one unit of risk *vis-à-vis* the EU integrated model.

The parameters of equation (10.3) are estimated at each sub-period $s$ separately by:

$$\alpha_{i,s} = E(R_{ec,s} - R_{f,s}) - \beta_{i,s}\,E(R_{i,s} - R_{f,s}) \tag{10.5}$$

$$\beta_{i,s} = \text{cov}(R_{i,s} - R_{f,s}, R_{ec,s} - R_{f,s})/\text{var}(R_{ec,s} - R_{f,s}) \tag{10.6}$$

The Fama–MacBeth two-step procedure is adopted to estimate the risk premia in the EU capital markets.[8] The expected returns (i.e. the computed average returns, empirical counterpart of the expected returns) are regressed against the portfolio sensitivity coefficient, the betas, to obtain the risk premia estimates for the relevant range of the data using the cross-sectional regression specified by equation (10.4).

*Hypothesis testing* Our underlying hypothesis is that capital assets (stocks) traded in EU equity markets are priced according to an international model. That is, we test the validity of the hypothesis that an integrated European Union composite market model – as opposed to a segmented model for each member state's equity market – prices the risk.

Alternatively, the hypothesis that the assets are priced in an integrated (European) market against the null hypothesis of no relationship is tested. The hypothesis is outlined below:

$$H_0 : \mu_i = 0$$
$$H_1 : \mu_i = 0 \tag{10.7}$$

where $\mu_i$ is (are) the estimated risk premium (premia) associated with the $i$th sub-period under consideration.

The total risk factor in a given market is measured by:

$$E(r_i^2) = \beta^2 E(r_{ec}{}^2) + E(\epsilon^2) \tag{10.8}$$

whose empirical counterpart is:

$$\sigma_i^2 = \beta^2 \sigma_{ec}{}^2 + \sigma_\epsilon{}^2 \tag{10.9}$$

where: $\sigma_i^2$ = measure of market portfolio specific (total) risk
$\beta^2\sigma_{ec}{}^2$ = measure of systematic (composite) risk
$\sigma_\epsilon{}^2$ = measure of unsystematic (idiosyncratic) risk

The time-series regression of equation (10.3) estimates the sensitivity coefficients. The risk premia are estimated by the following cross-sectional regression:

$$E(r_i) = \delta_i + \mu_i \beta_i + u_i \tag{10.10}$$

where $E(r_i)$ is the mean value of the $i$th market's rate of return. $\mu_i$ stands for the risk premium of the $i$th market. What we attempt to find out here is whether $\mu_i$ is priced by the data. Therefore, $\mu_i$ is estimated and tested to see whether it is statistically significant. If so, then the systematic risk associated with the market portfolio (i.e. the composite supranational market index) is priced. That is, markets are integrated. If, on the other hand, the composite index is not priced, then the markets are segmented.

Whether the composite model is priced examines the existence of integration (segmentation) in capital markets. However, it does not tell us about the sources of segmentation. In order to pinpoint the sources of segmentation, we attempt to look into the effects of capital controls on the pricing of capital assets. For that reason, the data are partitioned into several sections. The partitioning is based on major institutional developments in the EU towards either limiting or eliminating restrictions on capital movements. An acceptance of the null hypothesis implies that the risk premium is not priced and that the systematic risk of the international (European Union composite) model is not the proper systematic risk specification. It may also suggest that domestic factors are important for asset-pricing purposes in EU markets – at least as far as the stock markets are concerned. Further, a national pricing model wherein the systematic risk is represented by a purely domestic factor such as a market price index is likely to explain the variations in stock returns with some (greater than that of the composite model's) significance.

If the alternative hypothesis were to be adopted, then the international model would be priced. Capital assets are hypothesized to be priced according to an integrated European market model. That is, the integration of capital markets is said to be supported by the sample data of EU equity markets. The results of the time-series and the cross-section regressions as well as the empirical tests are evaluated in the next section.

*The F-test of risk premia differentials* We also perform the *F*-test of risk premia differentials for two sub-periods. The null hypothesis that risk premia of both sub-periods are equal to the full period's risk premia is tested both at 1 per cent and 5 per cent confidence intervals. That is, the null hypothesis that

$$H_0 : \mu_i = \mu_0$$
$$H_1 : \mu_i = \mu_0 \qquad (10.11)$$

where: $i = 1$ for the sub-period 1981/4–1983/12,
$i = 2$ for the sub-period 1984/1–1986/9, and
$\mu_0$ = risk premia of the full period 1981/4–1986/9

is tested by way of the *F*-test of risk premia differentials.

The tests that we employ here are tests of the integration of capital markets. An alternative to this would be a test of segmentation, where a segmented national model specified for asset-pricing is required. Our model can be translated in words in an attempt to estimate the risk premia independently before and after a certain European Commission directive on capital controls, to see whether the legislation amounts to a true regime switch.

We select two (institutionally) significant dates. Although some of the directives mentioned in the text do not bring about clear regime switches, it is still of empirical importance to identify these periods with different asset-pricing models. That is, one can still be concerned about whether it is possible to identify the sub-period with an integrated European composite model better than with a segmented model where the local systematic risk is the appropriate source of risk.

Essentially what we expect is that, if the year when a liberalization act or a major directive to limit capital controls over EU equity markets changes the way we define the market price of risk *vis-à-vis* specifying the correct systematic risk measure in a given market, capital markets should then become less segmented after the particular cut-off date. Empirically, the data after the cut-off year are expected to price the EU composite systematic risk, but not those before.

Two important dates for financial integration in the Community were the years 1983 and 1985. The risk premia in the EU equity markets are estimated both before and after the data- cut-off years of 1983 and 1985.[9] We also estimate the risk premia for the late 1970s and compare the estimates with those of the early and late 1980s. If the years that we select amount to regime switches, then there should be notable risk premia differentials between the sub-period before and the sub-period following the critical cut-off years.

One sample problem emerges due to the fact that in the 1980s there were a series of directives to limit or abolish capital controls. In order to keep the sample size large in each section of the data set, we allow the sections to overlap, but each period is compared only with the period that precedes or follows it.

If, as we expect, the composite index is priced after the cut-off year but not before, this will suggest that capital market segmentation is created by national governments' impediments to foreign investment in the EU member states. If the index is priced both before and after the cut-off year, then markets may be said to be integrated irrespective of capital controls. If the index is never priced – neither before nor after the selected cut-off year – this suggests that purely national factors are (still) important for asset-pricing purposes and that capital controls are not the real source that creates market segmentation.

We use stock market indices as the principal data. Using market price indices as reported by the IMF and adopting the same model described above, we evaluate the possible sources of capital market segmentation in an alternative way.[10] This is simply to look at the sources of market segmentation in this model by comparing the risk premia differentials across EU markets both before and after the cut-off year. Similarly, if capital controls are the only reason for segmentation, then the two risk premia should tend to become closer after capital controls are lifted, given that the risk premia in the two markets were different before the cut-off year.

If capital controls are unimportant for asset-pricing purposes, then the risk premia before and after the cut-off year should not differ from one another significantly. This can be tested through a standard $F$-test of linear constraint or through the Fama–Macbeth methodology. We perform the $F$-test of risk premia differentials. The $F$-test compares a given sub-period to a full period; that is, any given sub-period is compared with the full period from which the sub-period is selected on the basis of estimated risk premia. The standard $t$-statistics test whether or not a particular asset-pricing model is the correct model for pricing purposes.[11]

*Test results*

*Table 10.3: Computed average monthly rates of return*[a]

| Country | 78/7–81/3 | 81/4–83/12 | 84/1–86/9 | 81/4–86/9 |
|---|---|---|---|---|
| UK | 0.11543 | 0.14565 | 0.18098 | 0.16332 |
| Germany | –0.03168 | 0.13760 | 0.19273 | 0.16517 |
| France | 0.14681 | 0.09197 | 0.26020 | 0.17609 |
| Netherlands | –0.13662 | 0.16665 | 0.21021 | 0.18843 |
| Belgium | 0.14713 | 0.14059 | 0.22674 | 0.18366 |
| Denmark | 0.07118 | 0.03829 | –0.03951 | 0.17173 |
| Italy | 0.03422 | –0.10028 | 0.04845 | 0.02327 |
| Spain | –0.19940 | 0.02887 | 0.04426 | 0.02357 |

| Country | 72/1–86/9 | 83/4–84/12 | 85/1–86/9 |
|---|---|---|---|
| UK | 0.10826 | 0.17441 | 0.16383 |
| Germany | 0.06282 | 0.12521 | 0.02798 |
| France | 0.11190 | 0.02339 | 0.03334 |
| Netherlands | 0.07362 | 0.20497 | 0.23412 |
| Belgium | 0.06685 | 0.21563 | 0.25548 |
| Denmark | 0.12980 | 0.10678 | 0.06552 |
| Italy | 0.13006 | 0.05190 | 0.06875 |
| Spain | 0.06596 | 0.21437 | 0.05090 |

*Note*: [a] Returns are calculated using *IFS* adjusted share price indices

Computed monthly average returns are reported in Table 10.3. Estimated factor loadings (the results of the time-series regression 10.2) are reported for all countries in the sample in Tables 10.4 to 10.11. The cross-sectional risk premia estimates are reported in Table 10.12. Independently summarized are the results of sensitivity coefficients to demonstrate the strength of a particular EC market portfolio to the EC composite market index in Table 10.13. In this table estimated factor loadings are rounded for clarity. (Tables 10.4–11.13 are grouped at the end of the chapter.)

The results of the model suggest that systematic risk *vis-à-vis* the European Community composite model is not priced for the period 1978–81. This implies that European Community capital markets were segmented in the late 1970s. Domestic markets appear to be the major factors explaining the variations in stock returns. Thus, the local market index is the principal source of systematic risk in the period of late 1970s. Alternatively, the European Community composite index is unimportant for asset-pricing purposes for this period.

Several reasons can be given for dominance of a local market return over a composite European index in terms of asset-pricing. The most important characteristic of the 1970s was instability. As a result of the two major oil shocks, businesses as well as capital markets were regulated in this decade. Domestic policies outweighed policies to overcome difficulties in order to complete the single (common) market in Western Europe.

Most notably, this was the period when government impediments to equity markets within the EC were in existence, including in the UK and Germany. Macroeconomic policies conducted by individual states were far less interdependent. This was a period when productivity shocks still shaped monetary policies throughout Europe. Further, because the European Monetary System came into being in 1979, there was also an exchange rate risk in this period that could not be easily disregarded.

The systematic risk based on the same model for the periods 1981/4–1983/12 and 1984/1–1986/9 are priced. Both the standard $t$-test and the $F$-test of risk premia differentials support the view that EC equity markets became more integrated in the first half of the 1980s than they had been in the 1970s. The $t$-test of significance shows that the integrated asset-pricing model is priced between 1981/4 and 1986/9. Further, the null hypothesis that the risk premia in the EC composite market model for each sub-period – i.e. both 1981/4–1983/12 and 1984/1–1986/9 – are equal to the risk premia of the full period (1981/4–1986/9) is accepted with 1 per cent confidence based on the $F$-test of linear constraint (Table 10.14).

These results would apparently translate into the belief that the 1980s displayed a tendency towards greater integration across the Community markets. However, the null hypothesis that the EU composite market model is priced after our first cut-off year of 1983 but not before is not accepted by the data. That is, capital controls over stock markets do not seem to affect asset-pricing, at least in the early 1980s, although there is evidence to believe that the EC equity markets were more integrated between 1981 and 1986 than they had been prior to 1981.

Thus, we cannot conclude that restrictions on capital imposed by national governments are the only sources of segmentation. Other reasons appear to be important as well. These reasons are those that we have classified as 'indirect barriers', such as language difficulties and difficulties concerning information about markets or financial assets. It is important to restate that there seems to be a clear difference between the two decades, although we have been unable to attribute this result specifically to the presence of capital restrictions.

As far as our second cut-off year is concerned, there is little evidence that the year of the White Paper did indeed contribute to the integration of capital markets within the EC. The results concerning 1985 are more supportive (a greater $t$-value) of the hypothesis that government impediments are the only source of segmentation in equity markets than those concerning the first cut-off year, 1983. Yet the composite model for the period 1985/1–1986/9 still is not priced. Therefore, the data do not provide evidence for the role of restrictions on capital as the primary source of segmentation. This partially conclusive result is reached because, before and following the first cut-off year 1983, risk premia across EC capital markets did not differ significantly (see Tables 10.12 and 10.13).

**An alternative approach**[12]

Consider the single-index EU capital asset-pricing model that we have developed in this chapter.[13] In such a model, national capital markets contribute to the EU-wide systematic risk in proportion to their sensitivity coefficients (betas) *vis-à-vis* the value-weighted EC market portfolio. If a Union market contributes proportionally more to EU systematic risk than to total EU market value, it can be taken as a signal that the market at hand is integrated to the benchmark EU market portfolio. That is, any proportion of systematic risk in total risk *vis-à-vis* the EU market portfolio over and above the respective share in EU market value should give us *a priori* an idea about the status of integration. The proportions of systematic risk in total risk are computed as

$$\beta_i^2 \text{var}\ (R_w)/\text{var}\ (R_i) \qquad (10.12)$$

where $\beta_i$ is the sensitivity of rate of return on a national market's portfolio, $R_i$, to the EU benchmark rate of return, $R_{ec}$.

This is an alternative way of evaluating capital market integration based only on the times-series regression results of our standard model developed in this chapter. We report in Table 10.14 the proportion of systematic risk of portfolio returns explained by the single-market factor. Here, the difference in percentage between the proportion of a given market's systematic risk and the market's share in total EU capitalization is a relevant measure of equity market integration. Any systematic risk proportion that is higher than the market capitalization of a given country should imply integration.

In Table 10.14, it is clear that for the last and the most recent period, all market portfolios in the sample exhibit high proportions of systematic risk as explained by the single EU composite factor model. It is also clear that each member state's proportion of systematic risk in total risk is larger than the share of each market in total EU market capitalization. Thus, all markets appear to be integrated.

What seems to be true also is that each market's proportion of systematic risk as explained by the integrated model in proportion to its market capitalization share has increased through time in the entire decade of the 1980s. A close examination of the last period relative to the previous periods for which we have estimated the measures of systematic risk appears to suggest that the integrated model explains the variations in equity returns in each market in the sample better now than it did in the 1970s and even in the early 1980s.

This result provides partial evidence for the acceptance of an integrated model against a segmented model. That is, there is at least partial evidence that the systematic risk in the EU equity markets is priced in an integrated EU model. The interpretation of Table 10.14 seems to give different but more consistent results about capital market integration in EU. They are more supportive of the existence of an integrated model than the results based on the standard tests that are provided.

However, this approach does not particularly address the sources of segmentation in equity markets. All we can say, based on the results of this model, is that an integrated European Union model explains an increasingly greater proportion of variations in share prices. Yet we fail to attribute this to specific legislation eliminating or limiting capital restrictions; that is, we cannot in this approach select a year that represents a regime switch.

## Notes

1. All these three studies showed that interest rate parity holds almost identically in short-term Eurocurrency markets. See also Dooley and Isard (1980).
2. Greece and Portugal are not included in the empirical model.
3. Specifying the type of imperfection before undertaking any test is also recommended by Solnik (1974a, 1977).
4. If there is greater risk aversion than the logarithmic investor or if there are deviations from the purchasing power parity, then the equilibrium rate of return on any asset also depends on its correlation with the inflation rates in other countries (Adler and Dumas, 1983).
5. Gultekin *et al.* (1990) argue that generalized tests of capital market integration are usually uninformative and that individual 'event study' should be the approach to capital market segmentation. They attribute the difficulty of generalization to the complexity of governments' impediments to capital movements.
6. The EU capital markets can serve as an excellent sample to test integration. First, capital controls have been eliminated over EU exchanges. Second, exchange rates across the member states can float only within small margins. Third, indirect barriers, such as language difficulties, can be more easily assumed away for the EU investors who trade in EU markets than for other international investors who trade in other parts of the world. Hence, our utility theoretical assumptions about the existence of a mean-variance efficient portfolio in the EU context are more relevant than those in other world markets.
7. Because we use local market indices to proxy national portfolios, it is empirically impossible to run domestic CAPMs for each country in the sample. Hence, we only consider an international (i.e. European) CAPM to test integration.
8. As we saw in Chapter 5, the Fama–MacBeth procedure is based on two regressions. First, the time-series behaviour of returns is monitored in a linear regression and portfolio betas are found accordingly. Second, expected returns (i.e. mean returns in empirical work) are regressed cross-sectionally against portfolio betas to estimate the risk premium (premia). Refer to Chapter 5 for details of the procedure.
9. The selection of a cut-off year is not arbitrary. It is a date after which capital controls over equity markets are either lifted entirely or when a tendency in that direction has begun. In selecting these years as cut-off dates, we are motivated by their importance for the institutional framework of the Community. The year 1983 was the year of the first EC Commission initiative on liberalizing capital markets. The year 1985 is when the breakthrough White Paper

was introduced. We have assumed that there should be significant differences in the price of systematic risk across EC capital markets before and after the years of 1983 and 1985. Thus, the data are divided into three, and each period is expected to display different risk premia.

10. An explanation of the data and details of the sample are provided later in text.
11. *F*-test of linear constraint is also employed to test for integration. The results of this test are reported in Table 10.14. The Fama–MacBeth procedure is an alternative that requires that the risk premia for the EU are estimated each month (monthly data are used) of the two sub-periods. Thus, one can obtain two time-series of risk premia differentials that ought to have zero mean if capital markets are perfectly integrated and employ the Hotelling $T^2$ statistics to test the mean differentials.
12. This section draws largely on earlier work (Akdogan, 1992a).
13. Note here that the basic difference between the single-index international capital asset-pricing model and the standard CAPM of Sharpe (1964) and Lintner (1965) is the inclusion of a world market portfolio as the source of systematic risk in the former. The standard CAPMs are based on a market portfolio of domestically traded instruments.

*Table 10.4: Estimated sensitivities: single-index time-series regression estimates: United Kingdom*

| | 1978/7–1981/3 | 1981/4–1983/12 | 1984/1–1986/9 |
|---|---|---|---|
| Intercept | –0.4009242 | 0.2066939 | –0.2444835 |
| St. error | 0.4154918 | 0.3912069 | 0.4516421 |
| *t*–value | –0.9649389 | 0.5283493 | –0.5413214 |
| Portf. beta | 1.7243370 | 0.9935408 | 0.9140238 |
| St. error | 0.1047049 | 0.1231848 | 0.1190098 |
| *t*–value | 16.4685400 | 8.0654470 | 7.6802380 |
| | **1981/4–1986/9** | **983/4–1984/12** | **1985/1–1986/9** |
| Intercept | –0.7426724 | –0.2814495 | –0.5776732 |
| St. error | 0.2942565 | 0.4476616 | 0.6242966 |
| *t*–value | –0.2523894 | –0.6287104 | –0.9253185 |
| Portf. beta | 0.9360156 | 1.1935780 | 0.8487626 |
| St. error | 0.8409470 | 0.1434069 | 0.1572703 |
| *t*–value | 11.1305000 | 8.3230180 | 5.3968390 |
| | **1989/10–1990/12** | **1972/1–1986/9** | |
| Intercept | 0.2634756 | –0.3672665 | |
| St. error | 0.4713052 | 0.2183398 | |
| *t*–value | 0.5590339 | –0.6820870 | |
| Portf. beta | 0.8821814 | 1.4916730 | |
| St. error | 0.1237045 | 0.4770830 | |
| *t*–value | 7.1313590 | 31.2665400 | |

*Table 10.5: Estimated sensitivities: single-index time-series regression estimates: Germany*

| | 1978/7–1981/3 | 1981/4–1983/12 | 1984/1–1986/9 |
|---|---|---|---|
| Intercept | –0.5880780 | 0.6375008 | 0.5455773 |
| St. error | 0.3662375 | 0.5423070 | 0.8340432 |
| *t*–value | –1.6057290 | 1.1755350 | 0.6541356 |
| Portf. beta | 0.3006875 | 0.5870890 | 0.6147647 |
| St. error | 0.9229267 | 0.1707639 | 0.2197743 |
| *t*–value | 3.2579780 | 3.4380170 | 2.7972540 |
| | **1981/4–1986/9** | **1983/4–1984/12** | **1985/1–1986/9** |
| Intercept | 0.5993182 | 0.9305237 | 0.1407992 |
| St. error | 0.4736566 | 0.6997622 | 0.1330763 |
| *t*–value | 1.2600340 | 0.1329771 | 1.0580340 |
| Portf. beta | 0.6003950 | 0.6829956 | 0.5324518 |
| St. error | 0.1359308 | 0.2241665 | 0.3352404 |
| *t*–value | 4.4169180 | 3.0468230 | 1.5882680 |
| | **1989/10–1990/12** | **1972/1–1986/9** | |
| Intercept | 0.6473074 | 0.2346596 | |
| St. error | 0.9925177 | 0.2268501 | |
| *t*–value | 0.6521872 | 1.0344260 | |
| Portf. beta | 1.2240720 | 0.4049412 | |
| St. error | 0.2605083 | 0.4956785 | |
| *t*–value | 4.6987830 | 8.1694340 | |

*Table 10.6:* *Estimated sensitivities: single-index time-series regression estimates: France*

| | 1978/7–1981/3 | 1981/4–1983/12 | 1984/1–1986/9 |
|---|---|---|---|
| Intercept | 0.9103222 | –0.1316722 | –0.1430508 |
| St. error | 0.8997158 | 0.1420078 | 0.1568216 |
| *t*–value | 1.0117890 | –0.9272181 | –0.9121885 |
| Portf. beta | 0.6184443 | 1.7778520 | 1.7941910 |
| St. error | 0.2267304 | 0.4471602 | 0.4132322 |
| *t*–value | 2.7276640 | 3.9758730 | 4.3418460 |

| | 1981/4–1986/9 | 1983/4–1984/12 | 1985/1–1986/9 |
|---|---|---|---|
| Intercept | –0.1366209 | 0.2476871 | –0.1906887 |
| St. error | 0.1032462 | 0.8723501 | 0.2580409 |
| *t*–value | –1.3232540 | 0.2839309 | –0.7389866 |
| Portf. beta | 1.7841020 | 1.2327700 | 2.0074870 |
| St. error | 0.2950641 | 0.2794544 | 0.6500463 |
| *t*–value | 6.0464880 | 4.4113470 | 3.0882220 |

| | 1989/10–1990/12 | 1972/1–1986/9 |
|---|---|---|
| Intercept | –0.3568180 | 0.3349992 |
| St. error | 0.8680490 | 0.5796161 |
| *t*–value | –0.4110575 | 0.5779673 |
| Portf. beta | 1.1783350 | 0.8066024 |
| St. error | 0.2278387 | 0.1266489 |
| *t*–value | 5.1717920 | 6.3688070 |

*Table 10.7: Estimated sensitivities: single-index time-series regression estimates: The Netherlands*

| | 1978/7–1981/3 | 1981/4–1983/12 | 1984/1–1986/9 |
|---|---|---|---|
| Intercept | –0.5140414 | 0.4734072 | 0.8189706 |
| St. error | 0.4285786 | 0.4594578 | 0.7240978 |
| *t*–value | –1.1994100 | 1.0303600 | 1.1310220 |
| Portf. beta | 0.4184784 | 0.9484045 | 0.5709149 |
| St. error | 0.1080028 | 0.1446760 | 0.1908032 |
| *t*–value | 3.8747010 | 6.5553700 | 2.9921660 |

| | 1981/4–1986/9 | 1983/4–1984/12 | 1985/1–1986/9 |
|---|---|---|---|
| Intercept | 0.5830349 | 0.4286381 | 0.1888285 |
| St. error | 0.4179706 | 0.6954468 | 0.9073204 |
| *t*–value | 1.3948950 | 0.6163492 | 2.0811670 |
| Portf. Beta | 0.7424139 | 1.1825630 | 0.1734591 |
| St. error | 0.1194506 | 0.2227840 | 0.2285685 |
| *t*–value | 6.2152410 | 5.3081140 | 0.7588930 |

| | 1989/10–1990/12 | 1972/1–1986/9 |
|---|---|---|
| Intercept | –0.5701217 | 0.2347349 |
| St. error | 0.4884353 | 0.2398540 |
| *t*–value | –1.1672410 | 0.9786574 |
| Portf. beta | 0.6291375 | 0.5159886 |
| St. error | 0.1282007 | 0.5240926 |
| *t*–value | 4.9074420 | 9.8453700 |

*Table 10.8: Estimated sensitivities: single-index time-series regression estimates: Belgium*

| | 1978/7–1981/3 | 1981/4–1983/12 | 1984/1–1986/9 |
|---|---|---|---|
| Intercept | –0.4791878 | 0.1847870 | –0.5761634 |
| St. error | 0.6357684 | 0.1006925 | 0.7946960 |
| *t*–value | –0.7537144 | 0.1835162 | –0.7250111 |
| Portf. beta | 0.3681812 | 0.9706863 | 1.0344740 |
| St. error | 0.1602151 | 0.3170646 | 0.2094060 |
| *t*–value | 2.2980440 | 3.0614780 | 4.9400270 |
| | **1981/4–1986/9** | **1983/4–1984/12** | **1985/1–1986/9** |
| Intercept | 0.8295849 | 0.6624953 | –0.2761122 |
| St. error | 0.6396995 | 0.1006163 | 0.1159955 |
| *t*–value | 0.1296835 | 0.6584377 | –0.2380370 |
| Portf. beta | 1.0005300 | 0.8802533 | 1.0842880 |
| St. error | 0.1828178 | 0.3223208 | 0.2922112 |
| *t*–value | 5.4728240 | 2.7309850 | 3.7106290 |
| | **1989/10–1990/12** | **1972/1–1986/9** | |
| Intercept | –0.1062812 | 0.1074893 | |
| St. error | 0.7732933 | 0.3339039 | |
| *t*–value | –1.3743970 | 0.3219170 | |
| Portf. beta | 0.6604527 | 0.5771838 | |
| St. error | 0.2035618 | 0.7295960 | |
| *t*–value | 3.2539740 | 7.9110060 | |

*Table 10.9: Estimated sensitivities: single-index time-series regression estimates: Denmark*

| | 1978/7–1981/3 | 1981/4–1983/12 | 1984/1–1986/9 |
|---|---|---|---|
| Intercept | 0.7316912 | 0.3204602 | –0.1649363 |
| St. error | 0.8081036 | 0.9829183 | 0.1236955 |
| *t*–value | 0.9054423 | 3.2602940 | –1.3334060 |
| Portf. beta | –0.2200766 | 0.4969225 | 0.5580221 |
| St. error | 0.2036439 | 0.3095054 | 0.3259434 |
| *t*–value | –0.1080693 | 1.6055370 | 1.712022 |
| | **1981/4–1986/9** | **1983/4–1984/12** | **1985/1–1986/9** |
| Intercept | 0.1014695 | 0.6876041 | –0.9421071 |
| St. error | 0.8361408 | 0.1946853 | 0.1477983 |
| *t*–value | 1.2135460 | 0.3531874 | –0.6374276 |
| Portf. beta | 0.4008379 | 0.5887002 | 0.6118087 |
| St. error | 0.2389582 | 0.6236679 | 0.3723275 |
| *t*–value | 1.6774400 | 0.9439322 | 1.6234000 |
| | **1989/10–1990/12** | **1972/1–1986/9** | |
| Intercept | 0.9453095 | 0.1028969 | |
| St. error | 0.7755554 | 0.4118849 | |
| *t*–value | 1.2188810 | 2.4981960 | |
| Portf. beta | 0.8094964 | 0.2767334 | |
| St. error | 0.2035618 | 0.8999883 | |
| *t*–value | 3.9766630 | 3.0748560 | |

*Table 10.10:* *Estimated sensitivities: single-index time-series regression estimates: Italy*

| | 1978/7–1981/3 | 1981/4–1983/12 | 1984/1–1986/9 |
|---|---|---|---|
| Intercept | 0.3343144 | –0.1502715 | 0.1515785 |
| St. error | 0.1224530 | 0.1153278 | 0.1347445 |
| *t*–value | 2.7301440 | –1.3029950 | 1.1249330 |
| Portf. beta | 0.8778798 | 1.1148560 | 1.4812830 |
| St. error | 0.3085843 | 0.3631489 | 0.3550581 |
| *t*–value | 0.2844862 | 3.0699680 | 4.1719450 |
| | **1981/4–1986/9** | **1983/4–1984/12** | **1985/1–1986/9** |
| Intercept | –0.9072659 | –0.6824736 | 0.2317981 |
| St. error | 0.9042106 | 0.8929859 | 0.1992873 |
| *t*–value | –0.1003379 | –0.7642603 | 1.1631350 |
| Portf. beta | 1.4052810 | 0.7080263 | 1.7456040 |
| St. error | 0.2584116 | 0.2860650 | 0.5020367 |
| *t*–value | 5.4381500 | 2.4750540 | 3.4770440 |
| | **1989/10–1990/12** | **1972/1–1986/9** | |
| Intercept | –0.1712307 | 0.7481255 | |
| St. error | 0.9871288 | 0.5125931 | |
| *t*–value | –1.7346330 | 1.4594920 | |
| Portf. beta | 1.2287870 | 0.5683483 | |
| St. error | 0.2590939 | 0.1120041 | |
| *t*–value | 4.7426330 | 5.0743540 | |

*Table 10.11: Estimated sensitivities: single-index time-series regression estimates: Spain*

| | 1978/7–1981/3 | 1981/4–1983/12 | 1984/1–1986/9 |
|---|---|---|---|
| Intercept | –0.1450432 | –0.1756576 | 0.1976120 |
| St. error | 0.1108411 | 0.9014430 | 0.1332036 |
| *t*–value | –0.1308569 | –0.1948738 | 1.4835330 |
| Portf. beta | –0.2050036 | 0.3691667 | 1.0902060 |
| St. error | 0.2793222 | 0.2838501 | 0.3509978 |
| *t*–value | –0.7339325 | 1.3005690 | 3.1060200 |
| | 1981/4–1986/9 | 1983/4–1984/12 | 1985/1–1986/9 |
| Intercept | 0.8879304 | 0.2655490 | 0.7067049 |
| St. error | 0.8226306 | 0.1311308 | 0.1760418 |
| *t*–value | 1.0793790 | 2.0250690 | 0.4014416 |
| Portf. beta | 0.8384763 | –0.3015933 | 1.6792140 |
| St. error | 0.2350971 | 0.4200731 | 0.4434774 |
| *t*–value | 3.5665100 | –0.7179544 | 3.7864000 |
| | 1989/10–1990/12 | 1972/1–1986/9 | |
| Intercept | –0.7776593 | 0.3246724 | |
| St. error | 0.1670131 | 0.4481497 | |
| *t*–value | –0.4656279 | 0.7244731 | |
| Portf. beta | 1.2865640 | 0.3446308 | |
| St. error | 0.4383629 | 0.9792286 | |
| *t*–value | 2.9349290 | 3.5194110 | |

*Table 10.12: Estimated risk premia: single-index*[a]

| | 1978/7–1981/3 | 1981/4–1983/12 | 1984/1–1986/9 |
|---|---|---|---|
| Intercept | 0.6146511 | –0.3784168 | –0.1366721 |
| St. error | 0.1684089 | 0.2421567 | 0.2194486 |
| *t*–value | 0.3649753 | –0.1566503 | –0.6227978 |
| Premium | 0.6322328 | 0.3284932 | 0.3346064 |
| St. error | 0.2216570 | 0.2421684 | 0.2011396 |
| *t*–value | 0.2852300 | 1.3564663 | 1.6635530 |

| | 1981/4–1986/9 | 1983/4–1984/12 | 1985/1–1986/9 |
|---|---|---|---|
| Intercept | 0.1743709 | 0.2257366 | 0.3155492 |
| St. error | 0.2694151 | 0.9345241 | 0.1408185 |
| *t*–value | 6.4722020 | 2.4155240 | 2.2408230 |
| Premium | 0.1581887 | –0.1857003 | 0.7809283 |
| St. error | 0.2567258 | 0.1034935 | 0.1257862 |
| *t*–value | 0.6161775 | –0.1794319 | 0.6208376 |

| | 1989/10–1990/12 |
|---|---|
| Intercept | 0.6527848 |
| St. error | 0.3381792 |
| *t*–value | 0.1930293 |
| Premium | –0.2940588 |
| St. error | 0.3316612 |
| *t*–value | –0.8866240 |

*Note*: [a] The risk premia are estimated cross-sectionally running the mean values of market portfolio returns against the sensitivity coefficients (betas).

*Table 10.13:* *The F-test of risk premia differentials* ($\mu_1 = \mu_0$, vs. $\mu_1 = \mu_0$, and $\mu_2 = \mu_0$, vs. $\mu_2 = \mu_0$)

| Period | |
|---|---|
| 1981/4–1983/12 vs. 1981/4–1986/9 | Null hypothesis accepted at both 5% and 1% confidence levels |
| 1984/1–1986/9 vs. 1981/4–1986/9 | Null hypothesis accepted at both 5% and 1% confidence levels |

*Notes:*
$\mu_1$ = the risk premium of the sub-period 1981/4–1983/12
$\mu_2$ = the risk premium of the sub-period 1984/1–1986/9
$\mu_0$ = the risk premium of the full period 1981/4–1986/9

*Table 10.14:* *Proportion of systematic risk of portfolio returns explained by single market factor*[a]

| Market | 78/7–81/3 | 81/4–83/12 | 84/1–86/9 | 86/10–89/9 | 89/10–90/12 |
|---|---|---|---|---|---|
| UK | 0.897 | 0.677 | 0.655 | 0.786 | 0.809 |
| Germany | 0.255 | 0.276 | 0.201 | 0.253 | 0.647 |
| France | 0.193 | 0.337 | 0.378 | 0.302 | 0.691 |
| Netherlands | 0.326 | 0.580 | 0.324 | 0.441 | 0.667 |
| Belgium | 0.145 | 0.232 | 0.440 | 0.492 | 0.468 |
| Denmark | 0.000 | 0.076 | 0.086 | 0.128 | 0.568 |
| Italy | 0.002 | 0.233 | 0.359 | 0.408 | 0.652 |
| Spain | 0.017 | 0.051 | 0.237 | 0.286 | 0.417 |

*Note:* [a] The single market factor is the EU composite market return. Proportions reported are the share of systematic risk in total portfolio risk (i.e. $\beta^2\sigma_{ec}^2/\sigma_i^2$). Proportions are rounded.

# 11 A multifactor model

**Single-index versus multifactor**

We have tested for integration using a single-index capital asset-pricing model. We shall now adopt a multifactor return-generating model to estimate the risk premia to test for integration. A prespecified bifactor model approach is adopted. In a prespecified multifactor model the appropriate question is: What economic variables, other than the EU composite market index cause systematic variations in stock returns in the EU stock markets?

In a standard single-index CAPM, identifying the sources of risk is unnecessary since the only source of systematic risk is a market index or a market portfolio. As long as we can set or select a domestic (or international) market portfolio, a model of integration in this context consists of two cross-sectional regressions in the first stage, one with a single local and the other with a single international index. Within a multifactor asset-pricing framework, factors should be prespecified if a statistical method is not employed to extract the relevant factors. In order to capture the movements in the term structure of interest rates relevant for systematic risk we use a long-term interest rate. We have selected German government bond yields as a proxy for long-term interest rates.[1]

The following multifactor return-generating process is adopted:

$$E(r_i) = a_i + \sum_{k=1}^{k} \beta_{ik} q_{kt} + v_{it} \qquad k = 1, \ldots, K \qquad (11.1)$$

where:

> $E(r_i)$ is time-series mean value of the $i$th market portfolio's return;
> $\beta_{ik}$ is the $k$-factor sensitivity coefficient of the $i$th market portfolio as estimated by the regression (10.10);
> $q_{kt}$ is cross-sectionally estimated $k$-factor risk premium;
> $v_{it}$ is the residual of the regression.

The time-series estimates of systematic risk coefficients for country by country are reported in the Tables 11.1 to 11.8. The risk premia estimates of the cross-sectional regression are reported in Table 11.9. (All tables are at the end of the chapter.) The EU composite market return is priced for the first sub-period 1983/1–1986/1. This is consistent with the result of the single-index model. The other source of systematic risk, i.e. long-term bond yields, is also a priced factor for the same sub-period. However, the second sub-period, 1986/2–1989/1, does not contain any source of systematic risk priced. Neither the EU composite return index nor the German long term bond yield is a priced source of systematic risk based on the prespecified bipriced sources of systematic risk based on the prespecified bifactor return-generating model.

That both single-index and multifactor models price the EU composite return for the sub-period of early 1980s can be partially explained by the large market shares of the UK and German equity markets within the EU market. These two eliminated capital controls just before this sub-period in which we have the priced sources of systematic risk. Therefore, the impact of this was greater equity market integration within the EU in the first half of the 1980s because the British and German markets together account for almost 70 per cent of total EU market capitalization. That assets are not priced in an integrated European Union composite model in the second half of the 1980s until the first month of 1989, on the other hand, can be attributed to the 1987 stock market crash.

## Data

As in the previous chapter, the major data source for the empirical work presented here is *International Financial Statistics* (*IFS*) published by the International Monetary Fund (IMF). The IMF provides adjusted monthly share price indices of stock exchanges. The data are limited to outstanding shares traded on a given exchange. We take the monthly rate of depreciation and appreciation in stock price indices as a proxy for actual returns. These proxies are assumed to represent market portfolios in a given EU member state.

We have had to exclude some EU stock markets because of lack of data. The *IFS* does not publish share price data on Ireland, Portugal and Greece, simply because these are the countries that are in the process of developing official stock markets as well as liberalizing their financial sectors. Moreover, the data on the Luxembourg official stock exchange do not exist for the period before 1980. Therefore, equity markets of these four EU member states are excluded from the sample.

The government bond yields used in the multifactor model are obtained from Morgan Guaranty Trust Company of New York. The Morgan Bank regularly issues US dollar yields for international debt securities. The German government bond yields are taken as proxy for long-term interest rates. The yields are end-of-month yields and calculated semi-annually.

## Alternative models

This section outlines some other alternative models that can be employed in the context of European capital markets. We shall discuss several possible alternatives to our benchmark model proposed earlier. Some of these alternatives arise from the very nature of European integration, such as trying other data cut-off years to test for the role of capital controls in segmentation, or partitioning data into more divisions. These models can well be employed to test the issue of integration.

*Single-index alternatives*

There are a number of single-factor alternative models. For instance, the same model can be repeated with the micro data, and securities are pooled from EU markets. The composite index would then be set by individual securities. Individual returns are run against this composite market index both before and after the preselected cut-off year, such as the year of the Single European Act. If capital controls are the only reason for segmentation, then we expect the composite index to be priced after but not before the cut-off date. If the composite index is always priced, then the role of capital controls is neutral. If it is never priced, this suggests that other market imperfections are the cause of market segmentation.

Alternatively, if the risk premia of identical or similar securities differ in the two markets before but not after the cut-off year, this also implies that capital controls are the cause of market segmentation. If the risk premia do not differ significantly before or after the cut-off, then the likelihood that a purely domestic factor (or factors) is (are) priced is high. The same tests are employed.

Another alternative is to adopt a segmentation model where the validity of domestic versions of standard single-index CAPMs can be tested. Such models do not differ essentially from the integration models where the validity of integrated models are tested. Empirically speaking, the composite market index could be compared to domestic indices. In general, if the domestic factor is priced, the markets are segmented; if not, the composite index model may be more appropriate.

The procedure from this point is as follows: domestic versions are run both before and after the cut-off year. The necessary condition for the proposition to be justified that capital controls are the only source of segmentation is that the domestic index should have explanatory power – i.e. it is priced – before the cut-off year but not afterwards. The sufficient condition for the argument to be true is that the composite market index is priced after but not before the cut-off year. Therefore, regressions are run with micro data having individual stock returns, as in the second model.

Yet another way repeats all the above-specified models both with the macro data (stock market indices) and with the micro data (returns to individual securities pooled) by introducing several composite indices. Three other alternatives are an EC-5 composite index, an EC-9 composite index, and a Switzerland domestic market index.[2] The EC-5 consists of the core EU nation states, namely Germany, France, Netherlands, Belgium, and Luxembourg. The EC-5 is known for its homogeneity. It might be expected that an EC-5 composite index is priced relative to any domestic index that can be defined within these five countries.

The second option is the EU stock markets excluding Spain, Portugal, and Greece. The third option is suggested as a peculiar case study.

Finally, a model based on interlisted stocks similar to those adopted by Jorion and Schwartz (1986) can be adopted. Those stocks that are listed in EU markets are selected. This selection then is used as an index. First, the interlisted stock index is run against an EU composite index such as the ones mentioned above. Next, 'purely' domestic stocks, stocks that are registered in one market only are run against the same EU composite index.

Two conditions must hold for the argument of capital controls over markets to be justified. The necessary condition is that the domestic factor is not priced. The sufficient condition is that EU composite index is priced. If these two are satisfied then the government impediments such as capital controls are the sources of market segmentation. If neither factor is priced, then other market imperfections such as inability of a class of investors to trade and cost of obtaining information in order to invest in foreign markets may be the sources of segmentation.

*Multifactor alternatives*

The above-specified and tested models are single-factor capital asset-pricing models wherein the returns are assumed to be generated by a composite market index. In actuality, however, the linear stochastic process by which equity market returns are generated is a multifactor process. In a multifactor return-generating process, factors can also be variables that are not portfolio-related. Several macroeconomic variables ranging from interest rates to oil prices can be taken into consideration in specifying the asset-pricing model. If, on the other hand, a multi-beta CAPM based on mean-variance efficiency is adopted, factors will be confined to market portfolios (or market indices which serve the same purpose). In any event, the return-generating process is a multifactor one as in the following:

$$r_{it} = \alpha_i + \sum_{k=1}^{k} \beta_{ik}\delta_{kt} + \epsilon_{it}$$

where: $r_{it}$ = rate of return to the security or portfolio at time $t$;
$\beta_{ik}$ = $k$th factor specific sensitivity coefficient of the $i$th security or portfolio – i.e $i$th asset sensitivity to the $k$th factor, $k = 1,2,..K$;
$\delta_{kt}$ = the $k$th common factor as a source of systematic risk at time $t$;
$\epsilon_{it}$ = security or portfolio specific (diversifiable) stochastic residual risk at time $t$.

In bi-beta CAPMs, that is when $K = 2$, one domestic index and one international index are taken as factors. Estimated beta coefficients in that case give one national and one international risk premium. Depending on whichever is priced, segmentation or integration can be discovered. In an APT multifactor return-generating model, $K$ is normally greater than 2.

We should however remember that there is a major drawback in adopting APMs such as the one given above. As we studied earlier in the text, empirical works that have adopted arbitrage pricing theory, in general, extract the factors using statistical factor analysis. Although Chen (1983) suggests variables, which is justifiable by economic theory, this method still displays a major problem in asset-pricing. The problem is that there is no guarantee that the factors selected by factor analysis will have economic justification as determinant sources of the variations in security returns. A second problem, as we pointed out earlier, is how many factors, in addition to what factors, should be considered for pricing purposes (Chen, 1983; Ehrhardt, 1987; Trzcinka, 1986).

*Orthogonalizing the market portfolio*

Integration cannot be tested by running a univariate regression on betas because of the possible correlation between the local market portfolios and the world portfolio. One way of dealing with this problem is to orthogonalize the returns by isolating in the domestic market portfolio the component independent of the benchmark world market portfolio. Thus, that part of the domestic market portfolio that is orthogonal to the world portfolio is taken as an explanatory variable along with the world portfolio in a regression where the dependent variable is the rate of return to individual securities or portfolios.[3]

In passing, we shall underline an important point that should be considered in empirical research. Market portfolios are better than individual securities because the latter are a major cause of bias in the estimators. When the time-series of individual returns from a sample are used, it is implicitly assumed that the risk characteristics of the securities remain unchanged, say, between a period of regulation and deregulation. One problem with this approach is that the consistency of the risk premium estimates is jeopardized because both the factor loadings and the risk premia are estimated. The second problem is the stationarity of the factor loadings.

## Notes

1. German government bond yields are end-of-month semi-annual yields. We have assumed flat term structure. We wish to thank David Maslin of Morgan Guaranty Trust who has supplied the data.
2. Both EU composite indices are the weighted averages of the national stock market indices, weights being the percentages of total market capitalization.
3. Such a projection is not necessary in our case of European integration where small European markets have low correlation coefficients with the European composite index.

*Table 11.1: Estimated factor loadings: multifactor time-series regression estimates: United Kingdom*

| | 1983/1–1986/1 | 1986/2–1989/1 |
|---|---|---|
| Constant | 0.7151261 | 0.9366581 |
| St. error | 0.7569570 | 0.1102141 |
| *t*–value | 0.9447380 | 0.8498531 |
| β (EU comp.) | 0.9504365 | 1.0818920 |
| St. error | 0.9362513 | 0.1034103 |
| *t*–value | –10.1515100 | 10.4621300 |
| β (gov.-bond) | –0.6988369 | –0.1460369 |
| St. error | 0.9840485 | 0.1717220 |
| *t*–value | –0.7101650 | –0.8504260 |

*Table 11.2: Estimated factor loadings: multifactor time-series regression estimates: Germany*

| | 1983/1–1986/1 | 1986/2–1989/1 |
|---|---|---|
| Constant | 0.2794749 | –0.1267196 |
| St. error | 0.7806759 | 0.1634268 |
| *t*–value | 3.5799090 | –0.7753909 |
| β (EU comp.) | 0.1843874 | 0.8308380 |
| St. error | 0.9655883 | 0.1533381 |
| *t*–value | –19.0958600 | 5.4183410 |
| β (gov.-bond) | –0.3236724 | 0.1795708 |
| St. error | 0.1014883 | 0.2546315 |
| *t*–value | –3.1893580 | 0.7052186 |

*Table 11.3: Estimated factor loadings: multifactor time-series regression estimates: France*

| | 1983/1–1986/1 | 1986/2–1989/1 |
|---|---|---|
| Constant | 0.6289458 | –0.1589140 |
| St. error | 0.1888659 | 0.2774250 |
| *t*–value | 0.3330118 | –0.5728179 |
| β (EU comp.) | –0.2105332 | 1.1260260 |
| St. error | 0.2336011 | 0.2602990 |
| *t*–value | –9.0125100 | 4.3258950 |
| β (gov.-bond) | –0.4139999 | 0.2605715 |
| St. error | 0.2455268 | 0.4322495 |
| *t*–value | –0.1686170 | 0.6028267 |

*Table 11.4: Estimated factor loadings: multifactor time-series regression estimates: The Netherlands*

| | 1983/1–1986/1 | 1986/2–1989/1 |
|---|---|---|
| Constant | 0.1065366 | –0.6498519 |
| St. error | 0.9072522 | 0.1497007 |
| *t*–value | 1.1742780 | –0.4341008 |
| β (EU comp.) | –0.1648521 | 0.8059499 |
| St. error | 0.1122146 | 0.1404593 |
| *t*–value | –14.6907900 | 5.7379590 |
| β (gov.-bond) | –0.1003009 | 0.9539495 |
| St. error | 0.1179433 | 0.2332451 |
| *t*–value | –0.8504162 | 0.4089901 |

*Table 11.5: Estimated factor loadings: multifactor time-series regression estimates: Belgium*

| | 1983/1–1986/1 | 1986/2–1989/1 |
|---|---|---|
| Constant | 0.5044466 | 0.1748097 |
| St. error | 0.1042554 | 0.2316439 |
| *t*–value | 0.4838566 | 0.7546485 |
| β (EU comp.) | –0.2130826 | 0.3079265 |
| St. error | 0.1289495 | 0.2173440 |
| *t*–value | –16.5244900 | 1.4167700 |
| β (gov.-bond) | –0.3410427 | –0.2553846 |
| St. error | 0.1355326 | 0.3609190 |
| *t*–value | –0.2516314 | 0.7075954 |

*Table 11.6: Estimated factor loadings: multifactor time-series regression estimates: Denmark*

| | 1983/1–1986/1 | 1986/2–1989/1 |
|---|---|---|
| Constant | –0.5308877 | –0.1054416 |
| St. error | 0.1481852 | 0.1614159 |
| *t*–value | –0.3582595 | –0.6532295 |
| β (EU comp.) | –0.1603324 | 0.3087845 |
| St. error | 0.1832847 | 0.1514513 |
| *t*–value | –8.7477270 | 2.0388370 |
| β (gov.-bond) | 0.3457977 | 0.1629744 |
| St. error | 0.1926417 | 0.2514983 |
| *t*–value | 0.1795030 | 0.6480141 |

*Table 11.7: Estimated factor loadings: multifactor time-series regression estimates: Italy*

| | 1983/1–1986/1 | 1986/2–1989/1 |
|---|---|---|
| Constant | 0.3391990 | –0.1386265 |
| St. error | 0.1157415 | 0.2623824 |
| *t*–value | 2.9306600 | –0.5283375 |
| β (EU comp.) | –0.2233027 | 1.1101290 |
| St. error | 0.1431569 | 0.2461850 |
| *t*–value | –15.5985200 | 4.5093290 |
| β (gov.-bond) | –0.3917582 | 0.2202296 |
| St. error | 0.1504646 | 0.4088120 |
| *t*–value | –2.6036560 | 0.5387064 |

*Table 11.8: Estimated factor loadings: multifactor time-series regression estimates: Spain*

| | 1983/1–1986/1 | 1986/2–1989/1 |
|---|---|---|
| Constant | –2.9982650 | 0.2176828 |
| St. error | 1.5316440 | 0.2756962 |
| *t*–value | –1.9575480 | 0.7895751 |
| β (EU comp.) | 27.7829300 | 1.0885450 |
| St. error | 0.1894432 | 0.2586768 |
| *t*–value | 146.6557000 | 4.2081290 |
| β (gov.-bond) | 0.3157626 | –0.3097868 |
| St. error | 0.1991146 | 0.4295580 |
| *t*–value | 1.5858330 | –0.7211796 |

*Table 11.9: Estimated risk premia: multifactor cross-sectional regression estimates*

| | 1983/1–1986/1 | 1986/2–1989/1 |
|---|---|---|
| Constant | 0.4763949 | 0.3711497 |
| St. error | 0.1286386 | 0.4806332 |
| *t*–value | 3.7033580 | 0.7722098 |
| Premium (EU) | 0.3448660 | 0.2831606 |
| St. error | 0.1224161 | 0.5365525 |
| *t*–value | 2.8171620 | 0.5277407 |
| Premium-bnd | 0.8771327 | –0.4710336 |
| St. error | 0.8778906 | 0.4638140 |
| *t*–value | 0.9991367 | –1.015566 |

# 12 Market size and the issue of segmentation[1]

## Introduction

As we have repeatedly noted earlier, many empirical studies in the literature have tested either the hypothesis that assets are priced according to their local systematic risk source(s) or the hypothesis that assets are priced in an integrated model against the null hypothesis of no relationship.[2] This chapter will explore the role of market size in the segmentation of capital markets. There has been no research conducted concerning the relation between market size and the integration of capital markets, therefore the objective of this chapter is to incorporate the size of capital markets measured as total capitalization into the capital asset-pricing theories of integration. We shall first describe the sample and data.

*Table 12.1: Market values of European equities as of February 1992 (US$bn)*

| Countries | $ | % Europe index |
|---|---|---|
| Belgium | 39.6 | 0.026 |
| Denmark | 26.7 | 0.017 |
| France | 208.7 | 0.137 |
| Germany | 231.5 | 0.152 |
| Netherlands | 100.4 | 0.065 |
| Italy | 77.1 | 0.050 |
| Spain | 77.1 | 0.050 |
| United Kingdom | 609.7 | 0.401 |
| **EC total** | **1 370.8** | **0.900** |
| Austria | 18.1 | 0.011 |
| Norway | 9.5 | 0.006 |
| Sweden | 21.8 | 0.015 |
| Switzerland | 102.3 | 0.067 |
| **EFTA total** | **151. 7** | **0.100** |
| **EC + EFTA = Europe** | **1 522.5** | **1.000** |

*Sources*: *Morgan Stanley Capital International*, and the author's calculations.

As previously, monthly rates of return on local (national) market portfolios are computed as appreciation or depreciation in share price indices. The share price indices are taken from *International Financial Statistics* (*IFS*) published by the International Monetary Fund (IMF) for the period from January 1972 to February 1992. We include in this chapter more recent data as well. The IMF calculates share price indices based on local market indices. The European market index return, $R_e$, is computed as the value-weighted average of local market returns in the sample. Table 12.1 exhibits the market values of twelve European countries. The risk-free rate, $R_f$, is taken as the one-month Treasury bill rate in the United Kingdom, published in the *World Financial Markets* by the Morgan Guaranty Trust of New York.

**Test methodology**

We attempt to test for the integration of international capital markets employing a version of the standard international CAPM. Here the international market portfolio is replaced by the European portfolio. A European model for securities should be mean-variance efficient and the systematic risk *vis-à-vis* the European index should be priced. Purely European CAPM implies

$$E(R_i) = \gamma_0 + \gamma_1\beta_1 \qquad (12.1)$$

where $R_i$ is the excess return, that is the actual return minus the risk free rate, on asset (portfolio) $i$, and $\beta_i$ is the $i$th local market's beta.

Adopting the international CAPM given by (12.1), we devise an empirical test as follows. Given the probability distribution of the rate of return to local and international market portfolios, the stochastic return-generating process is given by:

$$R_{it} = \alpha_i + \beta_i R_{et} + U_{it} \qquad (12.2)$$

where: $R_{it} \equiv$ the nominal excess (the actual minus the $R_f$) rate of return on market $i$'s portfolio;
$R_{et} \equiv$ the nominal excess rate of return to European market index;
$U_{it} \equiv$ the residual term associated with the idiosyncratic risk.

All returns are expressed in a common currency, the US dollar. Standard assumptions about the distribution of the error term follow. That is, $E(U_i) = 0$, $E(U_i, U_j) = 0$ when $i \neq j$, $E(U_i, U_j) = \sigma_U^2$ when $i = j$, and $E(U_i, R_e) = 0$ for the relevant range of $i$ and $j$. According to (12.1) and (12.2), the systematic risk relative to the European composite portfolio should have explanatory power for the pricing of portfolios if integration is the correct model.[3]

The time-series regression of equation (12.2) estimates the security sensitivity coefficients, i.e. the betas. The risk premia are estimated by the following cross-sectional regression:

$$\bar{R}_k = \delta_k + \mu_k \beta_i + V_k \qquad (12.3)$$

where $\bar{R}_k$ is the mean return in the $k$th model and the letter $k$ is the index for the model and assumes values from 1 to 9. The models that we employ contain different baskets of local markets. The contents of each basket are selected in terms of market value. We first consider the large markets and gradually include the small ones. Explicitly, we deal with nine different models as shown below:

1. $k = 1$ when all 12 European markets are in the sample;
2. $k = 2$ when only the seven largest markets are in the sample;
3. $k = 3$ when only the five largest are in the sample;
4. $k = 4$ when only the three largest are in the sample;
5. $k = 5$ when all but the largest are in the sample;
6. $k = 6$ when all but the three largest are in the sample;
7. $k = 7$ when only the seven smallest are in the sample;
8. $k = 8$ when only the five smallest are in the sample;
9. $k = 9$ when only the three smallest are in the sample.

We look to see whether the $\mu_k$, the risk premium of the $k$th model, is priced by the data. If so, the systematic risk associated with the market portfolio (i.e. the composite European market return) is priced. If, on the other hand, the composite index is not priced, then the markets are segmented. As a matter of course, the implications in terms of the pricing of each model will differ. In particular, whether the last three models are priced by the data is of critical importance, since these three include only the small markets.

**Test results**

The hypothesis that assets are priced in an integrated (European) market against the null hypothesis of no relationship is tested. When we include all twelve nations without discriminating between them on the basis of market size, we reject the null hypothesis of no relationship. This rejection implies that the risk premium is priced in an integrated European model and that the systematic risk of the international (European composite) model is the proper systematic risk specification.[4]

We repeat the same procedure for all $k$s. Estimated betas for all countries in the sample are reported in Table 12.2. The time-series beta estimates cover the period 1972–92. Estimated risk premia and their test statistics for all $k$s are reported in Table 12.3. We reject the null hypothesis of no relationship for the third, fourth and the fifth models, where the markets included make up at least 60 per cent of the total European market capitalization. As we start excluding the large markets from the sample the test statistic becomes less significant. In the seventh, eighth and ninth models, where the shares in total market capitalization are far less than 20 per cent, the integrated composite model is not priced, for the risk premia in these three models are fairly insignificant.

*Table 12.2: Estimated betas: single-index (Europe composite) time-series regression estimates (12 markets)*

| National market | β | *t* |
|---|---|---|
| Belgium | 0.577 | 7.911 |
| Denmark | 0.276 | 3.074 |
| France | 0.806 | 6.368 |
| Germany | 0.450 | 8.169 |
| Italy | 0.568 | 5.074 |
| Netherlands | 0.515 | 9.845 |
| Spain | 0.344 | 3.519 |
| United Kingdom | 1.494 | 31.266 |
| Austria | 0.384 | 4.217 |
| Norway | 0.462 | 3.608 |
| Sweden | 0.205 | 3.990 |
| Switzerland | 0.620 | 8.046 |

There is a clear difference between the last three models and the rest. The first five models price the systematic risk *vis-à-vis* the composite European market. The only model whose test result is ambiguous is the sixth, where the included markets make up 31 per cent of the total European market value of securities. The results overall imply that the small securities markets are segmented from a benchmark European market. This result is of further importance at a time when direct barriers are being removed from security exchanges in Europe. Even though capital controls on the security exchanges are absent, capital assets may still be priced according to their local risk source(s).[5]

It seems that the domestic sources of risk – i.e the local market index in our model – may become idiosyncratic at world (Europe) level and therefore unimportant in the equilibrium pricing of assets. This point has been raised earlier in the previous chapters and is also well-covered in the literature.[6]

Hence, we provide further evidence in this chapter that a small country's risk is diversified away by the world market because it becomes unsystematic in an international context; hence, the (local) markets do not offer premia for domestic sources of systematic risk. Yet they do offer premia for international (European) sources. The pervasive European source(s) of systematic risk as embodied in the European composite market portfolio receive premia above the riskless rate in a small market.[7]

*Table 12.3: Nine models tested*[a]

| Model ($k$) | Markets included | Share in total capitalization | Risk premia ($\mu_k$) | $t$ value | Remarks |
|---|---|---|---|---|---|
| 1 | UK, Germany, France, Italy, Switzerland, Netherlands, Spain, Austria, Denmark, Sweden, Norway, Belgium | 1.000 | 0.39064 | 1.90092 | All 12 markets |
| 2 | UK, Germany, France, Italy, Switzerland, Netherlands, Spain | 0.922 | 0.37839 | 0.83780 | The seven largest |
| 3 | UK, Germany, France, Switzerland, Netherlands | 0.822 | 0.67489 | 4.07045 | The five largest |
| 4 | UK, Germany, France | 0.690 | 0.63200 | 3.87493 | The three largest |
| 5 | All but the UK | 0.599 | 0.45293 | 2.23777 | All but the largest |
| 6 | Switzerland, Netherlands, Italy, Spain, Belgium, Denmark, Norway, Sweden, Austria | 0.310 | 0.20935 | 0.678229 | All but the three largest |
| 7 | Italy, Spain, Belgium, Denmark, Norway, Sweden, Austria | 0.178 | 0.00237 | 0.020340 | The seven smallest |
| 8 | Belgium, Denmark, Norway, Sweden, Austria | 0.078 | -0.3564 | -0.12861 | The five smallest |
| 9 | Norway, Sweden, Denmark | 0.038 | 0.15673 | 0.001023 | The three smallest |

*Note:* [a] Mean returns of the markets in each model are regressed against the betas.

## Chapter summary

In this chapter the role of market size in deciding whether international capital markets are integrated or segmented is examined empirically. A sample of European equity markets is used to test for integration. We fail to accept the hypothesis that in small size (in terms of market capitalization) stock markets capital assets are priced according to an integrated market model. Local markets seem to be important sources of systematic risk. Small European markets are highly segmented from a benchmark European market. One explanation of this result is that the investors on small markets diversify away most of the local systematic risk. That is, the European market seems to be able to diversify a small country's domestic risk. On the other hand, large markets, namely the British, German and French securities markets, are integrated with the European market.

## Notes

1. This chapter is based on earlier work by the author (Akdogan, 1992b).
2. Here we are referring to the body of studies on international asset-pricing starting with Solnik (1974a, b, c, d, 1977) and including Stehle (1977) and Stulz (1981a, 1981b). The issue was a subject in the literature later in the mid-1980s. As we previously discussed in Chapter 6, Errunza and Losq (1985, 1989), Jorion and Schwartz (1986) and Wheatley (1988) are among more-recent applications of international asset-pricing theories.
3. Integration cannot be tested by running a univariate regression on betas because of the possible correlation between the local markets and the European composite portfolio. Hence, as Stehle (1977) first suggested, the orthogonalized returns should be taken into account by isolating in the domestic index the component independent of the composite index. Part of the domestic index that is uncorrelated to the European (world) index should then be taken as an explanatory variable along with the world index in a regression that attempts to explain rates of return. However, such a projection is not particularly necessary in our model where we deal with the issue for small securities markets that have fairly low shares in the value-weighted composite market index. Indeed, the correlation coefficients between the small markets of Europe and the composite market have been observed to be low.
4. See, for discussion, Akdogan (1991a, 1992a, 1992b).
5. Akdogan (1991a, 1992a) reports that European Union capital markets have gradually become more integrated as capital controls are removed. The role of capital controls on segmentation has been studied by Stulz (1981b).
6. Among those who have raised this issue are Solnik (1974 a, b, c, d, 1977), Stehle (1977), Stulz (1981a, 1981b), Errunza and Losq (1985, 1989) and Jorion and Schwartz (1986).
7. Our results could also be interpreted in the framework of a single-factor arbitrage pricing model where the factor is prespecified.

# 13 Geographical asset-pricing

## Regional integration

The proposition that the world capital markets are internationally integrated is too elusive to capture the true nature of integration. It could be argued that integration is taking place regionally but not internationally. Indeed, today's world consists of a couple of economic blocs, so-called trade areas that try to set up the institutions compatible with regional integration. The European Union (EU), the European Free Trade Association (EFTA), the North American Free Trade Agreement (NAFTA) are very well known economic integration attempts. Such economic blocs have already dismantled most barriers against free trade and finance across the member states within their respective regions. European integration is now on the verge of full monetary union. The Union states have been scheduled to accept a single currency by 1999 at the latest.

This is the current state of affairs; we take into account elsewhere (Akdogan, 1993) the underlying characteristics of such ventures toward regional integration. We argue that it is questionable that some international market portfolio will be mean-variance efficient in a world of economic blocs promoting free trade and finance among members yet discriminating against non-members. Based on Akdogan (1993), our task in this chapter is to compare regional and international asset-pricing models. This task eventually requires that we specify a regional benchmark portfolio to see whether the capital assets traded in the markets of a given geographical region can be modelled according to a selected benchmark. Following Akdogan (1993), we shall call the asset-pricing model that utilizes a regional market portfolio *geographical asset-pricing*. The chapter as a whole deals with the issue of regional (geographical) integration. After introducing the model we develop a procedure to test the validity of the geographical integration of capital markets using a large sample set.

## Geographical asset-pricing

The geographical asset-pricing model divides the world capital markets into regional trade blocs including free trade areas and a customs union (in the case of EU). From an empirical standpoint, the world market portfolio of standard international CAPM applications becomes a regional market portfolio in a geographical asset-pricing framework. Using some regional portfolio as a benchmark, we attempt to see whether the capital assets of selected regions are priced according to a regional CAPM as opposed to an international one. As we have done with the international CAPM in Chapters 9 and 10, the regional market portfolio is based on value weights.

*Hypothesis development*

As we have pointed out in previous chapters, if the world capital markets are integrated, the risk associated with identical securities traded in different locations should carry the same price. That is, identical risk characteristics will amount to identical expected returns in a world of integrated capital markets. If, on the other hand, markets are segmented and barriers to arbitrage exist, securities with the same risk content must be associated with different expected returns. Note that this definition applies to both regional, or what we call geographical, and international (worldwide) integration.

We know from the works of Sharpe (1964) and Lintner (1965) that a market portfolio, domestic or international, is assumed to be efficient in terms of expected return and variance. In this respect, a test of the Sharpe–Lintner asset-pricing model is also a test of the mean-variance efficiency of the given portfolio. In an international context, testing the validity of an international benchmark portfolio *à la* Sharpe–Lintner amounts to testing the mean-variance efficiency of the portfolio defined as the international benchmark.

Based on the underlying asset-pricing model that we shall develop in the next section, we test whether the international as opposed to the geographical capital asset-pricing model holds. The null hypothesis that the selected world market portfolio is mean-variance efficient (i.e. the selected pricing model holds) and that world capital markets are integrated are tested jointly. The test is an unconditional mean-variance efficiency test of the world market index portfolio. The index is constructed as the value-weighted average of the stock price indices from 26 national exchanges.

We divide 26 countries into four regions on the basis of the geographical blocs that these nations belong to. The four regions that we select are the EU, the EFTA, the Americas and the Pacific. We see each of these geographical blocs as a move towards an institutionally more integrated regional market.[1] Our objective here is to examine whether regional market share price indices (portfolios) are superior to the global index from an asset-pricing standpoint. This objective requires a pricing model that links the differences in country risk exposure to differences in expected return. We investigate below whether the country index portfolios are priced according to a global market as opposed to a regional one. The regional price indices are constructed as the value-weighted averages of the national stock market price indices in a given region.

*Data and preliminary analysis*

*Sources* Monthly rates of return on local (national) market portfolios, are computed as appreciations or depreciations in share price indices. The share price indices are taken from *International Financial Statistics* (*IFS*), published by the International Monetary Fund (IMF), for the period from January 1972 to January 1990. Both the world market index excess return and the geographical regional market excess return are computed as value-weighted of all (relevant) local market returns in the sample. The weights are the shares of local markets in the total world market and regional market capitalization, respectively. The weights adopted are the proportions of the local equity market capitalizations in the total world market and regional market respectively at the end of the mid-date of the data. The excess rate of return in a country is calculated as

$$R_{it} = \ln P_{it} - \ln P_{it-1} - R_{f,t} \tag{13.1}$$

where $P$ stands for share price index, $t$ is the time index, $i$ is the country index, and $R_{f,t}$ is the risk-free rate of return. We divide 26 markets into four geographical regions as follows:

1. European Union (EU): UK, Germany, France, the Netherlands, Italy, Belgium, Denmark, Spain, Ireland;
2. European Free Trade Association (EFTA): Switzerland, Sweden, Norway, Finland, Austria;
3. The Americas: US, Canada, Venezuela, Colombia and Peru;
4. The Pacific: Japan, Australia, New Zealand, India, Pakistan, the Philippines and South Africa.

*Table 13.1: Market values at the end of 1980 (US$bn)*[a]

| Market | Value | Share(%) |
|---|---|---|
| United Kingdom | 190.0 | 8.12 |
| Germany | 71.0 | 3.03 |
| France | 53.0 | 2.26 |
| Switzerland | 46.0 | 1.96 |
| Netherlands | 25.0 | 1.07 |
| Italy | 25.0 | 1.07 |
| Spain | 16.3 | 0.69 |
| Sweden | 12.2 | 0.52 |
| Belgium | 10.0 | 0.42 |
| Denmark | 4.0 | 0.17 |
| Norway | 2.6 | 0.11 |
| Austria | 1.9 | 0.08 |
| Canada | 113.0 | 4.83 |
| Australia | 60.0 | 2.56 |
| Japan | 357.0 | 15.26 |
| United States | 1350.7 | 57.77 |

*Note:* [a] Shares in total world market capitalization are used as weights. Market values of other countries in the sample were less than US$1 billion. We have assumed that their weights in total world market value are zero.

Table 13.1 exhibits market values at the end of 1980 – the middle year of our sample – of all countries in the sample that we have assigned as weights to set the value-weighted world portfolio. The market capitalizations in this table are taken from Ibbotson *et al.* (1982). The risk-free rate of return, $R_f$, is taken as the short-term time deposit rates for each country, as published in *International Financial Statistics* (*IFS*).

*Summary statistics*[2] Unconditional means, i.e. the average monthly rates of return to national market indices in our sample, are provided in Table 2.6. The rates of return reported in this table are computed as depreciation or appreciation in monthly share price indices for the whole sample period January 1972–January 1990. The highest mean returns are observed in Austria, Sweden, Finland, Italy and Denmark.

Table 2.5 reports cross-correlation coefficients as computed using the same data set for the period January 1972–January 1990. The cross-correlation coefficient between any two developed markets has been found to be in the range 0.2 to 0.5. The USA, the UK, Germany, Switzerland, the Netherlands, Japan, Canada and France have considerably high correlation coefficients among themselves and other developed markets, exceeding in many cases 0.4. Developing capital markets, on the other hand, have low correlations to their developed counterparts. Venezuela and the Philippines have consistently negative correlations to the other markets.

Variances and autocorrelations of the monthly excess returns are shown in Table 2.7. The largest variances are reported in Austria, the UK, France, Norway, Ireland, South Africa, Peru, the Philippines and Colombia. On the other hand, monthly excess returns in Japan, India, Germany, the Netherlands, Switzerland and Pakistan display small volatility. They have the lowest variances in the sample.

Most countries in the sample exhibit high positive first-order autocorrelations. High positive autocorrelations of virtually all degrees are reported for the markets of the UK, Germany, the Netherlands, Denmark and Italy. Meanwhile, negative autocorrelations of both low and high degrees are observed in Austria, South Africa and France. Negative autocorrelations seen in these three markets may be due to price overreaction to value changes or transitory price disturbances such as bid–ask spreads and pricing errors.

*A preliminary investigation of integration*[3] Consider a single-world-index international capital asset-pricing model according to which all tradeable securities and portfolios available to investors are priced. In such a model, national capital markets contribute to world systematic risk in proportion to their sensitivity coefficients (betas) *vis-à-vis* the value-weighted world market portfolio (VWWMP). If a market contributes proportionally more to world systematic risk than to world market value, then it can be taken as a signal that it is integrated to a benchmark international market portfolio. That is, any systematic risk proportion in total risk *vis-à-vis* the world market portfolio over and above the respective share in world market value should give us *a priori* an idea of the status of integration.

*Table 13.2: Proportion of systematic risk to total risk* vis-à-vis *the value-weighted world market portfolio (VWWMP)*

| Market | Proportion $\beta^2 var(R_W)/var(R_i)$ | Market value share |
|---|---|---|
| United Kingdom | 0.3251204 | 0.0812 |
| Germany | 0.1941126 | 0.0303 |
| France | 0.1411403 | 0.0226 |
| Netherlands | 0.3687071 | 0.0107 |
| Belgium | 0.2053407 | 0.0042 |
| Denmark | 0.0441251 | 0.0017 |
| Italy | 0.1085851 | 0.0107 |
| Spain | 0.0507453 | 0.0069 |
| Switzerland | 0.3418866 | 0.0196 |
| Austria | 0.0024531 | 0.0008 |
| Norway | 0.1158124 | 0.0011 |
| Sweden | 0.0901734 | 0.0052 |
| Ireland | 0.0895367 | 0.0001 |
| Finland | 0.0153405 | 0.0000 |
| Canada | 0.3569226 | 0.0483 |
| Australia | 0.3875519 | 0.0256 |
| United States | 0.5785282 | 0.5777 |
| Japan | 0.1863285 | 0.1526 |
| India | 0.0235667 | 0.0000 |
| New Zealand | 0.0783057 | 0.0001 |
| Pakistan | 0.0004379 | 0.0000 |
| South Africa | 0.0450402 | 0.0001 |
| Venezuela | 0.0009632 | 0.0000 |
| Peru | 0.0037740 | 0.0000 |
| Philippines | 0.0294163 | 0.0000 |
| Colombia | 0.0010461 | 0.0000 |

*Note*: [a] Systematic risk proportions are calculated from equation (13.2). Market capitalizations are based on the figures given in Table 13.1. The computation covers the sample period of 187 months, from January 1972 to January 1990.

Computed proportions of systematic risk in total risk relative to the VWWMP in all markets for the entire sample period January 1972-January 1990 are reported in Table 13.2. The proportions of systematic risk in total risk are computed as

$$\beta^2 \mathrm{var}(R_W)/\mathrm{var}(R_i) \tag{13.2}$$

where $\beta^2$ is the sensitivity of the rate of return on a national market's portfolio, $R_i$, to the international benchmark rate of return (VWWMP), $R_W$. Table 13.3 displays the proportions computed from the monthly data for 18 years. As is clear from the table, the computed proportions of systematic risk as explained by the common world factor in all markets are well above their respective shares in total world capitalization.

*Table 13.3: Time-series behaviour of the proportion of systematic risk in total risk* vis-à-vis *the VWWMP*[a]

| Market | 1972–4 | 1975–7 | 1978–80 | 1981–3 | 1984–6 | 1987–9 |
|---|---|---|---|---|---|---|
| UK | 0.153424 | 0.163829 | 0.283964 | 0.393764 | 0.637652 | 0.728361 |
| Germany | 0.178245 | 0.116728 | 0.152100 | 0.156472 | 0.298132 | 0.307822 |
| France | 0.092833 | 0.052330 | 0.122231 | 0.187451 | 0.241908 | 0.467219 |
| Netherlands | 0.173652 | 0.227837 | 0.279281 | 0.403769 | 0.682763 | 0.762541 |
| Belgium | 0.165234 | 0.145263 | 0.189223 | 0.209384 | 0.235616 | 0.312974 |
| Denmark | 0.002827 | 0.007275 | 0.019028 | 0.017237 | 0.105286 | 0.238799 |
| Italy | 0.018931 | 0.067253 | 0.056298 | 0.030490 | 0.128751 | 0.387045 |
| Spain | 0.000567 | 0.000634 | 0.002874 | 0.093937 | 0.107254 | 0.100452 |
| Switzerland | 0.189264 | 0.263981 | 0.182563 | 0.526819 | 0.752631 | 0.629513 |
| Austria | 0.000078 | 0.000025 | 0.000097 | 0.000192 | 0.001762 | 0.000971 |
| Norway | 0.006632 | 0.009926 | 0.092739 | 0.132902 | 0.242637 | 0.210928 |
| Sweden | 0.000298 | 0.000652 | 0.067110 | 0.141888 | 0.192011 | 0.220862 |
| Ireland | 0.001977 | 0.002837 | 0.073510 | 0.092713 | 0.176219 | 0.361201 |
| Finland | 0.000127 | 0.000869 | 0.007209 | 0.006152 | 0.022791 | 0.102873 |
| Canada | 0.178263 | 0.182934 | 0.367292 | 0.489201 | 0.762913 | 0.829310 |
| Australia | 0.273810 | 0.276310 | 0.426991 | 0.567922 | 0.872619 | 0.889621 |
| US | 0.427891 | 0.567234 | 0.652739 | 0.659842 | 0.782332 | 0.762519 |
| Japan | 0.002911 | 0.012768 | 0.092719 | 0.293874 | 0.342719 | 0.464212 |
| India | 0.002354 | 0.006735 | 0.006893 | 0.034093 | 0.156277 | 0.102428 |
| N. Zealand | 0.001872 | 0.008263 | 0.004390 | 0.082931 | 0.102983 | 0.138994 |
| Pakistan | 0.000025 | 0.000056 | 0.000043 | 0.000069 | 0.007219 | 0.061829 |
| S. Africa | 0.000928 | 0.000823 | 0.102939 | 0.162551 | 0.092833 | 0.145393 |
| Venezuela | 0.000231 | 0.000378 | 0.092821 | 0.072652 | 0.025695 | 0.092855 |
| Peru | 0.000082 | 0.000064 | 0.000009 | 0.018273 | 0.082775 | 0.099821 |
| Philippines | 0.002935 | 0.017266 | 0.009273 | 0.012876 | 0.097621 | 0.128972 |
| Colombia | 0.000267 | 0.000844 | 0.000983 | 0.001994 | 0.002689 | 0.005421 |

*Note*: [a] The systematic risk proportions reported here are computed as in Table 13.2. Here, the sample period is partitioned into six equal segments, each having three years of observations.

We also report the time-series behaviour of the systematic risk proportions in Table 13.3. The data set is first divided into six equal partitions, each of which consists of 36 observations. Systematic risk proportions *vis-à-vis* the single-index international CAPM are computed for each segment of the data.[4]

The shares of systematic risk in total risk as computed from a single value-weighted world index model increase over time. This is true for virtually all the markets in our sample. Furthermore, both Table 13.2 and the last column of Table 13.3 demonstrate that the proportions in all 26 markets exceed their respective market shares. This should also be taken as a signal that the capital markets in our sample may be integrated into a benchmark international market.

## Model specification

### *An international CAPM for country index portfolios*

We assume that world capital markets are perfect and frictionless and that the expected utility of each investor, irrespective of the country of origin, can be represented as a function of the expected value and the variance of the returns on the investment portfolio. The returns are assumed to be normally distributed. We shall assume that there is perfect correlation between the world market portfolio and world consumption.

Under these assumptions, a purely international CAPM for country index portfolios should follow

$$E(R_t) = \beta_w E(R_{Wt}) \qquad t = 1,\ldots,T \tag{13.3}$$

where $R_t$ is the excess return to national index portfolios, that is the actual rate of return minus the risk-free rate, $R_{Wt}$ is the excess rate of return to the world market index at time $t$, and $\beta_W$ is the local market's (true) beta *vis-à-vis* the VWWMP. Here, the beta coefficient measures the sensitivity of the rate of return on the national index portfolio to changes in the benchmark rate of return. It is given by $E(R, R_W)/E(R_W^2)$ which is empirically equivalent to the ratio of the covariance between $R$ and $R_W$ to the variance of $R_W$.

### *A geographical CAPM for country index portfolios*

Under the assumptions described for the existence of an international CAPM of equation 13.3, a regional (geographical) CAPM follows

$$E(R_t) = \beta_G E(R_{Gt}) \qquad t = 1,\ldots,T \tag{13.4}$$

where $\beta_G$ is the sensitivity of the excess rate of return on a national market index portfolio to the excess rate of return on the value-weighted regional market portfolio index (VWRMP), $R_{Gt.}$

*Empirical test*

Given the multivariate probability distribution of the rates of return to local and international market index portfolios, the hypothesis that the assets are priced in an integrated market against the null hypothesis of no relationship is tested. In order to make operational the international and geographical CAPMs described in expressions (13.3) and (13.4), we shall devise an empirical test by first formulating[5]

$$R_i = \beta_{i0} + \beta_{iG}R_G + \beta_{iW}U_W + e_i \tag{13.5}$$

where: $R_i$ ≡ excess rate of return on market *i*'s index portfolio;
$R_G$ ≡ excess rate of return to the geographical market index portfolio computed as the value-weighted average of the excess returns to the relevant national index portfolios;
$\beta_{i0}$ ≡ the intercept term.
$\beta_{iG}$ ≡ cov $(R_i, R_G)$ /var $(R_G)$
$e_i$ ≡ the residual term.
$U_W$ ≡ the component of the world index portfolio that is uncorrelated to the geographical index portfolio. This term is obtained (by projection) as the residuals from the following regression:

$$R_W = \alpha_W + \alpha_{WG}R_G + U_W \tag{13.6}$$

where: $\alpha_W = E\,(R_W) - \beta_{WG}E\,(R_G)$;
$\alpha_{WG} = \text{cov}\,(R_W, R_G)/\text{var}\,(R_G)$

Thus $\beta_{iW} = \text{cov}\,(R_i, U_W)/\text{var}\,(U_W)$ .

We have by construction:

$$E(e_i) = \text{cov}\,(e_i, R_G) = \text{cov}\,(e_i, U_W) = 0.$$

Equation (13.5) is a bi-beta representation. Following Fama and MacBeth (1973), we estimate the risk premia cross-sectionally by the regression

$$R_i = \gamma_0 + \gamma_G\beta_{iG} + \gamma_W\beta_{iW} + \epsilon_i \tag{13.7}$$

where $R_i$ is the 26 × 1 vector of mean rates of return to the national market index portfolios, and $\beta_{iG}$ and $\beta_{iW}$ are 26 × 1 vectors of sensitivity coefficients. This regression attempts to explain the cross-sectional variations to find out whether the local markets have their sensitivity coefficients with respect to the geographical and international index portfolios in order to determine the behaviour of expected returns.[6]

In terms of (13.5) and (13.7), the asset-pricing model imposes the following restriction:[7]

$$H_0: \gamma_W = 0 \tag{13.8}$$

If $\gamma_W$ is significantly different from its theoretical value, zero, then the segmented market hypothesis will be rejected.[8]

**Test results**

The results of 26 time-series regressions are reported in Table 13.4. This table gives the beta estimates based on the regression (13.5). The first column reports the country betas with respect to the value-weighted world index portfolio (the part of the world portfolio's rate of return that is uncorrelated to the rate of return to the regional index portfolio. The second column exhibits the country betas *vis-à-vis* the value-weighted regional index portfolio.

The null hypothesis of (13.8) is tested using the estimated risk premia from regression (13.7). The results of this cross-sectional regression, the second step of the standard Fama–MacBeth procedure, is reported in Table 13.5. The table reports risk premia estimation in three different sample periods. The first line in the table displays estimates for the entire sample period of 1972:1–1990. The data are then divided into two equal segments. The second line of Table 13.5 shows the risk premia estimates obtained using the data from the period 1972:1–1981:1. The third line reports the estimates based on data from the period 1981:2–1990:1.

The null hypothesis is rejected when we have employed only the data from the 1980s (line 3 in Table 13.5). Evidence from the decade supports the view that the systematic risk *vis-à-vis* a value-weighted world market portfolio (VWWMP) is priced. On the other hand, we fail to reject the hypothesis when we use only the first period of the sample (the 1970s). The second line displays the estimated risk premium from the period 1972:1–1981:2. The 1980s, indeed, represents a period of liberalization in world capital markets while the 1970s is a period of financial protectionism.

*Table 13.4: Estimated market betas: time series regression estimates in 26 world markets (t values in parenthesis)[a]*

| National market | $\beta_{iW}$(VWWMP)[b] | $\beta_{iG}$(VWRMP)[c] |
|---|---|---|
| Belgium | 0.1525690 | 0.8118856 |
| (EC) | (0.077291) | (6.763727) |
| Denmark | 0.08239661 | 0.4071910 |
| (EC) | (0.504298) | (2.855142) |
| France | 0.2205426 | 1.108560 |
| (EC) | (0.684248) | (2.393241) |
| Germany | 0.07922673 | 0.5395028 |
| (EC) | (0.311356) | (2.527661) |
| Italy | 0.1610572 | 0.8298156 |
| (EC) | (0.284524) | (2.643371) |
| Netherlands | 0.1418355 | 0.8332354 |
| (EC) | (0.783292) | (2.016839) |
| Spain | 0.1144508 | 0.4791043 |
| (EC) | (0.914235) | (2.076485) |
| United Kingdom | 0.1992815 | 1.468746 |
| (EC) | (2.782507) | (1.234019) |
| Austria | 1.064740 | 0.05852027 |
| (EFTA) | (3.426380) | (0.01845584) |
| Norway | 0.3379444 | 0.8449927 |
| (EFTA) | (1.536603) | (1.015368) |
| Switzerland | 0.08588686 | 0.8080020 |
| (EFTA) | (2.218431) | (1.590257) |
| Sweden | 0.1096514 | 0.5472212 |
| (EFTA) | (3.346157) | (0.0189363) |
| South Africa | 0.05441364 | 0.6628694 |
| (Pacific) | (1.651792) | (0.1889729) |
| Ireland | 0.09111953 | 0.7350708 |
| (EC) | (1.312301) | (0.0172613) |
| United States | 0.3495065 | 0.9098640 |
| (Americas) | (3.873652) | (0.0281373) |

| National market | $\beta_{iW}$(VWWMP)[b] | $\beta_{iG}$(VWRMP)[c] |
|---|---|---|
| Canada<br>(Americas) | 0.08670930<br>(1.507996) | 1.217173<br>(0.9812523) |
| Australia<br>(Pacific) | 0.08854356<br>(1.732946) | 1.129326<br>(1.548433) |
| New Zealand<br>(Pacific) | 0.06744526<br>(1.668623) | 0.4014017<br>(1.878806) |
| India<br>(Pacific) | 0.05275470<br>(1.010786) | 0.1902565<br>(0.0070533) |
| Pakistan<br>(Pacific) | 0.05425047<br>(1.405507) | 0.09203294<br>(0.8981238) |
| Philippines<br>(Pacific) | 0.1013749<br>(1.138055) | 0.5388729<br>(2.316392) |
| Japan<br>(Pacific) | 0.01749131<br>(0.5222684) | 0.5093921<br>(6.367396) |
| Peru<br>(Americas) | –0.02675652<br>(–0.3783718) | 0.1530984<br>(.8193935) |
| Colombia<br>(Americas) | 0.01412736<br>(0.1631612) | 0.09812481<br>(0.4284630) |
| Venezuela<br>(Americas) | 0.03095726<br>(0.7734764) | 0.1388921<br>(1.315614) |
| Finland<br>(EFTA) | 0.03912472<br>(0.5530999) | 0.3089140<br>(1.661739) |

*Notes*

[a] The dependent variable is the excess rate of return to the local market portfolio, and the independent variables are the excess rate of return to the regional market portfolio and part of world market portfolio that is orthogonal to the regional portfolio. The rates of return in national markets are computed as appreciation or depreciation in local share prices as reported by the International Monetary Fund in its *International Financial Statistics*. The excess returns are computed by subtracting local short-term time deposit rates, published in *International Financial Statistics*, from the respective rates of return.

[b] The part of value-weighted world market portfolio uncorrelated to the regional index portfolio.

[c] The value-weighted regional index portfolio.

*Table 13.5: The estimated risk premium*

The risk premia are estimated by regressing cross-sectionally the average excess rates of return to local market index portfolios against the regional and international betas ($\beta_{iG}$, and $\beta_{iW}$ respectively) reported previously in Table 13.4 from the following regression:

$$R_i = \gamma_0 + \gamma_G \beta_{iG} + \gamma_W \beta_{iW} + \epsilon_i$$

Using this regression the following null hypothesis is tested:

$$H_0: \gamma_W = 0$$

We also provide in this table the risk premium estimates for the 1970s and 1980s separately to see the differential risk premia between a period of financial protectionism (the 1970s) and a period of financial liberalism (the 1980s). The *t*-values are in parentheses.

| Sample period | $\gamma_W$ | $\gamma_G$ |
|---|---|---|
| 1972:1–90:1 | 0.051607 | 0.073778 |
| | (1.20037) | (1.0352) |
| 1972:1–81:1 | 0.029736 | 0.042571 |
| | (1.13289) | (1.1272) |
| 1981:2–90:1 | 0.683203 | 0.452930 |
| | (2.3002) | (0.924931) |

In the 1980s most capital markets, including those in our sample, abolished to a large extent major barriers against the free movement of capital. In the US and Canada restrictions against foreign investment did not exist for several decades. The UK and Germany lifted controls over their capital markets in 1979 and 1981, respectively. Switzerland, the Netherlands, Belgium, Luxembourg and the Scandinavian countries removed major controls by the mid-1980s. The European Union has gradually abolished the impediments previously imposed by member states in the 1980s. The 1983 Commission directive, the White Paper of 1985, the Single European Act of 1987, the 1988 directive scheduling the removal of the remaining restrictions in relatively less-developed EC capital markets, including Spain, Portugal, Greece and Ireland, have prepared the EU for a single common capital market. The developing (emerging) capital markets have also undergone major changes in terms of financial liberalization. With a few exceptions, emerging markets opened up their markets to international investors in 1980s.

**Chapter summary**

This chapter has tested regional capital market integration. The results indicate that the world capital markets have become more integrated in the 1980s. We fail to reject the hypothesis that a value-weighted world market portfolio is mean-variance efficient in this period, while the same hypothesis is accepted when we use data from the previous decade. The model posits the existence of a single factor: the value-weighted world market index, our proxy for the world market portfolio. Each national market has a risk exposure to the world index portfolio and differential expected returns across countries are determined by the relative risk exposures. The local risk content seems to become at least partially idiosyncratic at world level and therefore unimportant in the equilibrium pricing of capital assets.

Consistent with reports of earlier research, we find that capital restrictions are important sources of segmentation. We have first shown that all 26 markets in our sample have gradually started to contribute more to world systematic risk than to world market capitalization. Next, the null hypothesis of international capital market segmentation is accepted when we use the market index data from the period 1972:1–1981:1 while the same hypothesis is rejected for the period 1981:2–1990:1.

**Notes**

1. Although the Pacific as a regional bloc is not a very safe choice, the countries within it have shown interest in forming more comprehensive free trade and finance blocs in the region. Moreover, we have observed relatively high correlations of returns across what we call the Pacific Region (see the data section).
2. Some of the statistics have been provided in tabular form in Chapter 2.
3. This section employs the approach that we have suggested elsewhere (Akdogan, 1992a).
4. The way in which we partition the data is arbitrary. Our only objective here is to monitor the time-series behaviour of systematic risk proportions in national markets with respect to the value-weighted world index portfolio.
5. The time index is dropped for convenience without loss of generality.
6. The covariance of the rate of return to a national market index portfolio and with the rate of return on the regional market index represents a systematic risk not only when world markets are segmented but also in an internationally integrated global market, when the rates of return on the regional and global market index portfolios are positively correlated. Moreover, rate of return to a national market index may well be correlated to those parts of the world market index portfolio that are uncorrelated with the regional index portfolio. The $\gamma_{iW}$ measures this non-regional international risk. It should be clear that a cross-sectional regression using only $\beta_{iG}$ as an explanatory would be misspecified.
7. The methodology adopted here is similar to that of Stehle (1977). Stehle, however, does not deal with regional integration.
8. An alternative to (13.5) would be the null hypothesis of integration, in which case $R_G$ is broken down into its components by projection. Part of $R_G$ that is orthogonal to $R_W$ is taken as an independent variable along with $R_W$ itself to explain the rate of return to the local market index portfolio.

# 14 Summary and conclusions

It has been well recognized by many portfolio investors that the opportunities to be exploited in international risk diversification are far greater than those available in local diversification. Indeed, facts clearly indicate the rapid expansion in international equity. The international equity flows defined as the sum of equity purchases and sales associated with portfolio investment almost doubled between 1986 and 1990. The equity flows from countries other than the US, Europe and Japan have quadrupled in the same period, indicating a sharp increase in the share of so-called emerging capital markets. The expansion in international equity flows across world capital markets stimulates further the debate about the integration (segmentation) of international equity markets.

This book has attempted to examine the issue of segmentation versus integration in world capital markets both theoretically and empirically. Existing theories of international asset-pricing, namely the international extension of the Sharpe–Lintner capital asset-pricing model (CAPM), and the international version of the Roll–Ross arbitrage pricing model (APM) have been studied in the context of integration. The standard approach in the finance literature to the question of capital market integration versus segmentation is to detect whether risk premia differentials between and across similar financial instruments disappear. Empirically, the issue is tested by looking into the pricing structure of international capital assets. If the assets are priced in an international model where the sources of systematic risk are of an international character, then capital markets are said to be integrated. If, on the other hand, local markets and domestic sources of uncertainty are important in pricing capital assets, then the markets are said to be segmented.

Therefore, the subject matter of this book is also of interest to practitioners and investors, in addition to scholars and students of finance. The issue whether there exists a global integrated market for securities has been of the utmost importance to investors who allocate their funds internationally. International asset-allocation strategies differ remarkably, depending on the degree of integration of the market in which investors trade. Internationally diversified portfolios are likely to exhibit risk-adjusted returns above national portfolios. The underlying idea here is that the domestic systematic risk may become idiosyncratic hence diversifiable in an international context while only the idiosyncratic portion of risk can be diversified in a segmented domestic market.

As we have seen throughout, the subject of this book is also important for corporations seeking international capital. Corporate financial strategies differ substantially, depending on whether world capital markets are integrated.

Domestic firms will encounter different optimal foreign borrowing versus optimal home borrowing decisions. If a company has no choice but to raise its capital in a segmented local capital market, it will probably experience a higher cost of capital than a firm with access to world capital markets. Typically, the required rate of return on the common stock of a firm with no exposure to international capital markets, and hence restricted to its segmented domestic market, would be higher than that rate required by investors resident in other capital markets in the world. Moreover, segmentation is likely to create incentives for firms to adopt countermeasures. Dual-listing of a stock becomes an important strategy for the corporation.

What makes the issue of capital market integration more appealing is the growing tendency toward regional, or what we call geographical, integration. The European Union (EU) has become a single market. Major restrictions against the free movement of capital within the EU have been greatly diminished. The same applies, though to a lesser extent, to the capital markets in the European Free Trade Association (EFTA) region. Likewise, barriers against the investor's country of origin were eliminated decades ago in the US and Canada. Critical capital and exchange controls have been removed in Japan, which had extremely tightly regulated markets prior to the 1980 Financial Liberalization Act. In a world where institutional barriers have started to disappear, it is important to see whether world markets, indeed, become more integrated as exchange and capital controls are gradually eliminated.

Under these circumstances, can we speak of a truly international integration of capital markets? Would it be fair to argue that there is now considerable integration in world capital markets? As we have seen throughout this book, the answer to this question is not clear-cut because an important aspect of worldwide financial liberalization seems to be that it is not quite worldwide. Rather, it is taking place regionally. Indeed, there has been an accelerating trend towards forming regional and bilateral trading blocs, customs unions and free trade areas. Such trading blocs generally come with important regional financial liberalization directives, as in the case of European Union. Regional financial liberalization aims at the free movement of capital within a region and generally discriminates against foreign investors by way of differential capital taxation or re-investment schedules imposed on the citizens of non-member states.

That financial liberalization has taken place regionally raises the following important question. Are national portfolios priced according to a model where risk is allowed to be diversified internationally (worldwide) as opposed to a model where only regional risk diversification is ruled in? We have studied geographical asset-pricing and extended the earlier tests of capital market integration by using a broader data set. Using the geographical asset-pricing model that we have developed, we have shown that compensation per unit of sensitivity is the world price of risk and hence regional asset-pricing is not, at least at this stage, the correct specification. Our results indicate that world capital markets have become more internationally integrated in the 1980s. The model posits the existence of a single factor: the value-weighted world market index, our proxy for the world market portfolio. Each national market has a risk exposure to the world index portfolio, and differential expected returns across countries are determined by the relative risk exposures. The regional risk contents as embodied in geographical market indices seem to become at least partially idiosyncratic at world level, and therefore unimportant in the equilibrium pricing of capital assets. Consistent with the reports of earlier research, we find that capital restrictions are important sources of segmentation.[1]

We also performed empirical tests for European capital market integration. The integration versus segmentation issue is examined in a sample of European Union equity markets. There, contrary to prior belief, no clear-cut conclusion can be drawn based on the asset-pricing models. Neither a segmented nor an integrated model has empirical superiority over the other. However, a European Union composite return (integrated model) appears to explain the variation in stock market returns better in the 1980s than in the 1970s. The systematic risk *vis-à-vis* the EU composite model consisting of eight representative member state markets is priced in the first half of the 1980s. That is, the hypothesis that assets are priced in an international (European) integrated model – as opposed to a segmented market model – for each EU member state equity market is accepted. The systematic risk of the same integrated market for the period of 1978–80 is not priced. This result suggests that there is movement towards greater integration in the EU capital markets. However, we fail to attribute this result specifically to the presence of capital controls. Evidence does not support the view that the year 1983, when an important EC Commission decision was taken, is a significant year after which risk premia differentials across EU markets tend to disappear. No significant difference between the pre- and post-1983 periods was noted. Rather, the movement towards greater financial integration seems to be related to a more general attitude on the part of investors who trade in European equity markets.

The results of the prespecified multifactor model are more consistent with our argument that capital controls are the only sources of segmentation in world equity markets. When we take representative European government long-term bond yields (Germany) as a second source of systematic risk in addition to the composite index, the composite returns a priced factor in both data groups. On the other hand, representative bond yields are priced in the period of 1983–6. However, the bond yield factor is not a priced source of systematic risk between 1986 and 1989. The trend of a proportion of portfolio-return systematic risk, as explained by the single-factor model relative to market capitalization share, consistently supports an integrated capital market within the European Union. Further, the proportion of portfolio systematic risk in total risk relative to the proportion of market capitalization in total EU market capitalization has consistently increased in every state in the sample. Even those member states with marginal market capitalization shares have substantially high systematic risk components as explained by the integrated single-index model. As a general view we have come to the conclusion that the pricing of European capital assets cannot be appropriate in a segmented model where each EU member state has its own identification of systematic risk. Therefore, the assumption of a perfectly segmented market wherein a domestic market index is taken as the only source of systematic risk no longer seems to be valid as far as European Union capital markets are concerned.

## Note

1. The role of barriers against the investor's country of origin as a source of segmentation in capital markets is well-documented. See, for instance, Black (1974), Stulz (1981b), Jorion and Schwartz (1986), Gultekin *et al.* (1990), and Akdogan (1992a).

# References


Adler, Michael and Bernard Dumas (1975). 'Optimal international acquisitions', *Journal of Finance*, 30: 1–19.

—— (1983). 'International portfolio choice and corporation finance: a synthesis', *Journal of Finance*, 38: 925–84.

Akdogan, Haluk (1990). 'Market imperfections, and the issue of segmentation in capital markets', *Hacettepe University Journal of Social and Administrative Sciences*, Winter.

—— (1991a). 'Empirical examination of equity market integration in European Community', unpublished PhD dissertation, City University of New York Graduate School.

—— (1991b). 'A test for capital market integration', *METU Studies in Development*, 1991(4).

—— (1992a). 'Behavior of systematic risk in a regionally integrated model for stock prices', *Economics Letters*, 39, (2): 213–16.

—— (1992b). 'Market size and the issue of segmentation in capital markets', *METU Studies in Development*, 19 (2): 181–96.

—— (1992c). 'The international price of risk: are world capital markets integrated?', Bilkent University Department of Economics Discussion Paper no. 92(12).

—— (1993). 'International versus geographical asset pricing: cross-country empirical evidence', Bilkent University Department of Economics Discussion Paper no. 93(3).

Alexander, Gordon J., Cheol S. Eun and S. Janakiramanan (1988). 'International listings and stock returns: some empirical evidence', *Journal of Financial and Quantitative Analysis*, 23 (2): 135–49.

Aliber, R.Z. (1973). 'The interest rate parity theorem: a reinterpretation', *Journal of Political Economy*, 81: 1451–9.

—— (1978). *Exchange Risk and International Corporate Finance*, London: Macmillan.

Balasa, Bela (1961). *The Theory of Economic Integration*, Homewood, Illinois: R.D. Irwin.

Beckers, Stan, Richard Grinold, Andrew Rudd and Dan Stefek (1992). 'The relative importance across the European equity markets', *Journal of Banking and Finance*, 16: 75–95.

Berges, Angel (1981). 'Test of arbitrage pricing theory in international capital markets', paper presented at the European Finance Association Meetings, Jerusalem, September, unpublished.

Black, Fischer (1972). 'Capital market equilibrium with restricted borrowing', *Journal of Business*, 45: 444–54.

—— Michael Jensen and Myron Scholes (1972). 'The capital asset pricing model: some empirical tests', in M. Jensen (ed.), *Studies in the Theory of Capital Markets*, New York: Praeger.

Blume, M. and I. Friend (1973). 'A new look at the capital asset pricing model', *Journal of Finance*, March: 19–34.

Brennan, M.J. (1970). 'Taxes, market valuation, and corporate financial policy', *National Tax Journal*, December: 417–27.

Burmeister, Edwin and Marjorie McElroy (1988). 'Joint estimation of factor sensitivities and risk premia for the arbitrage pricing theory', *Journal of Finance*, 43: 721–33.

Campbell, John Y. and Yasushi Hamao (1992). 'Predictable stock returns in the United States and Japan: a study of long term capital market integration', *Journal of Finance*, 47: (l): 43–69.

Cecchini, Paolo (1988). 'The costs of non-Europe; or, The economics of 1992', *European Economy*, March.

Chen, N.F. (1983). 'Some empirical tests of the theory of arbitrage pricing', *Journal of Finance*, 38 (5): 1394–1414.

Chen, N.F., R. Roll and S. Ross (1983). 'Economic forces and stock market: testing the arbitrage pricing theory and alternative asset pricing theories', Working Paper no. 20–83, UCLA, December.

Cho, Chinhyung, Eun Cheol and Lemma Senbet (1986). 'International arbitrage pricing theory: an empirical investigation', *Journal of Finance*, 41: 313–29.

Cumby, Robert E. (1990) 'Consumption risk and international equity returns', *Journal of International Money and Finance*, 9 (2): 182–92.

Dhrymes, Phoebus, Irwin Friend and Bulent Gultekin (1984). 'A critical reexamination of the empirical evidence on the arbitrage pricing theory', *Journal of Finance*, 39: 323–46.

Dornbusch, Rudiger (1988). 'Money and finance in European integration', in *Money and Finance in European Integration*, EFTA Seminar, Geneva, January, pp. 9–22.

Ehrhardt, Michael C. (1987). 'Arbitrage pricing models: the sufficient number of factors and equilibrium conditions', *Journal of Financial Research*, 10: (2): 111–20.

Errunza, Vihang and Etienne Losq (1985). 'International asset pricing under mild segmentation: theory and test', *Journal of Finance*, 40: 105–24.

—— (1989). 'Capital flow controls, international asset-pricing, and investors' welfare', *Journal of Finance*, 44: 1025–32.

European Commission (1989a). *Europe Without Frontiers–Completing the Internal Market*, Luxembourg: European Commission.

—— (1989b). *The European Financial Common Market*, Luxembourg: European Commission.

—— (1990). *European Unification*, Luxembourg: European Commission.

Fama, Eugene and James MacBeth (1973), 'Risk, return, and equilibrium: empirical tests', *Journal of Political Economy*, 81: 607–36.

Fama, Eugene and M. Miller (1972). *The Theory of Finance*, New York: Holt, Rinehart and Winston.

Francis, Jack Clark (1986). *Investments: Analysis and Management*, New York: McGraw-Hill.

Giovannini, Alberto and Philippe Jorion (1987). 'Interest rates and risk premia in the stock market and in the foreign exchange market', *Journal of International Money and Finance*, 6: 107–23.

—— (1989). 'The time variation of risk and return in the foreign exchange and stock markets', *Journal of Finance*, 44: 307–25.

Grauer, Frederick, Robert Litzenberger and Richard Stehle (1976). 'Sharing rules and equilibrium in an international capital market under uncertainty', *Journal of Financial Economics*, 3: 233–56.

Gultekin, Mustafa N., N. Bulent Gultekin and Alessandro Penati (1990). 'International capital markets segmentation: the Japanese experience', in E.J. Elton and M.J. Gruber, (eds), *Japanese Capital Markets*, New York: Harper & Row, pp. 193–222.

Hamao, Yasushi (1988). 'An empirical examination of the arbitrage pricing theory: using Japanese data', *Japan and the World Economy*, 1: 45–61.

—— (1990). 'The Japanese securities markets: an overview', paper presented at the Conference on Japanese Securities Markets, Leonard N. Stern School of Business, March.

—— Ronald Masulis and Victor Ng (1990). 'Correlations and price changes and volatility across international stock markets', *Review of Financial Studies*, 3: 281–307.

Hansen, Lars Peter and Robert J. Hodrick (1980). 'Forward exchage rates as optimal predictors of future spot rates: an econometric analysis', *Journal of Political Economy*, 88 (5): 829–53.

—— (1983). 'Risk averse speculation in the forward foreign exchange market: an econometric analysis of linear models', in Jacob A. Frenkel(ed.), *Exchange Rates and International Macroeconomics*, London: University of Chicago Press, pp. 113–52.

Harvey, Campbell R. (1989). 'Time-varying Conditional covariances in tests of asset-pricing models', *Journal of Financial Economics*, 24: 289–317.

—— (1991). 'The world price of covariance risk', *Journal of Finance*, 46 (1): 111–57.

Ibbotson, Roger G., Richard C. Carr and Anthony W. Robinson (1982). 'International equity and bond returns', *Financial Analysts Journal*, July–August: 61–83.

International Finance Corporation, *Quarterly Review of Emerging Stock Markets*, various issues.

—— (1991). *Emerging Stockmarkets Factbook 1991*, Washington, D.C.: International Finance Corporation.

International Monetary Fund (1986). *International Financial Statistics Supplement on Price Statistics*, Washington, D.C.: IMF Publications.

—— (1991, 1992). *International Capital Markets: Development, Prospects and Policy Issues*, Washington, D.C.: IMF, 1992.

Johnston, John (1984). *Econometric Methods*, New York: McGraw-Hill.

Jorion, Philippe and Eduardo Schwartz (1986). 'Integration vs. segmentation in the Canadian stock market', *Journal of Finance*, 41: 603–13.

Kim, S. Bae (1993). 'Do capital controls affect the response of investment to saving? Evidence from the Pacific Rim', *Federal Reserve Bank of San Francisco Economic Review*, no. 1: 23–39.

Korajczyk, Robert and Claude Viallet (1989). 'An empirical investigation of international asset-pricing', *Review of Financial Studies*, 2: 553–85.

Kraus, A. and R. Litzenberger (1976). 'Skewness preference and the valuation of risk assets', *Journal of Finance*, 38: 1085–1100.

Levy, H. (1978). 'Equilibrium in an imperfect market: a constraint on the number of securities in a portfolio', *American Economic Review*, 68: 643–58.

Levy, H. and M. Sarnat (1970). 'International diversification of investment portfolios', *American Economic Review*, 60 (4): 668–75.

Lintner, John (1965). 'The valuation of risk assets and the selection of risky investments in stock portfolios and capital budgets', *The Review of Economics and Statistics*, 47: 13–37.

—— (1969). 'The aggregation of investors' diverse judgements and preferences in purely competitive markets', *Journal of Financial and Quantitative Analysis*, 4: 346–82.

Litterman, Robert (1986). 'Forecasting with Bayesian vector autoregressions: five years of experience', *Journal of Business and Economics Statistics*, 4: 25–38.

Markowitz, Harry (1959). *Portfolio Selection: Efficient Diversification of Investment*, Cowles Foundation Monograph 16, New Haven: Yale University Press.

Martin, John D., Samuel H. Cox and Richard D. MacMinn (1988). *The Theory of Finance*, New York: Dryden Press.

McElroy, Marjorie and Edwin Burmeister (1988). 'Arbitrage pricing theory as a restricted nonlinear multivariate regression model', *Journal of Business and Economic Statistics*, 6: 29–42.

—— and Kent D. Wall (1985). 'Two estimators for the APT model when factors are measured', *Economics Letters*, 19 (3): 271–5.

Merton, R. (1973). 'An intertemporal capital asset pricing model', *Econometrica*, 41: 867–87.

—— (1987). 'A simple model of capital market equilibrium with incomplete information', *Journal of Finance*, 52: 483–510.

Micossi, Stefano (1988). 'The Single European Market: finance', *Banca Nazionale del Lavoro Quarterly Review*, no. 165: 217–35.

Morgan Guaranty Trust Company, *World Financial Markets*, various issues.

—— (1992). *Guide to Central Bank Watching*, New York: Morgan Guaranty Trust Co.

Mossin, J. (1966). 'Equilibrium in a capital asset market', *Econometrica*, 35: 768–83.

Obstfeld, Maurice (1986). 'How integrated are world capital markets? Some new tests', National Bureau of Economic Research, Working Paper no. 2075, Washington, D.C.: NBER.

Razin, Assaf and Efraim Sadka (1989). 'Integration of the international capital markets: the size of government and tax coordination', National Bureau of Economic Research, Working Paper no. 2863, Washington, D.C.: NBER.

——(1990). 'Capital market integration: issues of international taxation', *National Bureau of Economic Research*, Working Paper no. 3281, Washington, D.C.: NBER.

Reilly, Frank K. (1986). *Investments*, New York: Dryden Press.

Reinganum, M. (1983). 'The anomalous stock market behavior of small firms in January: empirical tests for tax-loss selling effects', *Journal of Financial Economics*, 12 (1): 89–104.

Roll, Richard (1977). 'A critique of the asset pricing theory's tests. Part 1: On past and potential testability of the theory', *Journal of Financial Economics*, 5 (4): 129–76.

Roll, Richard (1988). 'The international crash of October 1987', *Financial Analysts Journal*, Sept.–Oct.: 19–35.

Roll, Richard and Stephen Ross (1980). 'An empirical investigation of the arbitrage pricing theory', *Journal of Finance*, 35: 1073–1103.

Roll, Richard and Bruno Solnik (1977). 'A pure foreign exchange asset-pricing model,' *Journal of International Economics*, 7: 161–79.

Ross, Stephen (1976). 'The arbitrage theory of capital asset-pricing', *Journal of Economic Theory*, 13: 341–60.

Rubinstein, M. (1974). 'An aggregation theorem for securities markets', *Journal of Financial Economics*, 1: 225–44.

Sharpe, William F. (1964). 'Capital asset prices: a theory of capital market equilibrium under conditions of risk', *Journal of Finance*, 19: 425–42.

—— (1991). 'Capital asset prices with or without negative holdings', *Journal of Finance*, 46 (2): 489–509.

Solnik, Bruno (1974a). 'The international pricing of risk: an empirical investigation of the world capital market structure', *Journal of Finance*, 29: 365–78.

—— (1974b). 'Why not diversify internationally rather than domestically', *Financial Analysts Journal*, July–August: 48–54.

—— (1974c). 'An equilibrium model of the international capital market', *Journal of Economic Theory*, August: 500–25.

—— (1974d). 'An international market model of security price behavior', *Journal of Financial and Quantitative Analysis*, September: 537–54.

—— (1977). 'Testing international asset pricing: some pessimistic views', *Journal of Finance*, 32: 503–11.

—— (1978). 'International parity conditions and exchange risk', *Journal of Banking and Finance*, October: 281–93.

—— (1983). 'International arbitrage pricing theory', *Journal of Finance*, 38: 449–57.

Stehle, Richard (1977). 'An empirical test of the alternative hypotheses of national and international pricing of risky assets', *Journal of Finance*, 32: 493–502.

Stulz, Rene (1981a). 'A model of international asset-pricing', *Journal of Financial Economics*, 9: 383–406.

—— (1981b). 'On the effects of barriers to international investment', *Journal of Finance*, 36: 923–34.

—— (1985). 'Pricing capital assets in an international setting: an introduction', in D. Lessard, (ed.), *International Financial Management*, New York: John Wiley.

Trzcinka, Charles (1986). 'On the number of factors in the arbitrage pricing model', *Journal of Finance*, 41: 347–68.

Wheatley, Simon (1988). 'Some tests of international equity integration', *Journal of Financial Economics*, 21: 177–212.

Wieser, Thomas (1989). 'Price differentials in the European economic space (EES),' Occasional Paper no. 29, Geneva: European Free Trade Association.

World Bank (1991). *International Capital Markets: Developments, Prospects, and Policy Issues*, Washington, D.C.: World Bank Publications.

—— (1992). *International Capital Markets: Developments, Prospects and Policy Issues*, Washington, D.C.: World Bank Publications.

# Index